To my wife

For her patience and courage to climb all those stairs

VENTURES INTO ROCOCO

by

M.H.Maas B.Arch

First published in 2007

ISBN 978-1-84753-952-6

CONTENTS

Venturing into Rococo

When I was into my first or second year of secondary school my parents gave me a book on art. I do not recall the exact title; it was something like "Eeuwige Schoonheid" which translates to "Eternal Beauty" It had a red linen binding and as I recall it was an introduction into appreciating the visual arts and must have included something on Architecture, which is somewhat unusual. From the content I remember very little, a drawing by Rodin of a nude seen on the back; it was one line defining the contour and hair and a woodcut showing the head of Christ. It was a spiral cut starting at the tip of the nose and spiralling out formed the face by widening or narrowing the black line, very clever, very technical but even then I did not think much of the print itself. But it had also photos, a plan and lay out of the vaults and a long section of the "Vierzehnheiligen" church by Balthazar Neumann, which I studied over and over again. It made a deep impression on me but I am not going to state my interest in the architecture of the Austrian Empire between 1600 and 1800 started with that encounter with " Vierzehnheiligen".
It was a few years ago while researching some ideas on the History of Architecture it struck me that the period roughly from 1600 to 1800 has received a rather varied treatment in the various Histories of Architecture that I know. For those who are not so familiar with the styles in the History of Architecture I will elaborate.
When in the fifteenth century the Italians turned away from the examples of the North and decided to study and follow the great examples of their past something new happened. The Italians very quickly regarded their new method of building superior and what had gone between the late Roman times and now as barbaric. They recognised two modes of building the proper way reconnecting with the Roman past and the other way as by the Goth. This rather simple scheme of Roman, followed by barbaric or Gothic after the fall of the Roman Empire in the West and the Renaissance of the civilised style was the start of a system of styles following each other in nice clean sequence. This scheme has been gradually elaborated to something that round nineteen hundred looked very much like below.
Greek Architecture 800- 330 BC
Hellenistic 300 BC- 100 BC
Roman 100 BC-350 AD
Early Christian 350 – 800
Carolingian 800-1000
Romanesque 1000- 1200
Gothic 1200 – 1500
Renaissance 1500 1600 (in Italy 1400-1600)
Baroque 1600-1750 (sometimes subdivided in Baroque 1600-1700 and Rococo 1700-1750)
Classicism 1750-1850
Convenient as this may look it very quickly became clear that the matter was somewhat more complicated, and scholars started to distinguish sub styles and found that there were great variations in this scheme necessary to cover more local traditions. The period 1350-1800 covered by some as Renaissance gave a huge variety of dates and styles
The 1956 edition of Roger Bannister's History uses a rather broad brush classification: Renaissance Architecture and gives a different starting date for Italy 15 century which is also given for France while the rest of Europe it starts in the 16th century. For all the show ends in the 19th century when, conveniently, Modern Architecture starts.

Pevsner[1] is somewhat more varied: he divides a similar period into Renaissance and Mannerism (1420- 1600) and the following into two geographically defined regions: Baroque in the Roman Catholic Countries and Brittain and France from the 16th to the 18th century. Where in this picture of that period the architecture of Germany, the Netherlands, Denmark and Scandinavia fits is not quite clear. Professor Ter Kuile[2] has a more detailed vision. He recognises Renaissance in Italy (1420 – 1520) and Mannerism (1500- 1600) and further "The expansion of the Italian styles in the 16 century". He then proceeds with Baroque in Italy and German speaking countries (1600- 1750) and a separate style "Para baroque" which covers Brittain, France, the Netherlands. He is very reticent about what took place in Northern (Protestant) Germany Scandinavia and Denmark. The new edition of Bannister, the handbooks by Kostoff, Watkins and Furneaux Jordan all have different views on the period.
It became clear to me that it was not quite clear how all these building activities and styles fitted together and in diversity and in common ground as a European phenomenon. With Ter Kuile and others I could distinguish two very different approaches in Europe in the period 1600 – 1800 roughly confined to two regions. The Protestant North and West of Europe and to a great extent France and the Catholic and by the house of Habsburg dominated South-East.
When I was dealing with that period I felt fairly confident about my views on the North West of Europe. The South East I had little personal experience with. From the literature two things struck me. First the very different feel of the exuberant interiors of the churches in the South east compared with sober insides in the North West and on the other hand so much commonality in detail all derived from the Classical Architecture. Somehow there must be something the two regions of Europe have in common I felt and that needed closer scrutiny. I should really go out there and see for myself what was going on in these regions. An idea was born!
But there was another matter I wanted to clarify for myself.
It has often been said that the Il Gesu church built by Vignola for the Jesuits was the major influence for that part of Europe and a starting point for the development.
It seems a good idea not to debate the merits of this concept but have a good look at Vignola's creation and then with that as some yardstick in mind venture out into the Rococo of Austria and Southern Germany and see what we can find out.
We will start with a look at the Il Gesu by Vignola.
Not to putting too much on Vignola it is good to point out that what now is Il Gesu is only partly Vignola's work. He was commissioned by the Jesuits and produced a design that owed some and according to others a lot to Alberti's San Andrea in Mantova (started in 1470). As with Il Gesu it is not quite certain that the transepts and chancel are Alberti's design. The heavy barrel vaulted nave and the dome over the crossing are certainly by Alberti and these features are equally dominant in Vignola's concept of Il Gesu. The entrance façade was designed by Giaccomo della Porta.
In 1672- 1685 the present interior decoration of frescoes and stucco was executed. As the beginning of the Austrian and Southern German development started earlier than that we can safely ignore the later additions. Vignola's nave must have looked very similar to what the San Andrea now looks like. It is not clear what finish Vignola had in mind but it is safe to assume that he had something less exuberant and more structured in mind. Looking at the San Andrea all elements are clearly defined and separated. Columns and entablatures shaped themselves remain unaffected by

---

[1] Nikolaus Pevsner: An Outline of European Architecture. Pelican. Fourth edition 1953
[2] E.H. Ter Kuile: De Bouwkunst van Hellas tot Heden. Phoenix Pockets 46

decorations. Vignola's design must have looked similar. The later decorations do blur the clear separations of parts especially the division of the vault in bays and clearly show that they are of a much later date.

The church as it stands now has a four bay wall pillar nave covered by a barrel vault. The last bay before the crossing is slightly narrower. In each bay a large window cuts into the barrel vault providing light in the nave, very much like a basilica cross section. The transept does not extend beyond the nave. The chancel is one bay and a half round apse. The dominant feature in the interior is the dome over the crossing.

This concept of a nave combined with a dome can be viewed as a compromise between aesthetic ideals and practical requirements. All famous architects preferred the central dome over something like a Greek cross. Da Vinci played with the central dome in his design for the ideal church, Bramante and Michael Angelo's design for the San Pietro was a Greek cross dominated by a huge central dome. The design for the St Peter was extended during the building campaign by Modena to form a nave with a dome over the crossing at the request of the principal the Pope. He thought that the church needed more room for the worshippers.

As with all compromises this one also has a few problems. The sanctuary with the main altar is not under the spatial high point. It is a bit strange to have such a prestigious feature covering only part of the space for the worshippers. Very quickly the dome looks like an empty gesture, which rather than drawing the attention to the high altar takes it all up and reduces the liturgical centre of the building to a second rate feature. But architects could not help themselves; ever since the early Renaissance rediscovered the central dome it has been the problem to combine an oblong space with a centring shape like the dome. This would also be the problem that the Austrian and German architects of the 17th and 18th century tried to resolve if the scholars are right who support the view that Il Gesu was a major inspiration.

But there is more. Anyone who has had a look at the St Vaast[3] in Arras (ill. 1) or the St Philippe in Paris and has seen the Court Chapel[4] in the Residence in Würzburg (ill 2) by Balthasar Neumann will be puzzled how these so different buildings are all built in the same culture at very much the same time i.e. between 1735 and 1780.The Church in Arras you can in one glance see how it fits together. It is a rectangular space divided into three aisles by two rows of Corinthian columns which support a barrel vault. The central aisle ends in a sanctuary closed by a semicircle. There is a transept with a dome. All parts of the structure and the space are clearly separated from each other all is perfectly formed and separated. Whatever furnishing or decoration there is, is designed as thing in its own right and reads as furniture rather than furnishing and decoration.

How different is this all in the Chapel by Balthasar Neumann! It takes time to work out what the shape of the space is and how the construction all fits together. Upon entering one is overwhelmed by the abundance of shapes colours textures and light. Then you can discern Corinthian columns but it is not quite clear what they support. They are connected by a heavy entablature but does that carry the vaulting? Sometimes it does and sometimes it does not. Do the columns separate side aisles from the main body? It turns out they don't; they are some sort of a screen in front of the walls. The first impression is a central space that fades out between the columns and appears to open into the infinite space in the skies. The whole the structure sculpture decoration and colours, rich gold, red, grey blue and black, is one

---

[3] Architect Pierre Contant d'Ivry (1698-1777). Begun 1755.

[4] Ca 1730. Decoration by Hildebrandt

integrated mise en scene showing how the terra firma we live on at this spot connects with the outer world regions of miracles and light.
Yet, these buildings are conceived on locations barely 500 km apart in Europe, a Europe that barely 200 years ago created buildings that apart some local variants and idiosyncrasies were very much in the same vain and easily recognised as Gothic at places much further apart than Arras and Würzburg.
Further more the buildings have so much in common in forms and detail to be recognisable as part of one cultural tradition.
This all leaves us with two questions.
What is it that unites these buildings what is the commonality?
What is the difference what concepts make them so utterly different?
To find a satisfactory answer to those two questions and to asses the importance of the Il Gesu is what I set out to do.
Having an idea what to look for when travelling those parts of Europe, preparations could begin in earnest in 1999.
I had obtained a copy of J Bourke's Baroque Churches of Central Europe, and together with the books on the History of Architecture I began preparing a list of things to see, classifying them into " must see", "worth seeing" and "could if time permits". I transferred them onto large photocopies of the map of Northern Italy, Austria and Southern Germany[5]. I included Northern Italy to see how much building activity was going on in the 18th century. There is very little going on there during that period so I could include some of the things I wanted to see anyway like Guarini in Turin and further east Mannerists like Romano and Palladio and the must see sights in Ravenna and Venice. It also gave the chance to see the San Andrea in Mantova as a substitute for Il Gesu in Rome. Once all sights are plotted it is easy to divide them roughly in groups which can conveniently be visited from one centre and complete the planning by cutting up the copy of the maps and list the buildings with their classification for that part of the map. At the same time I made contact with Italian embassy and the Goethe Institute through the German Embassy and I am grateful for their help and the introductory letters they gave me. By the beginning of the Southern Hemisphere spring of 2000 (September) the details were sorted out and we went to our travel agent to put a schedule of flights together and organise a car through Eurodrive.
The idea was to fly to Holland visit some friends early April and from there fly to Lyon; pick up our Eurodrive[6] Peugeot and cross the Alps to Torino, hoping that early spring in Italy would be warmer than in Holland. We had some snow while we stayed in Holland between 13 and 20 April. We would gradually travel East to Venice and from there North to Wien and gradually north and West to Tirol and end up in Salzburg early June. Here my wife would fly back to Holland. I would continue first north to the Czech border, west from there to Würzburg, from there south to end up somewhere west of München. From there I would go to Ronchamps to visit Notre Dame du Haut by Le Corbusier and proceed to Strasbourg to hand in the Peugeot, take the train to Frankfurt and fly back to Holland. A few days later we would fly back to New Zealand. We had about two and a half month for the operation which was

[5] Michelin 419, 420, 926, 428, 429

[6] Scheme for tourist from outside Europe whereby you buy a new (French) car and resell at the end of your trip for a guaranteed price.

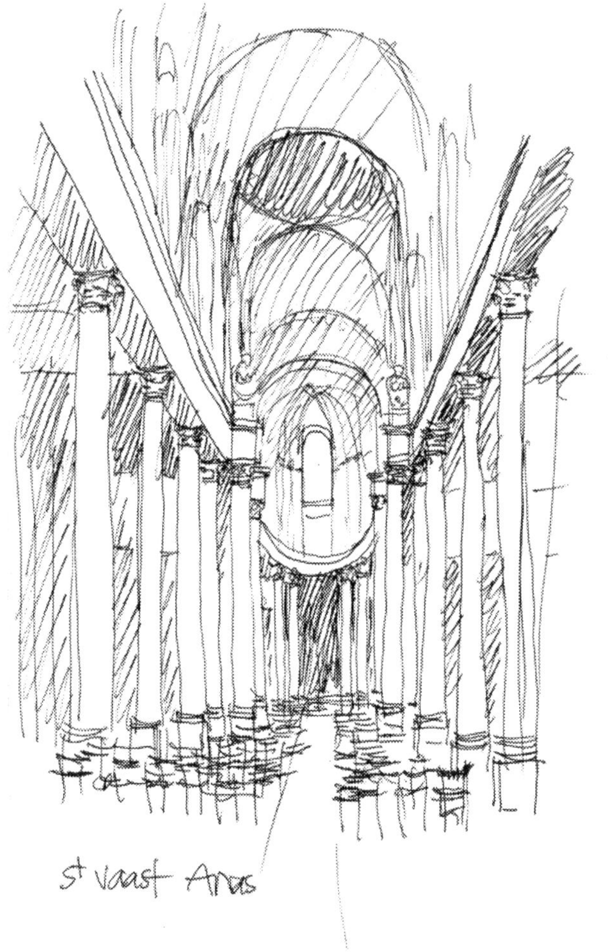

1. Saint Vaast in Arras France

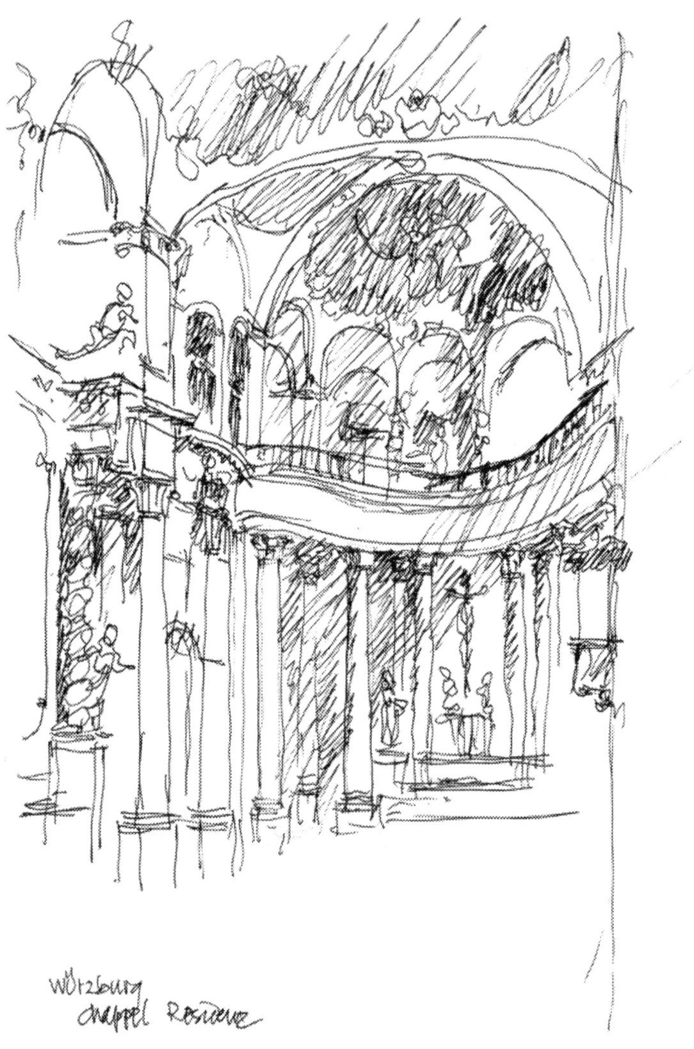

2. Chapel of the Residence in Würzburg

ample. We started on the trip on 20 April and I flew back to Holland on July 14 after our brand-new Peugeot 206 had clocked up 12000 km. It sounds a lot, but it averages out to about 225km per day which given that that includes long stretches as a trip to Ravenna from Verona (more then 200 km single trip) and one day from Leutkirch in Wurttemberg to Ronchamps through Switzerland and some other longer day trips is not too onerous a driving task. It left us with ample time to do other things like shopping and doing nothing but enjoying the land, landscape and people.
The idea to start in Italy worked well. It was still a bit chilly in Torino probably because of its closeness to the Alps that still had a lot of snow. Milano was warmer and very nice indeed. Verona was warm and so was the rest but not yet oppressively hot. The landscape I believe was on its best; the trees just in green with that invigorating freshness that wears off over summer to this weary smudged green of summer. The coo-coo was out and calling in the hills outside Verona and the tourist were still at home except Italian schools and busses with Japanese. So it was not crowded nowhere not in Verona, not in Ravenna and not in Venezia.
Wien was still early spring- the chestnuts in the Prater just in bloom, the evenings in the Wiener Wald where we had our lodging were still frosty: it was all fresh and new, spring.
The cold spell in Kufstein was the last of winter and further on it gradually went to early summer with those long warm summer evening when the sun does not seem to set and the warm day endless. I have fond memories of the evenings in Sommerhausen on the Main just South of Würzburg
The churches in Austria and Germany are invariably all still used as parish church sometimes combined with servicing a monastery. This means that from time to time you will find that there is a wedding (Maria Plain, Volders) or funeral or some other liturgical ceremony going on which restricts your viewing. You can wait till the end or restrict yourself a bit. Sometimes you will find that the grille in the West of the church under the gallery for the choir is locked and you have to take in the church from there if you don't want to go to the Pfarrhaus (the Vicarage) to seek further access. The smaller churches are generally one room, which can be appreciated from the West; it is the detailed look at sculpture and decorations that is not very well possible. I only found on a very few occasions that it was really too restrictive. Given that the above visits to those churches are free you should make a donation in the appropriate box in the back of the church for the upkeep. In most cases you will find a guidebook to the church in the back for a very reasonable price with lots of very useful information and photos.
This is not the case in Italy. Many churches close during siesta time (12.00 to 14.00) and on Festive Days which includes public Holidays like Liberation Day, Labour Day. It pays to check with the tourist office but that information might not always be fully relied upon. There generally is an entrance fee and there is very little information on the church and it's interior. So get that from the Tourist Information before you go. To complicate matters further there may be some reductions for Senior Citizens, Students, War veterans- you would probably not qualify for that- holders of European passports and furthers groups. It varies from site to site and it pays to ask and produce evidence.
Early 2001 all was organised; we only needed to find a house sitter to look after the house and our cats and eat the vegetables still growing in the garden.
It took some ringing around but in the end we had someone looking after the house the cats and the vegetable garden.
Nothing now stopped us and on 11 April 2001 we flew to Auckland to catch our flight to Amsterdam

Torino

21 April

We arrived around noon at the youth hostel. Getting to Torino had not been difficult. We had flown from Amsterdam to Lyon the day before and had no great difficulties in finding the young lady who was waiting for us to hand over our Peugeot 206. We had ordered a white one. The car that waited us was green. "Mais le vers c'est bien cool" she assured us, the "o" of cool charmingly lengthened. Some aspects of youth culture do seem to be universal and even the Academie Francaise cannot stop that. So we started our cooool Peugeot and turned on to the auto route towards the East. Lyon airport is east of Lyon so we had an easy escape. It was fairly early in the afternoon and we cruised to Chambery. With some local and very helpful assistance we found and booked in a Novotel just off the motorway. France is all too familiar, like home. So the holiday had not yet started; that would happen tomorrow when crossing the Italian border. When preparing for our trip our children and the Youth Hostel Organisation in New Zealand had convinced us that Youth Hostels are now no longer the bunks and barrack style accommodation but just another budget accommodation. We joined the club and were eager to give it a try. The Youth Hostel in Torino would be the first. It had E-mail, but whether our booking had been arranged we did not know. We had not received confirmation.

Getting to Italy and to the outskirts of Torino had been a real holiday trip. Getting into Torino and to the hostel had been a breeze until we crossed the river at the end of the Corso Vittorio Emanuele II. There the map we had bought in France and all other information started to fail and I had to try my best Italian to secure the assistance of a local who professed to speak English. His English appeared of the same quality as my Italian. His Italian was however a lot better and also faster so he ended up walking with us until we came in sight of the hostel. It appeared to be a late nineteen early twentieth century villa on a very steep site. But there was some parking at the back. So we parked the car and we found our way to the entrance and the door locked. The fore court was deserted the wind was cold and the door closed. At the far end a man sat on a retaining wall and watched our approach and our efforts to get in with great patience and interest. In the end he got to his feet and walked over. He turned out to be from Libyan or Abyssinian extraction and able to communicate in some English, some French, some Flemish and lots of Italian and possibly Arabic, but I did not get round to testing that. "It is closed, three o'clock," he informed us. Regardless of whether this was or was not in the book it was closed and it did not look as if anyone was inside. "She needed lunch" my wife said and so we asked him for a decent and not too expensive restaurant. He offered to take us to his favourite. I always rely on my instinctive judgement when accepting people's offer to help. I had my doubts about Omar-for that was his name. They were probably based on his black appearance; black yeans and a black leather jacket. In N.Z you are conditioned to think black: Black Power, Gangs, criminal background. I felt that my wife was feeling the same. But it was broad daylight he was a lot lighter than I and we were going into the centre with the "pullman" he said to a street just of the Vittorio Emanuele. I remembered that "il pullman" in Italian is just a bus, ordinary public transport. So we parked the car behind the hostel, locked it carefully and followed Omar down to the river to the half round square at the bridge at the end of the Vittorio Emanuele. We went on the bus and Omar got us off somewhere not too far from the station. He crossed the boulevard and turned into a narrow side street. About twenty meters into the street there was a compact mass of people all focussed on a shop on the right hand side. That was where we were to go Omar declared. We had great doubts that we would ever be able to get to the door let alone inside, but

Omar somehow got us in what appeared to be a lobby about 2.5 meter wide and 1.5 deep. The wall opposite the entrance was mostly taken up by a counter where all business of the restaurant was controlled. The lobby was filled to its absolute Italian maximum, which is more than twice what one normally would accept in New Zealand. Everybody was talking and trying to get something organised. Omar joined in and managed to get us a table that is the first one to become available. And turnover was fast we did not wait very long when Omar ushered us through a door at the right and manoeuvred us to a round table just behind the door and a window that looked out on the street. The room was filled to the absolute maximum with tables, all tables were occupied and the room was filled with noise. It later appeared that there was a similar room at the left-hand side of the lobby. Service was fast and simple like the menu. The meal was very good; the wine was an acceptable vin du pay and unlimited. A bottle was placed on the table and when empty replaced. Omar knew all about it. He went immediately for the Secondo, my wife ordered some pasta –the Primo – and I normally do not lunch so I had a chance to take it all in. The restaurant was about three tables wide and about four deep. On the left hand behind the counter in the lobby was the servery with direct access to the kitchen. It was warm and noisy, every body seemed to be in a hurry, service was very efficient so within half an hour or so we were out on the street again and waiting for the bus to take us back. When the hostel finally opened, Omar disappeared into the interior; he apparently used it as a permanent address for the duration of his stay in Torino. From the somewhat complicated conversation in English, Italian, French and Flemish we had made out that he drifted around a lot.

We joined the group in front of the counter trying to get a bed. We had E-mailed to the hostel from New Zealand with varying success, but never actually received a confirmation of a booking. We had made jokes about the person in charge of the establishment Anna Palmieri-a surname she shares with the Italian Ambassador to New Zealand at the time- Anna appeared to be a roundish woman somewhere in her thirties and not easily persuaded. When we finally got to talk to her she maintained that she never received any E-mail and that there was no room in the Hostel. She could see if she could get us in a hotel for similar cost. After some ringing she gave an address: Albergho Something on Via Berthollett, near the Railway station. There was little else we could do but try our luck there.

While I was trying to get something organized with Ms Palmieri my wife had made contact with an Aussie couple on their last leg of their European tour. They were in the same situation but for the fact that they did not speak very much else than English. How they had managed in France we did not ask. They decided to take the New Zealand lead and follow us in our tracks. With the maps we had finding Via Betholļet was not a problem, even getting into the street was no big deal although the area, as it consisted of narrow streets, was made somewhat inaccessible through an intricate one way system. We even found parking just outside the station in an area all parking and stopping was strictly prohibited. We just joined the multitude of Italians that ignored the rules. With my best Italian I had asked a respectable looking man what the round blue red-bordered disk with a red Andreas-cross meant. He was most emphatic in his answer: parking there was illegal and could attract horrendous fines. When I asked what about all those cars he raised his hand in a gesture of I don't know and went his way. We decided to take the risk like all the rest and went to find the hotel. It did not look like what we expected. It was just a glass door, locked and with little to indicate that it was the hotel. We had walked past it without noticing. I had rung the doorbell to ask where the hotel was when the young man announced that this was the hotel. "Are you the people sent through the hostel?" He did speak English. "Yes we are!" we said and explained that we would like to see the room. We briefly inspected the premises and the room. It was clean not luxurious but the price was about the same as the hostel and the amenities from what I had seen from the hostel certainly not less. So we booked and went to get the car and find a parking space near the hotel. Parking in the street was quite safe the young man in the Hotel had assured us; there are always people in the street, so nothing happens. We found out later what he meant. The neighbourhood housed or attracted a lot of North African people, a inheritance of the colonial past no doubt. The men stood around, conducting business or engaging in lengthy and agitated discussions. This began round five and only gradually diminished after midnight but it never died down completely to start up again early in the morning. Our room had windows overlooking the street with all advantages and disadvantages. The ongoing street noise was one of the things you had to live with. We found the Aussies - because they sneaked in while we were trying to turn- and our self a car park close to the hotel. But there is some justice in this world: the Aussies got punished. The antenna of their rental-Eurodrive Peugeot was snatched off and they had some scratches. They faced the task of writing a damage report by filling in the French form that comes with the car. We did not offer to help. Anzac cooperation must have limits, especially after their cheeky behaviour of pinching the car park we saw first. For diner we went back to the restaurant of the afternoon and as we were early by Italian standards we could go in without waiting. It was good and very reasonable in price. After the eventful day we turned in early to get a good night sleep. Apart from the North African discussions and the emptying of the glass-recycling container on the corner somewhere in the dark of night we slept well.

22 April

The next day, the sun was out, it felt like spring when we went to the centre of town. It was all well within walking distance. It is a very much 19 century and in many aspects like French Mediterranean towns: a gradation of boulevards to very narrow streets with a multitude of trees. Plane trees mostly, they were just in their first frail foliage. The fragile green together with the sun made it a pleasure. We found our way to the centre where there is very little left from any earlier building period beyond the nineteenth century. The public space is a bit large; the castle is a bit big for the Piazza Castello. So it acts as a fleeting open space, which on the west side reads as a forecourt to the piazzetta and the Palazzo Reale. Close to the fence defining the Piazzetta Reale on the west side is the San Lorenzo: a rather plain looking door in a flat façade. We were somewhat early so we sat in the sun and relaxed like the rest of the population. It was quiet. Not that I have anything to compare it with but we had plenty of empty space and nobody seemed to be in a hurry. When the door opened the San Lorenzo[7] was very much worth to wait for: it is a very exciting little church. It is a lot smaller than I had imagined based on the photos of the interior I had seen. It starts very heavy and agitated at ground level with very vehement movements in and out. There is an alternating of inward and outward directions of real material

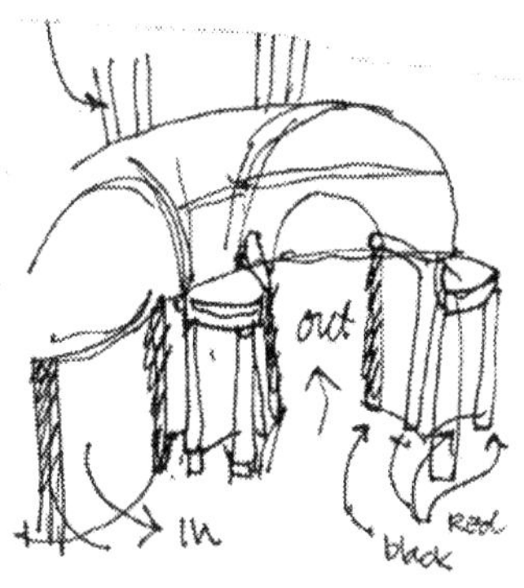

[7] Architect Guarini 1668

elements. This heavy material look is supported by strong colours black and red. The structure and the colour grow lighter and less material going up; the cupola is very light and almost weightless. It adds to the impression of height and an increased sense of light and lightness. The whole of the composition has a certain nervousness over it an agitation that diminishes with the height.

We went on to the Chiesa della Carmine[8]. The church has suffered from the development of the Via Roma, which forced the closure of windows at one side. The interior is now rather bland.

The Duomo is the usual collection of all periods. I liked the Crucifixion Altar. The Baroque side altars all looked a bit out of place. The Capella S. Sindone is another on the list of must see in Torino. Unfortunately it was closed to my great disappointment. It was the other work of Guarini I had been looking forward to. But we could have known. It had been in the papers that there had been a fire in the church, which had caused substantial damage. The famous shroud was undamaged but the Capella was still closed for restoration.

There is of course more to do in Torino but we were there to look at architecture from the mid 17th Century to about 1800. Baroque in Northern Italy is not very strong. Work from Guarini was together with work from Juvarra the things I really wanted to see. As the distance to Milano is not much we would have time to visit Stupinigi and Superga both from Juvarra and still have plenty of time to arrive early afternoon at the Youth Hostel. We had bought a map of Milano and identified how to get to the Hostel and that appeared on the map to be pretty straightforward. For the evening meal we consulted the young man in the hotel. He directed us towards a street off Vittorio Emanuele. On the approach we realised that we were sent to the same restaurant we had already discovered with the assistance of Omar. Turning into the street there was no one. The restaurant was closed. They had their weekly closure. It takes some getting used to when you come from new Zealand where everything is very much open all the time. We wandered around but the neighbourhood did not offer anything and it was getting late. My wife needs her food at very regular times so we had to do something. A station is usually a place where you should be able to find something to eat. We ended up eating a rather poor Pizza in the one of the outlets in the station; nothing to endears us to Torino

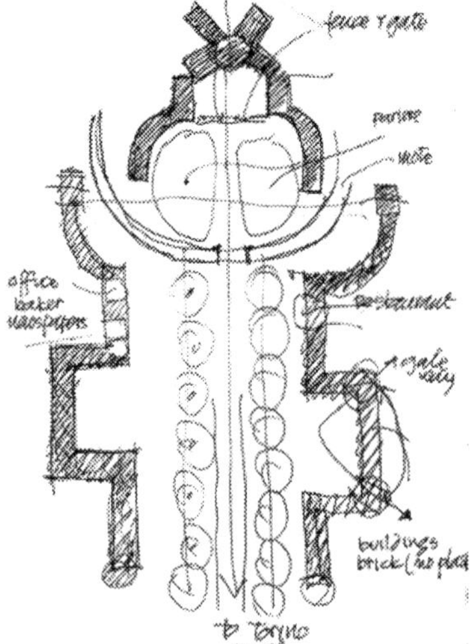

23 April.

The next morning we paid our bill and went off to Stupinigi.[9] It was a cold spring morning, grey with a cold wind. When we arrived we found out that it was still closed to the public. There was staff around preparing the buildings and gardens for the tourist invasion. But they could not be convinced. I did not think of my introductory letter of the Italian Ambassador. It worked miracles later that morning! We could walk through the gardens, which they were preparing for the summer season. It is an impressively large set up for

[8] Architect Philippo Juvarra

[9] 1729-1733

what is described as a hunting lodge. Along a very imposing approach that starts of in Torino are arranged in some cross shape extensive support building in the local brick. They are now partly empty, and partly, closer to the hunting palace itself used as shops, a restaurant, community hall and school. Some of it has been converted into private houses. The very wide approach starting at the outskirts of Torino is lined with trees and ends at the access onto the grounds proper. The complex is surrounded by a mote of some sort and the gardens at the back with a wall of the local brick. Across the mote is a vast forecourt roughly circular in form bisected by the approach to the forecourt proper closed of by an ornate gate. The areas left at both sides are taken up by large parterres. A service road leads along the perimeter serving the outbuildings which at the time served as stables staff quarters and the like. The weather did not encourage extensive walks. We tried to get a cup of coffee but again we were out of luck. Monday was their closing day, so no coffee. The baker however was open so we could find something warm to eat. To get some eye of what the weather was to be like I bought a newspaper. But we found that weather forecasts in Europe are rather parochial. They show only the region and seem to be designed for pre-schoolers. No intellectual nonsense as isobars and highs and lows or fronts. No, a simple graphic lay out of clouds and half covered sun discs and very stylised raindrops is all you get. The weather seems to be restricted to boundaries of the distribution of the newspaper. If you leave the district then you have to sort out yourself what it is going to be or take your chances. So there was little else we could do there after our walk about but to carry on to Superga[10] and from there to Milano. To get to the Basilica de Superga you have to go back to Torino as the Hunting lodge Stupinigi is at the end of the Corso De Unione Sovietico, which passes over the Tangentiale and changes name and character there. We did not want to do that so with the help of our Michelin map and some turning we found the bank of the Po and the way up to the Basilica. It is high up on the hills on the right hand bank of the Po. The forecourt gives a magnificent view over Torino. The weather had started to clear; the sun was out. The wind remained cold. The church itself was open to the public. For the rest of the complex there were guided tours; we had missed the last one of the morning. But the letter of the Italian ambassador proved a big help. One of the Signorinas reverted to her best English and gave us a full guided tour of the complex including the tombs of all the members of the house of Savoy which later was to be royal family of the united Italy. As a curious detail members of the House of Savoy although in exile are still buried in the church or rather in the crypt under the church.

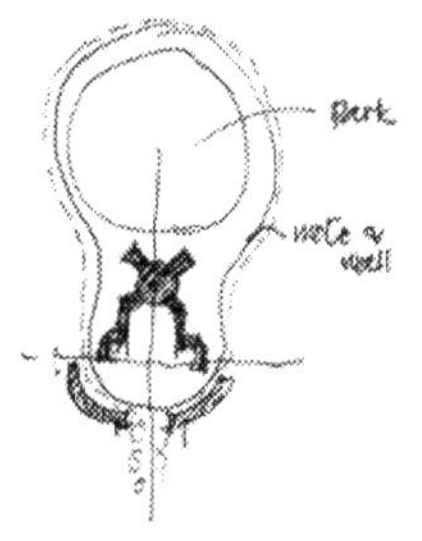

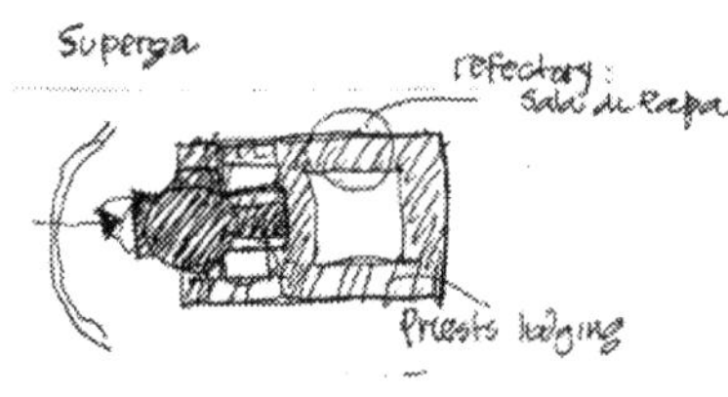

The most attractive part of the complex is the situation and the exterior. The interior with the dominating dome is somewhat cold and without surprise. The sculpture and in the church and of the Royal Tombs is

[10] 1717-1731

somewhat pathetic or sentimental as most of the sculpture of that period. Very expertly done but somewhat empty or cliché.
The road back to the main route to Milano wasn't difficult to find and we soon entered the Autostrada to Milano. The trip to Milano went without a glitch. It was an interesting ride. It is a rather flat country that sometimes vaguely reminded me of the Dutch landscape It leads through the dry and wet rice cultures some of us still remember from the film with Anna Magnani, Bitter Rice about the poverty of the people working the rice fields for the big owners; one of the masterpieces of the Italian Social Realism films of the fifties. On the outskirts of Milano the task of finding your way into town without getting lost in the maze of one way roads traffic regulation and road signs that seem to direct you everywhere except where you want to go we feared could be complicated. But Milano coming in from Torino wasn't too difficult and we arrived without any real hold ups.
We entered Milano early in the afternoon and found the youth Hostel easy enough. It is a large building with an institution look and feel over it. It reminded me of military lodgings. The foyer is a large oblong space with a long counter on the right, and what in New Zealand would have been a queue. Here it was people huddled in front of the counter trying to get ahead. The man in charge appeared to be not very interested in his task and did the checking in and handing out of bed linen in an almost mechanical way. I joined the people waiting to get us booked in. Price wise it was also a bit of a surprise. They have only "three-bed" rooms available and you have to pay for three beds whether or not you use them or take linen out. That brought the price per night well above what we paid for the hotel in Torino. The rooms are a bare minimum. The bed I slept in had a deep sag in the middle. The door had a large window with clear glass, which could not be covered. I found a way of hanging my jacket to cut out the light from the corridor and give us some privacy. The remainder of the facilities is very austere and extremely basic. While I was getting us sorted my wife became engaged in a conversation with Emma, a New Zealand girl. Her parents live in Napier not to far from our house. She had worked in Rome to get experience in speaking Italian. She was now offered a job with Tradenz (Trade New Zealand) in Milano and was to start work the next day. Her Italian was rapid and impressive we found out. She was a bit lost and down. She had planned on staying the Youth Hostel for the months that her job lasted but was now considering to go and look for other accommodation. While she was on the phone she also rang around and found us a hotel on the Via Tito Livio almost on the Piazza Salgari, which were to view the next morning, the Albergo Nina. We had diner and went to bed. After a noisy night – a Japanese group had invaded the facilities- we had a taste of the breakfast supplied, which we found in keeping with the basic austerity of the rest of the amenities. After we had seen Emma off to her new lodgings she was to view we found our way to Albergo Nina. It appeared to be a five-story building at the corner of the Piazza and Via Tito Livio The presentation was a bit flaky. It looked like a very much run down house which they were now doing up with the help of relatives. You had to climb one flight of stairs to arrive at the reception, which was downright out off a De Sicca film. Entering the door you were confronted with a short counter in a hole in a wall and beyond a room in total chaos. The outfit was run by a very skinny young man under the supervision of an enormous matron. Conversation was in Italian; given my knowledge of the language that did not allow for very much beyond the very basics. The room the young men showed was three flights of stairs up and overlooked the Piazza below It had no ablution attached ,but it was clean and we were the only guests on our floor so the ablution though communal was in fact for our only use. The price was very reasonable and the neighbourhood a definite improvement over the Hostel.

The Piazza, which our room overlooked, was densely shaded with trees and had a small well used playground. Around the square were shops and one or two restaurants; a normal urban residential area and not to far from the nearest underground station. After we had settled in and dragged the luggage up the stair we went to work and to town. After all this was a study tour.
We headed for the centre and started with the Duomo not really in the program but I had studied the history of the building to some extend in relation to the minutes of the lodge[11] that are fairly complete and give a great insight in the design considerations and process. I had formed my self some idea of what the church would be like and was not disappointed. The very detailed and busy grouping of verticals is right for the square. It apparently had been cleaned recently like so many monuments in Europe. The splendid white frilly mass fills and dominates the square. which features two rather repetitive long sides and an opposing end of similar texture. The Duomo draws all attention and is very much present at the other end. We sat there for a while to take it in.
The interior is also what I expected: dark and incoherent. Its only merit is the size. The proportions and detailing is chaotic and whimsical e.g. the oversized capital with saints incorporated. I was prepared for it. It is really not all that attractive a n interior. It lacks the structured coherence of the great churches north of the Alps. The light levels due to the side aisles having different heights are low, which combined with the vastness of the plan creates a feel of being lost in twilight It is of course packed with work of varying quality like any other major church. But on the whole the people of Milano must have felt cheated when they gradually saw the church they did end up with. At the time of the inception they wanted a church bigger and lighter than the Notre Dame in Paris[12]. And that is certainly not what they ended up with![13] We had a coffee on the Piazza in a big establishment on the North side near the entrance of the mall to get us prepared for the next sight.

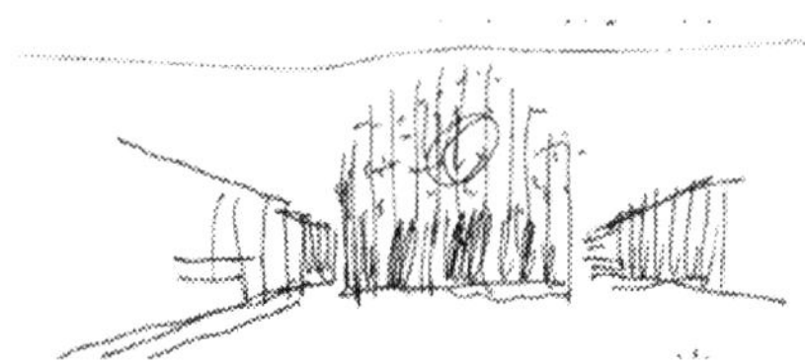

The old San Lorenzo dating to AD 370 or so, must have been impressive and the Renaissance additions are well in keeping except for the dome: it is too tall to lofty and vertical. I feel that the relation between the support and the dome is not right.
Going back to our accommodation we decided not to bother finding another place. Initially we considered finding a different hotel. The family running the Albergo Nina was a bit chaotic and somewhat eccentric. But as the Albergo Nina was about 15000 liras cheaper and its facilities better than the hostel, we decided to stay and not to look for other accommodation. After all we were not going to stay in Milano very long. There is a lot one might visit but Baroque and Rococo Architecture does not feature strongly on the list. As the nearest underground station was not too far away, we parked our Peugeot properly, Italian or Milano style: nosing in with the two front wheels on the footpath, leaving just a 1m wide little alley between the front of the car and the buildings. It does not look as if it is in the Italian road code as a proper

---

[11] See: James Ackerman: Ars Sine Scientia Nihil Est (Skill without knowledge is nothing)

[13]See: note 12

way of parallel parking but every body parked their car that way. So parallel parking is nosing in with front wheels on the footpath. You can get a lot more cars parked that way. We then noted that tomorrow night all vehicles needed to be clear of the streets, it was street cleaning day for the neighbourhood. We were just about to get concerned that all cars and there were quite a lot of them had to find an alternative spot for the night when we found out that in the evening you just parked your car fully with all its four wheels on the footpath and pulled it back the next morning. As long as you had no wheel on the carriageway you were legally not parked in the road and street cleaning would not have your car towed away. Street cleaning happened during the night. So no worries and we used the underground to get around in Milano and left our car safely parked near the hotel.

25 April

The next day we went to town to finish the program. Santa Maria della Grazie[14] a nice cupola and a well-proportioned cloister with column spacing on the square i.e. the distance between the columns is about the height of one column. When we tried the San Ambrogio[15] we had our first experience with the nightmare of closing hours. The sign on the church reads: Giorni feriale: 9-12, 3-7 Giorni Festivi: 9 –13, 3- 7. And it was 25 April, a public Holiday, La Liberazione d'Italia. But the San Ambrogio was closed at twelve and remained closed. So we had an early lunch and went back later the afternoon. It has been much altered with a roomy oblong fore court. The interior is open and spacious, very restrained. We had our first confrontation with what later appeared to be a regular feature in many of the Rococo churches we visited in Austria and Germany. The crypt contained a weird spectacle; three skeletons assembled and put in seating position, fully clothed and crowned: the three patron- saints of the church that is what is believed to be their mortal remains, safely behind glass of course. It did not inspire deeply devotional feelings towards the Saints, only a bemused look.

We had a look into the Castello Sforza to see the last work of Michael Angelo: the Pieta Rondiani an unfinished work and a reworking of a early unfinished work of Christ being taken down from the cross. It is in unfinished state an impressive work. The ability to rework a new concept in an old form and turn the constraints into an advantage is fascinating. The same day we made our first great step in understanding the Italian hospitality system. A Bar is a restaurant that serves meals only at messogiorno, lunchtime and a Ristorante serves meals at nights. Lunchtime meals are very competitively priced: unfortunately I do not eat lunch as I do want to do things in the afternoon and a good warm meal makes me very drowsy and sleepy. So we had to look for Ristoranti in the evening. We further discovered that the most expensive way to have coffee is to drink it outside in the furniture made available by the establishment, cheaper is it to have it inside sitting at one of the tables and cheapest is to have it standing at the long counter where one has the benefit of the paper. You learn all sorts of thing along the way! The neighbourhood restaurant was closed so we had Chinese around the corner. The Chinese are in Europe and possibly over the world a culinary alternative to Mc Donald: you know what to expect, the food is decent and the price always very good and to my mind highly preferable to anything Mc Donald has to offer. The next day we planned on going to Verona but not until we had tried the Lavanderia in the neighbourhood

---

[14] Church by Guiniforte Solari 1465,crossing and dome by Bramante 1493

[15] Cloister by Bramante 1490

Verona.

26 April

After we had found the Lavanderia and got the machine to do the washing and drying we were off to Verona. The weather started to improve gradually, partly because we were moving away from the Alps, which are that time of the year, and especially that spring still covered with snow. About half past eleven we got on to the SS11 to Brescia. It was sunny and the country was green, not much traffic on the road. Leaving Brescia behind we headed for the Lago di Garda where we would like to have a rest and the lunch. We found a very empty parking overlooking the lake. The view was splendid very little activity and the place was clean. From the lay out of the area we could see that it would be crawling with visitors and tourists in the season with all manner of boats and tourists attractions. But now it was the relaxed feel of an early morning with nothing very much to do. A man was doing some maintenance on his boat. People walked around with the calm of a little village. The population was slowly getting ready for the season. But not yet the hurry for the tourists as they are still some time away. We sat under the young trees fresh green and enjoyed the peace and quiet of the day. The lake was calm and almost like the mirror the brochures show you. The sun was warm and for the first time since we left for New Zealand in 82 we heard the coo- coo, the distant call so characteristic for spring in Europe. With some reluctance we packed our things and got in the car. We wanted to be in Verona in time to make sure that we found somewhere to stay. After the Milano experience we had decided to give away the idea of Youth Hostels and try our luck with the private sector through the Visitor Information Centers. They do provide ample information on all classes of accommodation. They do not make bookings for you like they do in Austria and Germany as we later found out. But the experience with Youth Hostels had given us enough incentive to try alternatives.

The only map we had of Verona was the street plan in our Michelin Guide. They worked for us when we visited France regularly and had to do it again. Using the little map of the Guide and following the signage pointing to the City Centre and the "I" of the Information Centre we should be able to get there and find somewhere to park the car long enough to get ourselves organized. The temperature was gradually increasing and on approaching Verona it was warm, really warm. Our entry into Verona was a bit of a gamble; none of the maps we had was much of a help but we must have had Fortuna herself looking after us. We found a car park right up against the post office within a stone throw of the Piazza d'Erbe where the Guide Michelin said was the tourist Information Office. A very helpful Signorina did not agree with Michelin and as she was running the shop that Michelin said was the office she had powerful arguments to convince us that she was right and Michelin wrong. "No, it was near the Arena" she said and was quite adamant, mostly in Italian. The map in the Guide Michelin was good enough to get us to the Arena and the vast open area around it. The Signorina in the Visitors Information was quite helpful, her English also. So we ended up with enough information to find us an economic place to stay. When we found our car, the telephone was next to it, we had a card—we had bought it from a somewhat different American in the Youth Hostel in Miilano for half the price- and I ventured into getting something organized over the phone in Italian. The first try was a place outside Verona, a farm. When I had the lady of the house on the phone she declared that she never did business over the phone. We should come out-a ten to 15 km run into the country along rather small roads said the Michelin map. We tried the next one. A former nun's institution: they were fully booked. So we ended up in a former Seminary: Casa di Monsignore Carera. It appears that Italy like

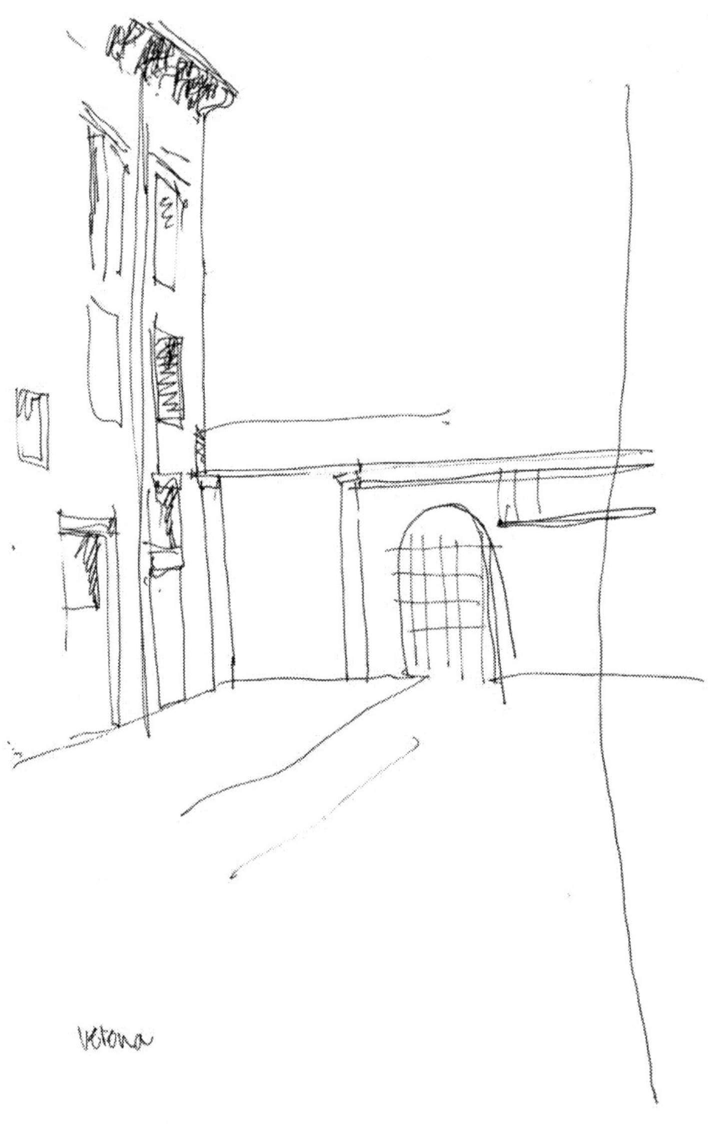

3. Courtyard near the dome in Verona

the rest of the world has seen a dramatic reduction in vocations for the priesthood and many of the substantial institutes designed for the training of the future clergy are empty. Our home had been converted in a accommodation with a wide enough mission statement to probably qualify religious and allow at the same time to cater for a wide range of custom. It appeared to be a large complex with extensive ground on the banks of the Adige not far from town. Quite good actually and so was the accommodation: high ceilings, roomy corridors with the empty sound that reminded me of the old boarding school I attended as day pupil, and a large room with a separate bathroom of decent proportion, all immaculately clean. Breakfast was included in the modest price and a possibility to have a simple but nutritious meal in the evening. The menu catered for Italians, pasta as Primo, meat as Secondo and salad bar for vegetables or Tertio, and generally fruit or yoghurt or some other desert and a bottle of table wine. We decided to stay a week. From Verona we could visit Mantova, Vicenza, Padova and possibly Ravenna. I used the Lettera d'Introducione of the Ambassador and management promised to find us accommodation somewhere near Venezia when we were ready to leave.

27 May.

The next day, the sun was out and it was getting warm. We started out to visit some of the sights. The Tourist information was very helpful in pointing out where the works of Sanmicheli were located. So we started out on the serious work. I will not reflect on individual buildings unless something that surprised me or was totally different from what I expected. Sanmicheli[16] lived up to my expectations. We visited Palazzo del Consiglio, palazzo iBerilagua, Palazzo Pompei. Palazzo Pompei was under restoration and covered with scaffolding from top to bottom. The scaffolding was covered with a mesh I assume for safety. On it they had painted the elevations of the palazzo, rather deceptive from a distance but at the corners it looks rather funny. The St Zeno Maggiore[17] impressed by the beautiful bronze doors. The panels are precise hard edged with an impressive degree of abstraction. The figures are clearly detached from the background that carries a very restraint overlay of almost decorative secondary elements to the scene depicted. The choice of episodes is Old Testament scenes on the right hand wing and scenes out of the life of Christ on the left wing. The Old Testament scenes all point to the future Salvation in Christ, the left wing showing the actual Salvation through the Life of Christ and His Crucifixion and Resurrection. The interior is impressive but for the Gothic choir. The calm static main body does not find a worthy culmination in the East. One thing that I had noticed in Greece struck me again in an early Christian Aedicule containing an altar. An aedicule normally consists of columns and a pediment. So did this one. The column however had a peculiarity that I had seen often in Iconostasis in Greece and more particular in the Byzantine Museum in Athens. The columns have a decorative knot half way up the shaft. It creates the impression that the columns are not so much there to support the heaven represented by the pediments but more to tie the heaven down and keep it present on earth. Given the Greek Orthodox view that the church was to keep God, his Grace and his kingdom here on earth rather than being a way of guiding us into heaven I thought the knots to be a natural decoration for a vertical element connecting heaven and earth. I did not recall the dates of the specimen I had seen in Athens and was surprised to see it in so early a construction and outside the Orthodox realm. Some the concepts currently regarded as Greek Orthodox could have been current in early Christianity and could explain the presence of this in the

[16] Sanmicheli 1484-1559

[17] 1045-1149

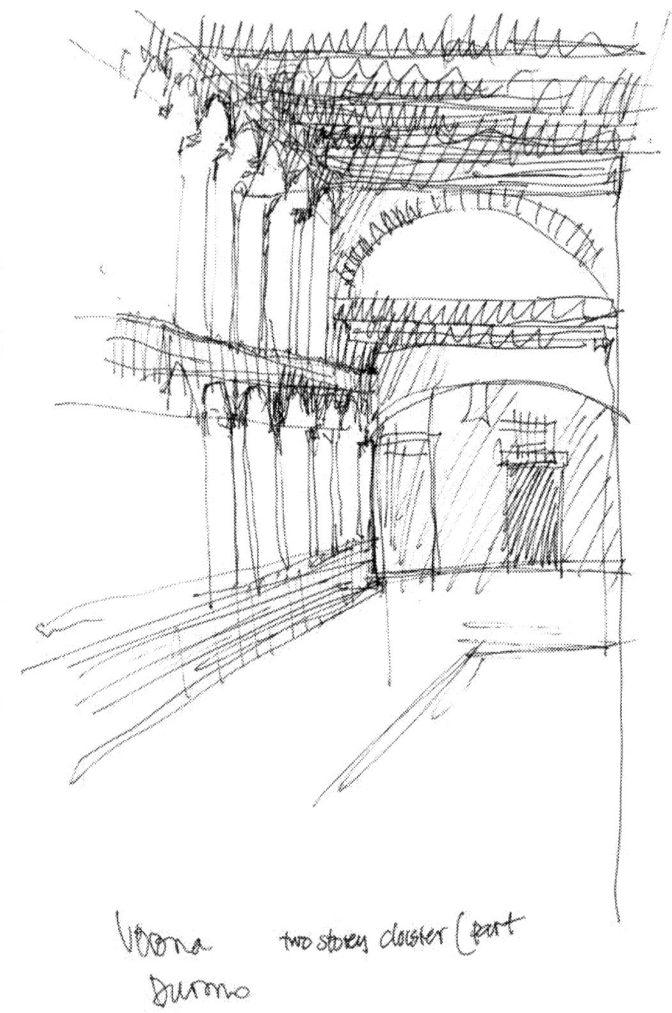

4. Cloister with double storey colonnade.

West unusual feature. We finished the work program with the Anastasia and a quiet walk through Verona and the Internet café near the castle, via Roma. We had a free parking just across the Adige in a little green area with a kindergarten. It is conveniently close to town and good exits to the route out to the north and Casa Mgr. Carera. Verona is of an easy scale. The average height is about three storey, the streets are relatively narrow and very recognizable. This makes the older part on the medieval plan much more intimate. It is near the arena, where the tourist information office is that the urban fabric starts to unravel. The large open area is not defined sufficiently to be related to any of the buildings. We decided to go to our lodgings. We had our simple meal in the former refectory. There some bar facility in the entrance hall; we had a good coffee and a Italian brandy which I prefer over French brandy. Just like the Greek brandy it generally is less sharp more velvety and somewhat sweeter.

28 April

We had plans to get on our way to Mantova early but we overslept and just managed to catch the tail of breakfast. So we arrived later than our plans. The "I" was easily found and a free car park close bye. It was now close to twelve so we had lunch first because everything would be closed till at least two if not longer. We wandered through town and visited the Casa Romano and the Casa Mantegna

I was very much looking forward to the Palazzo del Te. It is one of the most well know Mannerist[18] buildings and it displays in my view clearly what the Mannerists tried to achieve. After the classic Renaissance had mastered the use of the orders and the rest of the Roman forms and treated them rather in a static vein and often more as decorative scheme, the new generation wanted to understand the nature of the system and express that. Palladio[19] experimented with freestanding columns and engaged columns in one and the same façade (Palazzo Chiericati). Romano was very much in to expressing the supporting role of the columns and pilasters and the passive being supported character of the lintels. Even in his arches he gives the central position of the keystone an upward trust by lifting the large cover stones and leaving a gap. Those overdramatic details, familiar to me from photos worked as I expected. The Palazzo is gigantic and all is bulk expression and very, very empty. There is still a large part of the interior wall decorations and again the experiments with scale, foreshortening, dramatic gestures is a further indication that after the discovering and development of the motifs and means of a coherent artwork the Mannerist artists were experimenting to see what could be achieved by intensifying the accepted schemes and by visually interpreting the relations between the different elements. In that process they often went beyond the credible into the bizarre. But the experience gained gave the next generation the means to create the less extreme more balanced but certainly grandiose Baroque works. I enjoyed it but walking through and looking at those vast and empty monuments and there are so many monuments in Italy of the world first and second class, that I can not disregard the question of the cost of the constant upkeep and restoration. Who pays and is the vast expense worth it? Is it not a burden on the community that will increasingly be difficult to sustain? For most of the Palazzi there is no real use; you cannot turn them all into Museums. And the empty churches what are we to do with those? Seeing all this you start to question the fascination of our time with history. Someone once observed that if we had been so fascinated with history from roman times onwards

---

[18] Mannerism. Style current between 1500 and 1600 characterised by rather individual interpretation and application of the Classical style elements

[19] Andrea Palladio 1508- 1580

there would not be no place to build something anywhere. Shouldn't we pull down what can no longer serve a purpose rather than spent fortunes on painstakingly restoring monuments that we cannot find any use for? The historical importance is generally only appreciated by a few. Of course we need a certain measure of stability in our environment to be able to feel at home and connected, but are we not at the moment very much financing the hobbyhorses of the select few? To return to the Palazzo, I believe that to get some idea what Mannerist tried to achieve the Palazzo del Te is a good place to start. Romano's efforts now look farfetched but in his time he was quite "cool". We spent quite some time there until we were certain the Good Lord had opened his doors again and we could see the San Andrea[20]. I was disappointed, possibly because the interior is so much darker than the photos suggest. It is a big church with a cupola added by Juvarra, which does not distract but does not contribute very much either. I could not help wondering whether the between the wider bays with the side altars and the narrower bays with the double story arrangements is not very visible and consequently does not enliven the nave. Its main impact is the huge space and the articulation of the narrower and wider bays is not forceful enough to influence the main space. Our last visit took us to the Duomo by Romano an upgrading of an earlier Gothic church. I do not believe that the remake improved the general space. It is and remains a typical Lombard scheme. In the exterior one can see abundant indications what the original church was like. Going inside I was not convinced that the decision to upgrade was a wise one. The San Andrea was always that dark and all side chapels windowless. The contrast Church features a wide plan a high main nave and double aisle. The clerestory windows are small and reduced in size in the upgrading. The windows in the outer aisle again are smaller and less in number than in the Gothic original, hence the whole church is dark, and the size now is oppressing rather than uplifting. Mantua itself is very much less accommodating and geared up for tourists than Verona. It is not polished up and many houses are in need of some cleaning up and tender loving care. The streets often feature a paving in river pebbles with sidewalks of marble slabs that are worn, polished and slippery. The storm water drainage is predominantly towards the middle of the road draining through marble sump grates. It is a cross section for streets I favour; it creates a more intimate urban space

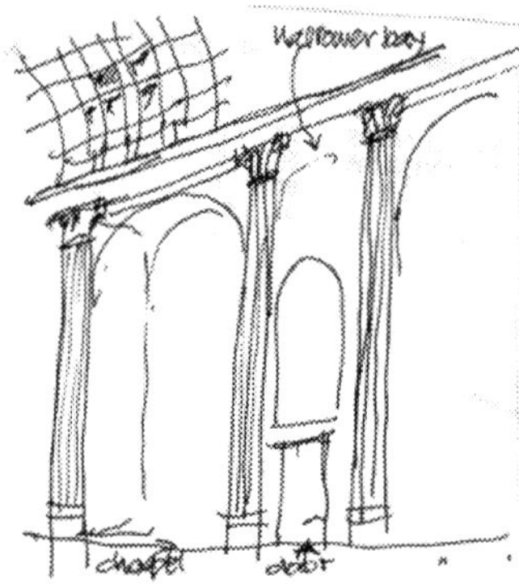

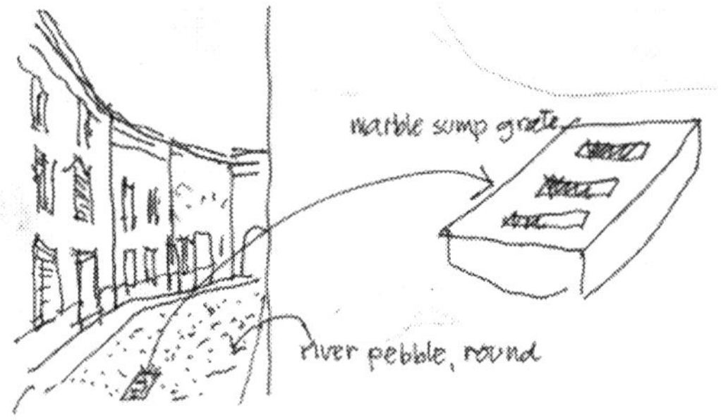

[20] Leon Battista Alberti 1404-1472

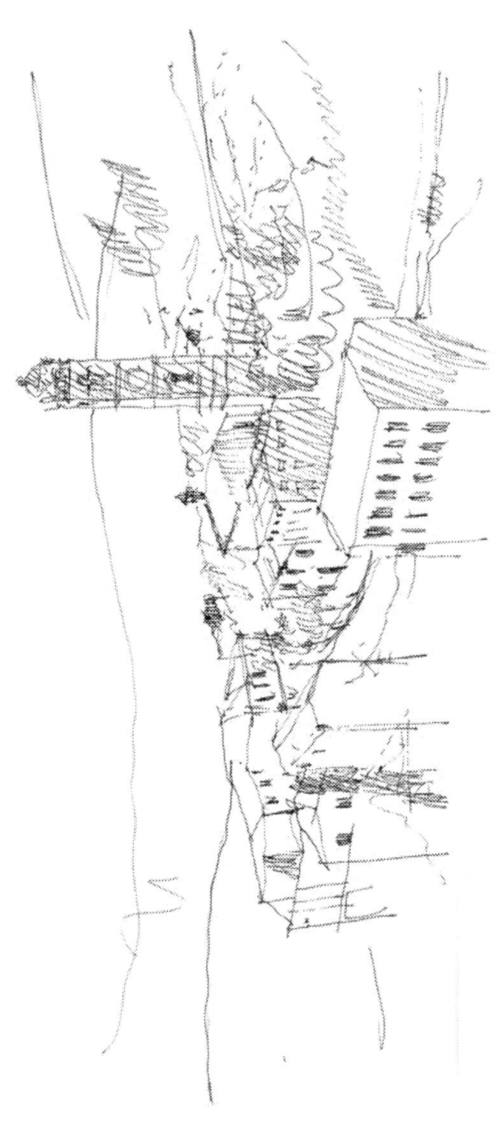

5.Bosco Chiesanuova

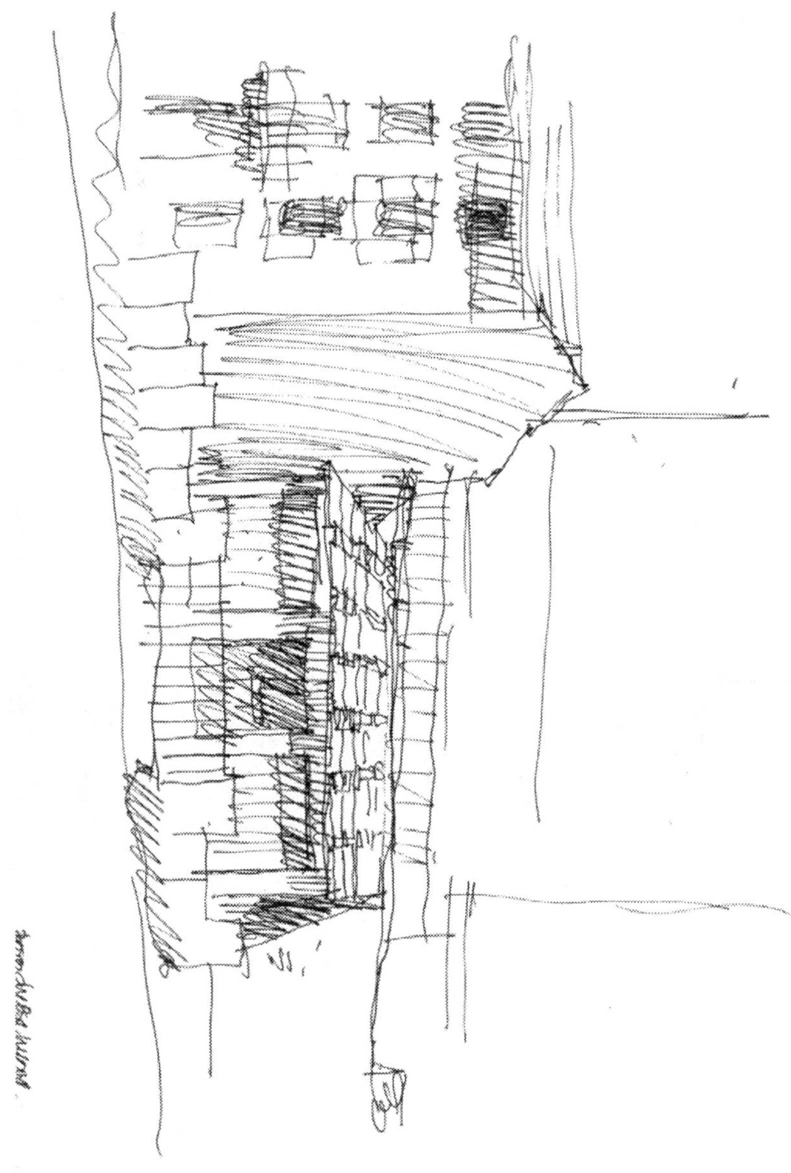

6. Bosco Chiesanuova

that relates better to the defining frontages. It also allows more interaction between the opposing street frontages across the street. But river pebbles are very hard to walk on for long; it really strains your ankles. You will get used to it I suppose and being born and bread Mantovian might give you strong and shapely ankles.

29 April.

Sunday. The plan was to go to Vicenza, but we heard that there was a bomb scare. A 550 kg WWII bomb was found and had to be disarmed or carried away. The authorities had advised against visiting the town. There were going to be all sorts of restrictions on and areas and routes closed of. Italians do make a drama out of many things and this could be one of them; so we decided not to risk driving there and find that it was not worth it and had a walk through Verona in stead. We wandered into the Duomo and the Giardini Giusti. On the walk back we had a cappuccino and a sandwich near the Ponte Nueva. The young lady was from Dutch extraction and managed Dutch complete with an Amsterdam accent. For the afternoon we drove into the hills north of Verona and ended up in Boscodichiesanuova. It was fascinating to see how early summer retreats into late spring and then into early spring with the gradually increasing altitude. When we parked the car just outside Bosco Chiesanuova it was what I remember from Holland as late March. The trees still without foliage or the first timid green showing. The fruit trees in the white veils of bloom. The suns quite warm, the wind still cool. We parked the car off the road on what looked like a forest track. My wife sat herself in the sun to read and I tried to do some drawings of the location of the village a bit below us. It is fascinating how the patterns of settlements explain and at the same time intensify the natural features of the land by just being practical about how to live on the land. It is only in very recent times that we have sometimes imposed patterns on the landscape regardless of the lay of the land. The orientation and relative position of the roofs of the little village intensifies and explains its location on the slopes of a hill. They use an interesting roof cover there-I suppose there is ample supply of easily split natural stone- It consists of large stone slabs1.2x 1.5 by 50 mm thick. They are butted against each other horizontally and overlapping in the downward direction. The joins are covered by narrow strips o the same material. I suppose that it has advantages in a mountain climate. It will be heavy so loosing tiles in strong winds will with this size of tiles not occur and there will be no eaves leaks in early spring when the snow on the roof starts melting. On the way back to Verona I noticed how the stone slabs gradually changed into tiles. The eaves and gable overhangs, possibly because they are very much exposed to uplift were the last areas to lose the slabs. There is also an advantage to have less joins in the roofing on the eaves and directly further up. In early spring the snow on the roof melts slower on the eaves where it does not receive heat from the interior. Water from the melting snow on the roof has a tendency to pond up against the snow and then finds its way into the structure through joins. Ceramic tiles have a lot of joins and the joins are not watertight at all. The slabs have only a few joins and this makes water tightness easier to achieve.

30 April.

The next day, we were on our way to Ravenna. The following day would be 1 May, Labour day on the Northern Hemisphere. So all Italy had a long weekend and many are on the road to see their treasures of the past before the tourists arrive and make it unpleasant. So we knew it
could be busy in Ravenna. It is about 220 km but we guessed that by taking the autostrada we would be able to get there well within two hours. We had not counted on getting on and of the motorway but still just two hours. We must have been lucky with the Senso Unico and all other traps that Local Authorities set to frighten vehicular traffic from penetrating the city by car. We had our 206 safely parked for

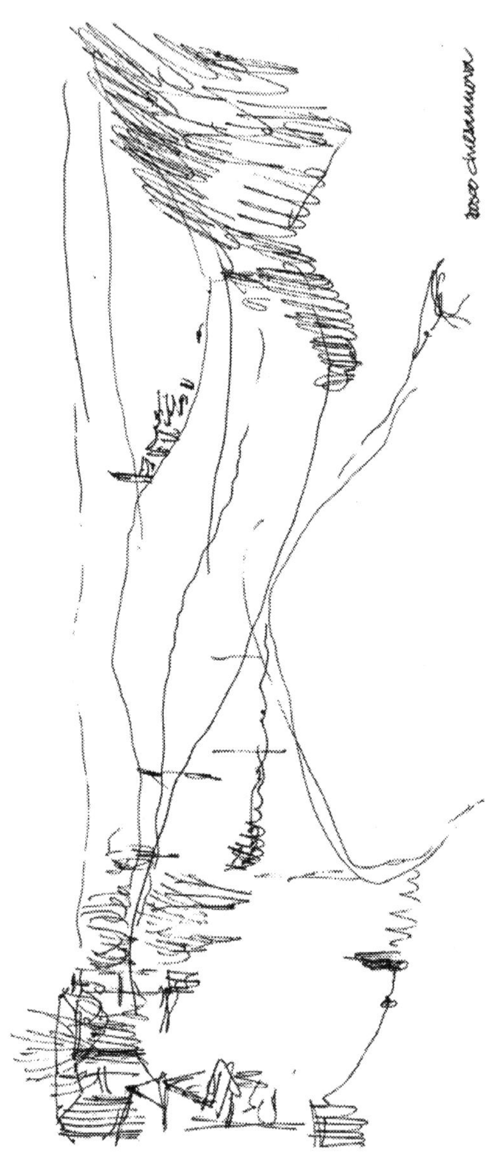

7. In the hills North of Verona

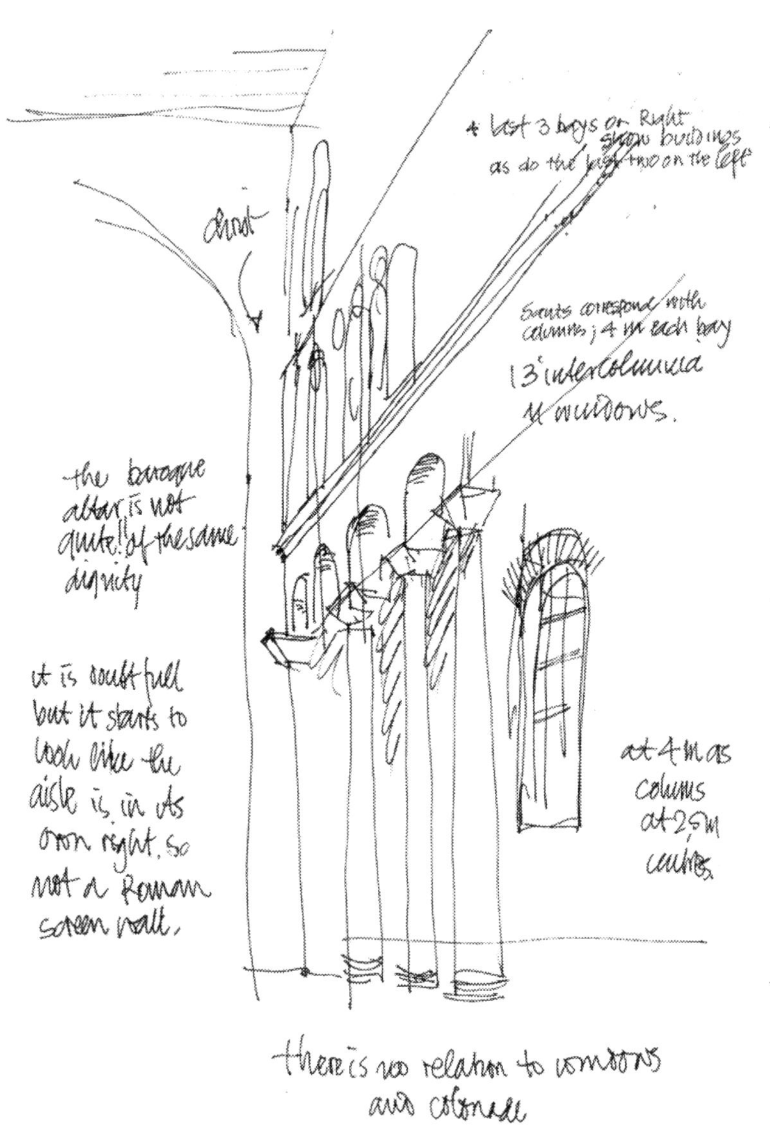

8. San Apollinare Nuovo

the day for 4000 liras just behind the Museo Archivesciville.
The Tourist information is just around the corner and the Signorina speaks English and does it well. Tickets to all sites are available at the Museo. There we found a queue that was at least two hours but luck did not desert us. I overheard an Italian conversation which informed me that tickets for all sites are also sold at the San Apollinare Nuovo [21]and that there was hardly anybody there. We with the maps of the Tourist Information found the San Apollinare no problem at all and the tickets were no problem either.
We all have seen photos of the treasures of Ravenna, times over, but to see them is different. The mosaics are splendid. The changing colour and light experience cannot be captured in a photo. The building itself is in perfect harmony with the mosaics. The Rococo addition of the chancel is insignificant in comparison. The calm dignity of the space is no competition for the Rococo chancel and altar. The abundance of detail and small scale frills loose out against the serene, simple and refined grandeur of the nave; it looks crude exaggerated and unconvincing. Christianity of the 6th century must have been quite different from the 18-century version. Leaving the church we went on to all sites. Although the two Battesteri are very similar in the themes of the mosaics I prefer the Battestero deghli Ariani[22] to the Neoniani[23]. The latter is more complete. It still has the big central basin with the elevated location for the celebrant. In both the whole interior is transformed from a material building into a stunning world of splendour, colour and mystery. The building is no longer material and any reference to the outside world is suppressed. Entering after having been confronted with the very plain brick exterior the effect is impressive. The interior does not in any way refer back to the outside and in a sense the place is not of this world but a world of a different order created by the mosaics. Leaving means with a shock coming back to reality of the every day world with sun, dust and in this case a loud bunch of Japanese tourists under the guidance of a rather brash Italian guide. I had been looking forward to the visit of the San Vitale[24] and in particular the relation between the central and secondary space I wanted to see for myself. From photos and drawings I had surmised that the secondary spaces would be not much more than an elaborate necessity of a Roman screen wall. I first had to overcome disappointment. If you know the building only from photos you have no idea that the structure is so battered. I knew the interior quite well from photos. Understandably in these photos the real condition of the interior had been carefully manipulated to show what it could have looked like, not the skeleton that has survived. The building

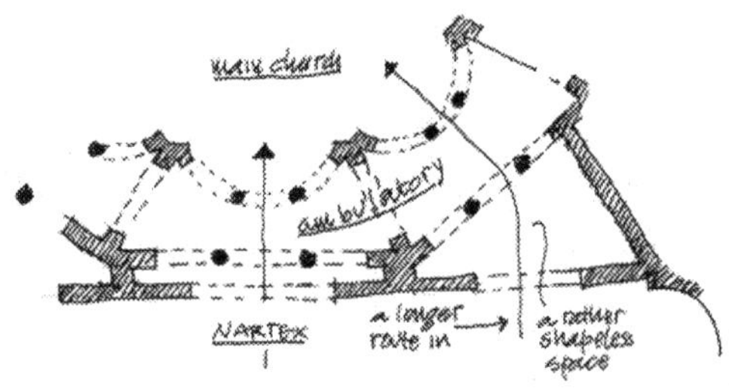

as it has survived is in its exterior the plain brick structure was as I expected. Going inside does not produce the transition into a new world like the baptisteries still do. There is too much destroyed of the mosaics and original furnishing to be able to

---

[21] Late 5th or early 6th century
[22] Late 5th century
[23] Also called Battestero deghli Ortodossi .Late 4th or early 5th century
[24] Consecrated in 548n AD

uphold splendour of the original. The frescos added do not sit well with the structure and it is at many angles hard to imagine the splendour and otherworld ness of the original. The material structure remains very visible and shows all the compromises and the not too well resolved details of the compositions. The connection of the church with the narthex is for me not convincingly resolved. The seemingly equal entrances to the main church from the narthex are in fact not equal at all. The two side entrances suffer from the somewhat shapeless space one has to go through before entering the ambulatory on a very awkward angle.

This creates a very ambiguous entrance experience. The somewhat longer route could have heightened the experience of entering a very special place by lengthening the entrance path; the unformed space and the angle of the entrance into the ambulatory only raises questions of what is what and devalues the entering. A further detail that does not show very clearly on photos is the not well-resolved irregularity of the conch containing the altar. It is slightly wider than the others and the necessary adjustment to the system is not resolved. And again as expected the central space is what the church is all about. The ambulatory is so little conceived as a space in its own right and so interrupted by the conches that it is fragmented into parts totally dependent on the central space and parts, that feel isolated, and without purpose, accidental to the concept of the central space. The light of the alabaster windows is very is very curiously yellow and dim; it must have been brighter originally, but entering the central space the effect of the mosaics must have been very much reliant on artificial lighting during the liturgy.

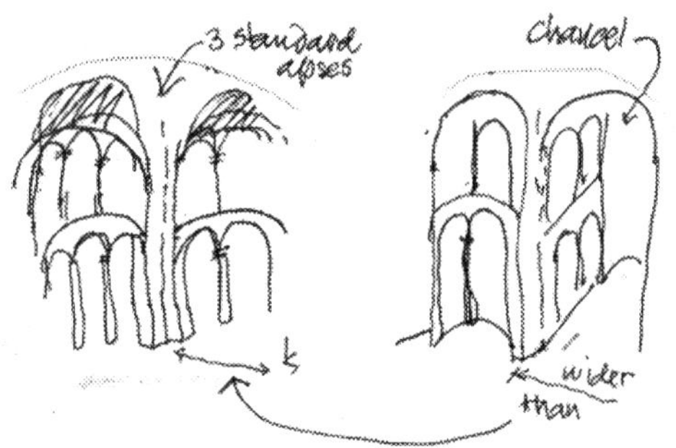

All together Ravenna is a wonderful place; you can experience space with no material definition. Covered by mosaics, the wall is no longer wall but part of a nowhere space. The splendour of the mosaic and their spatial effects is what I will always remember of Ravenna.

We went through Galla Placidia[25] and again the mosaics do make the experience, which is unforgettable, apart from a very disruptive crowd of

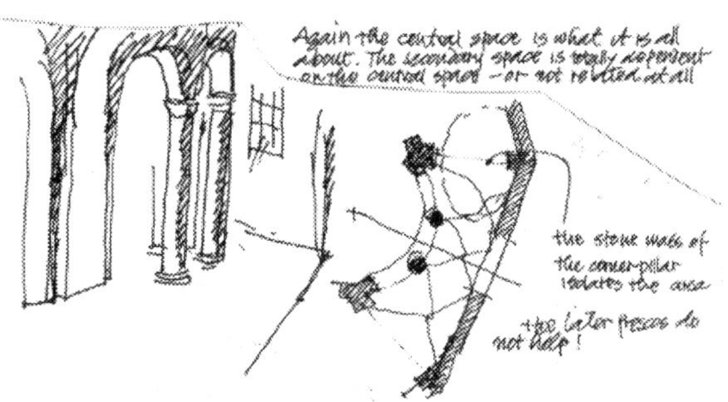

[25] 2nd quarter of 5th century

Japanese invaders under the guidance of a very rude Italian guide! How come a nation known for it formal politeness can be so rude. Wherever I have seen them on my visits this has been something that intrigued me. Are they only polite to countrymen and in their country? Do they believe that politeness is not owed to the barbarians of the West? Do they regard themselves as superior the Herrenvolk?
We ended the day in the San Apollinare in Classe with the mosaics in the apse in full glory. The relation between intercolumniation and windows is there but for some minor deviations. It is amazing how light roomy and optimistic the early Christian interiors look. The majestic peace of the apse with the green meadow, a flock of sheep under the protection of the Patron Saint of the church Saint Apollinare does suggest that Christianity then was somehow different more optimistic and cheerful Christian outlook on life, without hell, sin and the devil. There is nothing of the brooding half lit space of the Gothic or the heavy material presence of the Romanesque. We did not skip the Mausoleum of Theodoric but it is only curious for its monolithic vault and of interest for the scholar concentrating on that period; for an architect interested in the form of buildings and their interior and exterior detailing it is not a "must visit".

2 May

After a leisure day in the hills North of Verona- 1 May is Labour Day in Europe, in Italy everything closes- we finally were off to Vicenza the town of Palladio. After the Autostrada day to Ravenna we felt like a nice drive along a local road. So we decided to take the SS12 to Vicenza. This turned out to be a mistake of nightmare proportions. The distance is probably not more than 60 km. But instead of running trough a rural landscape the road is lined with industry with some houses predating the Italian industrialization dotted in. There is a constant coming and going of heavy trucks, extraordinary loads and a tremendous number of traffic lights. It took us about two hours to get there and it was gone 11 when we arrived at the Information Office. One goes to Vicenza for Palladio[26] and we were no exception. Palladio it was going to be today.
The Basilica shows that Palladio knew what he was doing. Very expertly he unifies two different buildings based on different modules into one complex. Very convincing, so much so that I do believe that most people would not notice the problem nor see how it was resolved. Palazzo Chiericati again is very convincing and it works exactly as I expected it to work. The play between engaged and freestanding columns together with the open and closed perimeter does look convincing. For lunch we went out of town towards Villa da Capra or a Rotunda on the off chance that it might be open during lunchtime. It wasn't! The villa sits on an enclave of rural peace and quiet indicated as such and protected (?); the sun was out and it was getting warm. We sat in the sun with our picnic and waited for the villa to open for the public. The villa is a surprise; its relation to the land is quite different from what I expected from all photos I have seen of it in the literature. Nowhere is the entrance, which I believe is original shown or mentioned. Nowhere is the relationship with the landscape captured let alone analysed. The setting I believe has not changed very much since it was built. I spent some time drawing to get the feel of the work. On closer observation the Villa is in need of restoration. The sculptural detail needs extensive work. I believe the villa is still privately owned but does the gate take pay for the upkeep and will it be able to pay for the cost of the restoration. It suddenly occurred to me that what would be so for the Villa Rotunda must be true for all the treasures of the past. They must be a burden. You cannot turn all palazzi into Museums. The vast expanse

[26] Andrea Palladio 1508- 1580

of the Pallazzo Del Te in Mantova, the taking of the entry tickets cannot come anywhere near the cost of the upkeep and ongoing restorations. And Italy is really covered with first rate relics of the past and not counting the sums needed to maintain the second and third class monuments-which anywhere outside Italy would be regarded as of major importance- the money involved in the upkeep must be a burden. Many of the churches- first rate monuments though they are- are still in use and maintained probably by the community and pilgrims. But Italy is almost covered with piles of stones gigantic buildings that serve no purpose and not very likely to serve a useful purpose in the future. Should the past be valued that much that it is allowed to suffocate the present and be a stone around the neck of the future?

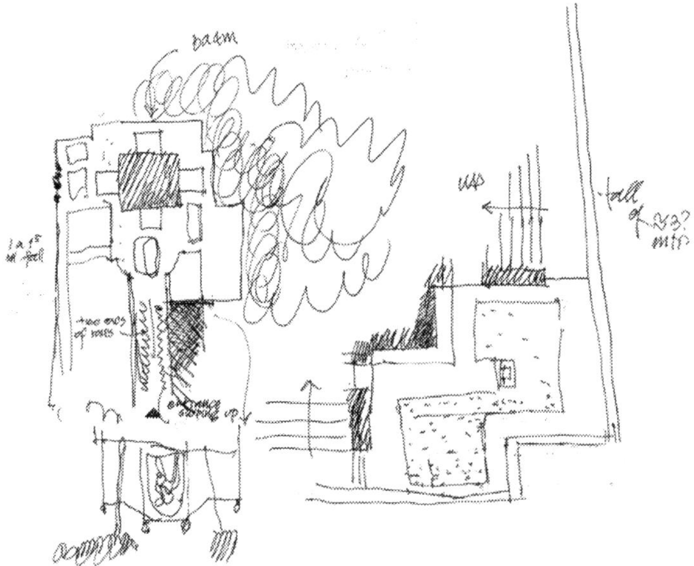

Villa da Capra. Site plan

4 May

Management of the Casa di Monsignore Carera had found us a hotel in Mirano; L'Albergo al Cinque Colonne, a bit more than the present accommodation but really close to Venice. We had decided to have a quiet day in Verona and get packed for the next shift on 4 May. The plan was to have a last look at Vicenza- the first visit had been cut short back by the experiment with the SS12- and than move on to Mirano to get us organized for Venice. On the map it looked only a short drive and that it turned out to be. We reached Vicenza in no time, proving that the Autostrada may be boring but it certainly a lot faster; we arrived at 9.30. We had not been in the Teatro Olympico[27] by Palladio. It is a curious interior trying to be an outdoor classical theatre. The scale of the stage with the foreshortening of the streets is very interesting. It suggests being ¾ full sizes, which has a strange interaction with the scale of the auditorium. The theatre is very small and has an intimate feel. I would

[27] 1530

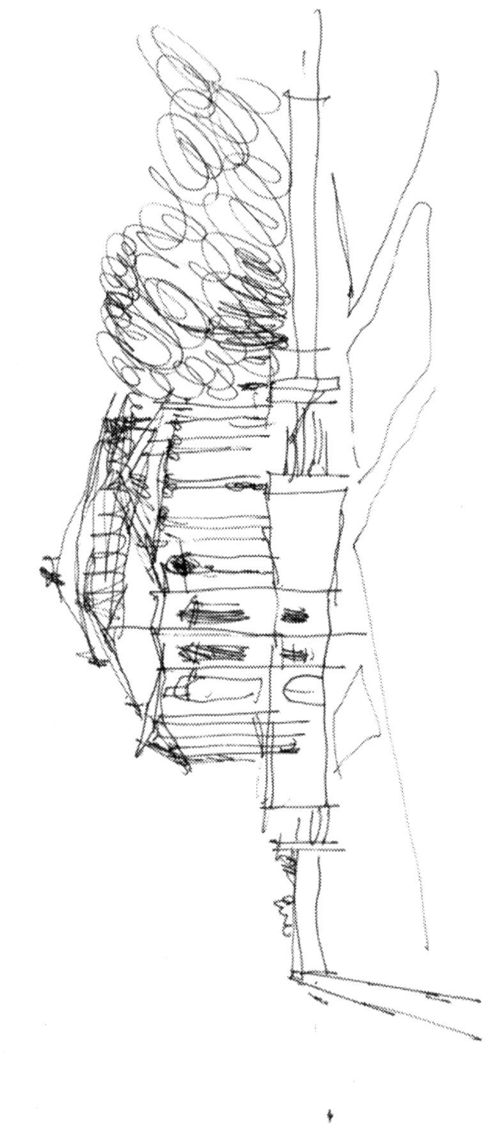

9. Villa da Capra or Rotunda

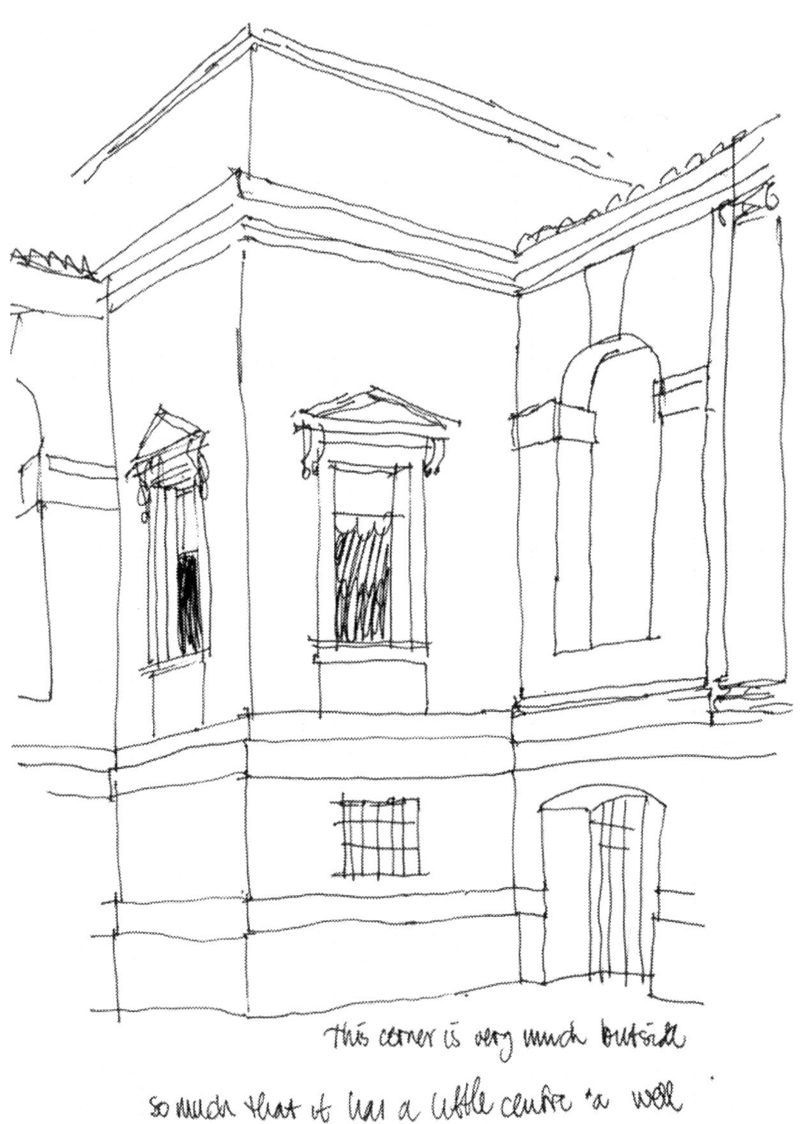

10. Villa da Capra. Corner

like to see a performance of a play there to experience how the make believe world of the play merges with the equally make believe world of the building. Empty it looks very much in waiting for something to happen. The palazzo Chiericati looked even better the second time around. The Basilica on second viewing is even more convincing. The clever way in which two existing structures with different structural bays have been seamlessly joined into one exterior is masterly. He certainly knew what he was doing

After lunch in the Giardini we went on our way to Mirano. All went like clockwork apart from some confusion after we left the Autostrada on the secondary roads to Mirano. Signposting seems like so often intended for those who already know their way. For first comers that poses some difficulties, but we got there in the end.

Mirano is a little town 10, 15 km from Venezia. It is relatively unknown and there is little to indicate that it is geared up for tour.

The hotel was quite attractive with a bar and a restaurant. Both looked and proved to be of a very decent standard. The town is big enough to support a few restaurants so we knew we did have to eat in the hotel every day Mirano has an excellent bus service that takes you straight to the piazza in front of the railway station in Venezia and the main station of the Venetian public transport is nearby. We bought tickets for the next day, had a walk through town and a meal and were prepared for Venezia.

So far Italy had not been that chaotic. It was early enough in the season to have only a few non-Italian tourists. Of course there was still quite a good many tourists but they were mostly Italian school parties or older people taking advantage of the relative calm and the by now quite agreeable weather. Apart from a few cold clear days in Torino and Milano the weather had been quite good

We had a meal in one of the restaurants somewhat above budget and were ready for Venezia.

Venezia

4May.

The trip to Vicenza taking the Autostrada was a pleasant surprise. We were there at 9.30 a.m., which gave us all the time we needed for the Teatro Olympico and another look at the Basilica and the other works of Palladio. After lunch in the Giardini we were on our way to Mirano, which wasn't to far. We managed the intricacies of road signage on secondary routes and booked into the Albergho and investigated transport to Venetia. The man in Verona had done a good job. The little town is big enough to support a few restaurants so that you don't have to eat in your hotel if you don't want to. Quiet and away enough from the tourist track to be reasonably priced and close enough to have an excellent connection wit Venezia. To celebrate the success of the shift to Venezia we indulged in a meal that was somewhat over budget. But it was worth it. Italian cooking is generally quite good. The amount of fatty stuff is minimal, the pasta variations are really god the attention to detail and service is good. We never went to expensive restaurants but modest restaurants provided good service and good food with high standard of presentation, and an attractive wine list.

5 May.

We had bought the tickets for the trip the day before. There is no ticket buying on the bus, you have to get those at outlets in town in a Tabacchi. We found the bus easy enough and it all went without a hitch. Moving around in Venezia is really easy. You don't have to decide anything. There is one option only. Buy tickets for the public transport system and work your way into town. The map we had bought in Vicenza was to small a scale to be useful but we found the ticket office. While I was queuing and we were working out what to buy a one-day free pass or a three-day. We were more or less deciding on one-day tickets when my wife was offered a three-day ticket with still one valid day. An American tourist did not want the ticket to go to waste; she was leaving and could not use it. It was valid till very late in the afternoon. With one-day ticket we were right. We took line 82 which takes you through the Canale della Giudecca city.

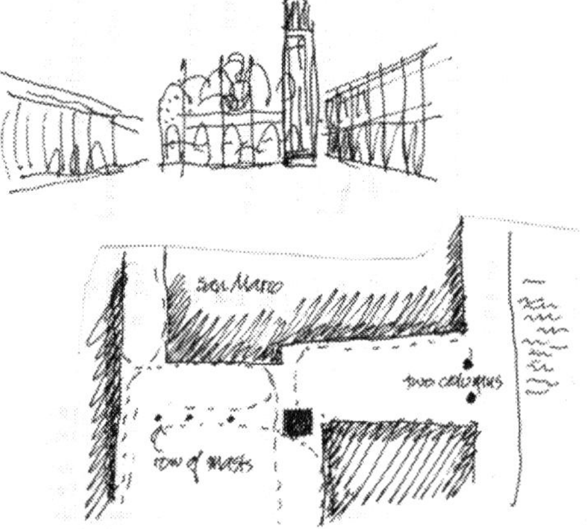

The entrance around the harbour and than from the open or seaside into the Canale Grande and on to the quay the Riva deghli Scavioni, a bit away from the Doge Palace near the Ponte dei Sosperi Marco and into the city. We walked up to the Ponte de Paglia onto the Molo and turned along the Palazzo Duccale into the Piazzetta and turned into the city. The entrance is magnificent, more impressive than I expected. The spatial composition is full of subtle detail. In relation to the Piazzetta and Piazza the San Marco has a situation very similar to the Duomo in Milan; a large rectangular square with very repetitive definitions and at the end a very massive but very frilly building. The Duomo works well; its size and very detailed exterior do dominate the large square and control the space. The San Marco is equally successful in dominating the Piazza San Marco and the situation has some additions that do articulate the large space. The Milan composition lacks the surprise and richness the Piazza San Marco has. The openings on both side of the Milan Cathedral are of similar size and lead up along the cathedral. This strict symmetry has nothing of a surprise. In Venezia the San Marco is connected to the mass of the Palazzo Duccale, the campanile narrows the Piazza and indicates the beginning of a screen wall and at the same time suggests a pivot in space. The screen indicated by the Campanile is completed by the four masts. It creates a smaller forecourt to the San Marco. The Campanile anchors the composition.

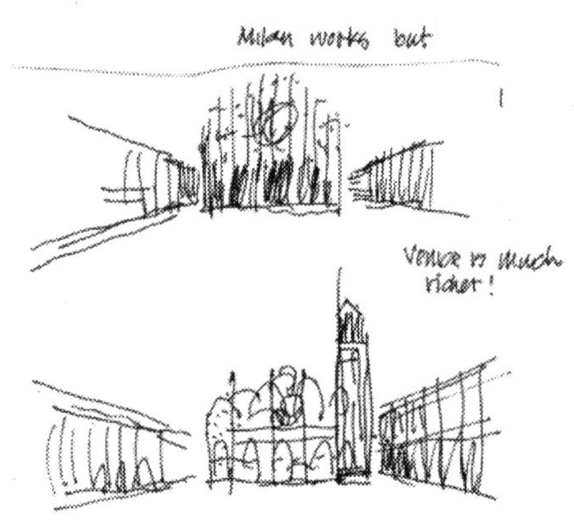

Rounding the campanile the city suddenly opens to the sea. The Palace of the Doge is just the building to do it; the smaller accessible scale at ground level and the grand gesture of the closed surface above to give it the impact and size required at that spot to achieve the grand scale opening the sea requires .The two columns are a secondary gate and show what Venice is all about, a gateway to the sea and the world beyond. The dome of the San Giorgo is distant enough to be over the sea and close enough to be a destination, symbol of all destinations reached by sea. The rather dull and repetitive wall opposite the Palace of the Doge has very little importance and it just needs to be there to define the space not demanding any attention, which would distract from the main experience the relation with the sea; the two columns and the sea beyond; the gate to the world. I had not expected it to be so moving and strong. The visit to the San Marco we managed to get in and the lights were on. We had a good look at the mosaics, which are of a varying quality. But it gives a good impression what a fully finished San Vitale would have looked like. From there we had a walk to the San Zaccaria. The intricacies of not loosing your ways in Venezia are not easy mastered, but we found the church, but unfortunately it was locked. God apparently had a day off.

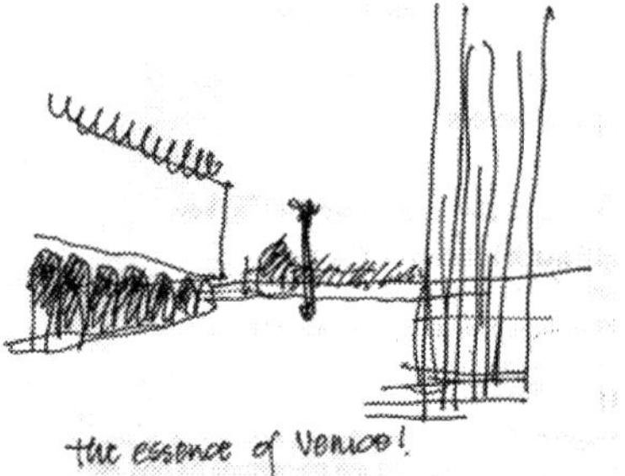

So back at the sea we boarded no 4 and sailed down the Canal Grande. It is a grand view. I will not count the different Palazzi, but Venezia, at least at this time of the year is a pleasant surprise. I had expected it to be one large tourist attraction a "ville morte" living of its past from the tourists. But that was not the impression at all. Public transport on water was busy very busy with ordinary people who live and work in Venezia. There was a lot of traffic on the Canale Grande and the water busses are real public transport with all the normal routine aspects of people pushing to get on or just missing the bus and fuss about awkward luggage and old ladies loosing things. We interrupted our trip at the Rialto Bridge. There were a lot of people but mostly Italians. It is of course completely oriented toward tourists, which is reflected in the prices for the usual horrible and mostly fake product associated with Venezia.

But at this time of the year Italians apparently take the opportunity to visit the sights in their country. So Venezia was still very much in Italian hands. I am not certain that the urban life is strong enough to take in the enormous influx of tourists in the summer. But it was May, the weather was nice and a smell of sea pervaded the city. It is exciting a thing to go back to. We had a last stop at the Marcolo an oasis of peace and quiet. We decided against walking to the Ghetto; it was Saturday, Sabbato in Italian and Sabbath, so all would be closed. Near the Piazzale Roma we had tea and beer watched the crowd until we felt it was time to go home.

6 May.

It's Sunday and all Italy closes down.

We decided to skip Venezia. We would have another day there. We tried our luck with Padova. It appeared to be a "Dominica Environmentale", a car less Sunday in the city center. We entered Padova near the San Giustina and the Prato della Valle and found a car park on large empty space along Via Carducci of the Prato della Valle. Michelin said that the Information office was there but a local said it was near the San Antonio. We found the San Antonio and had a look inside, for me from a Catholic background it was something from 40 to 50 years back. The devotion for the Saint and the expression of it was something I forgotten all about. But it is still alive and has taken on modern forms. You can still write your question for San Antonio on a piece of paper and put it in the box; Saint Anthony will look into it and help you if it is in your interest. Now you can also E-mail your cause to the Saint and pray for the best and his assistance.

The church was filled with people not tourists but pilgrims to San Antonio seeking his help. It looked authentic and very much alive. The church was packed there was a mass going on amidst the mass of pilgrims queuing for a glimpse of the Saints tomb It was noisy hot and we quickly went outside for lunch.. After lunch we found a small exhibition that was open during the dead hours. Donatello and his Contemporaries, mainly from the Padova region. There were a few pieces of Donatello some lesser know and a not too large collection of smaller bronzes.To see some lesser work of the great name and having that side by side by work of the lesser coryphées gives it all a sense of relativity. Even the master has bad pieces that do not stand up, and the lesser names do produce work of the same of quality as the master. It was an ideal exhibition enough to take in.

When we came out we went for the Duomo. A very clever design, but it could not convince me. The structure is clearly expressed in gray and white but the space does not come to life.

The Prato della Valle has me puzzled. It is an unusual arrangement of a vast Piazza with a definition that is not strong enough to contain it and an unusual feature in the middle; a very much designed oval with statuary in it. It is very formal with a moat around it, four bridges leading up to the treed lanes that follow the main axis of the oval. It floats in the middle of the vast space; going up to it and leaving it one has the distinct feeling of crossing a desert of no mans land. The whole piazza is too large and does not come together. On the west side the space gradually drifts out into emptiness. The bars and cafes etc and outdoor seating gradually can no longer fill the place. The relations between the central oval and the urban fabric are unclear. The triangle that could serve as a forecourt to the Santa Giustina is not formed; it is just a corner cut off by the road. The relation to the big park or green area on one side is unclear. I have given it much thought but still do not know what to make of it.

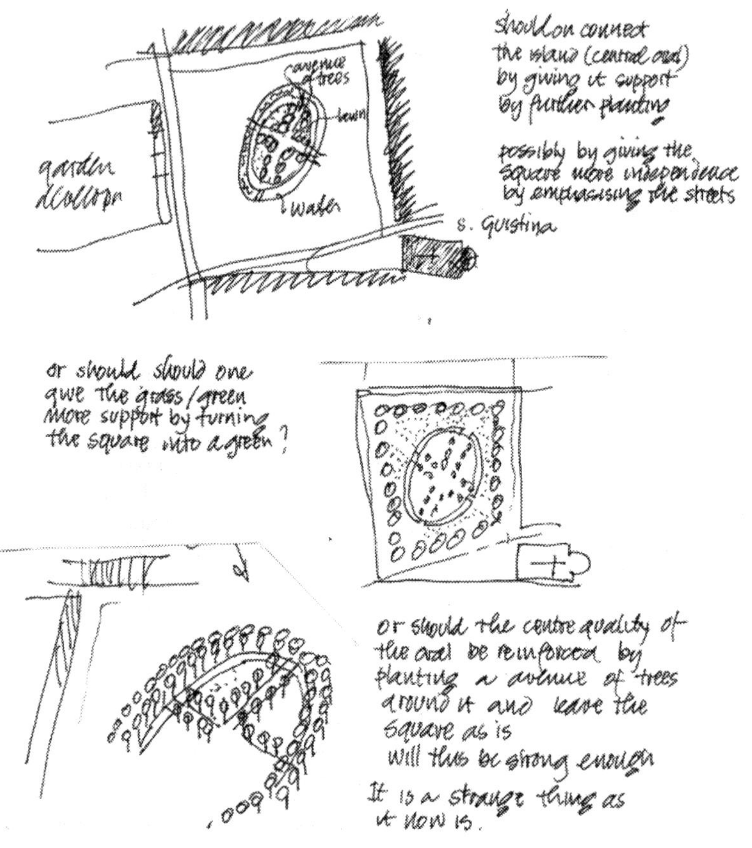

7 May

Venezia the next day did not disappoint. I found it more exciting than the first time. But there is too much to see. We only took in the general quality of the urban texture and the relation with the water. We visited the San Giorgio and the Santa Maria della Salute and ended the day with a walk through the ghetto. It is a fascinating city with many different aspects. A place to go back to! The arrangement with the hotel in Mirano was quite good; reasonable prices, a quiet town and good transport to Venezia.

8 May

We had a walk around on the market in Mirano-My wife bought an umbrella and I four pair of cotton socks, more suited for the hot climate, for about ten dollars, the best buy on the market and we were off to Villach Austria.

Wien

8 May

We find ourselves in Austria for the first time other than passing through. The difference with Italy is striking. Austria first impression is calm, quiet, well behaved, clean, and rural; pretty with an undertone of prettyish. Biedermeyer Gemütlichkeit, middleclass. Villach our overnight stop on the way to Wien has a large pedestrian area; mainly a low speed mixed area and everybody abides by the rules. There is no aggressive or expressive driving, no parking outside indicated areas, no two wheels on the footpath, all just as was intended by the law. It is all well designed, organised and clean, very clean. No instant signs on bits of cardboard, no litter, no noise, no smelly cars, all very polished. The tourist information in Austria is very helpful. Staff speaks English, they even books you in a Gasthaus or Bed and Breakfast. In Italy they only provide you with the information and you are on your own for the negotiations and the final deal. So we had a decent room on the Rennsteiner Strasse and enough time to have a walk around and a decent meal. After a good night rest we were ready for the next bit up to Vienna. We had decided not to go into the city itself, but to start at a smaller town outside Vienna that looks to be close enough to have good connections by public transport. Our search started in Baden south of Wien. The man in the Tourist information looked a bit unusual and uninterested, but was competent enough to organise some advertising for his pamphlets he was going to print and find us a room in Breitenfurt in the Wiener Wald. It was a bit of a search but we got there all right. It appeared to be a Gasthof, which is a local pub and restaurant with some accommodation. It is the perfect rural setting on a hilltop in an undulating countryside with very attractive views over a valley with some forests, very quiet and very close to Vienna. It was very early in the season and there was only one more guest, a young man who had to do a job in Wien. We settled in and made arrangements for our evening meal and went for a quick drive to Liesing to familiarise our selves with the situation around the nearest railway station, just within the boundary of the Vienna urban Transport system. Tickets valid on the Vienna Underground are also valid for the railways up till Liesing. For about $ 50 we had four days of free transport to Vienna and in Vienna itself. Not bad. And getting to Liesing was no problem. There was parking near the station free for all day. And being not very big and next to the station it was perfectly safe. The Frau Wirtin had assured us that it was absolutely safe and she was right

10 May.

Off to Wien. The tourist information office is very busy and Staff not very interested. They also have a big warning for art lovers in the form of a quotation of Kurt Kraus" Ich muss den Aestheten eine niederschmetternde Mitteilung machen: alt Wien war einmal neu." [28] With that in mind we are ready; we have a map of the town and public transport system and the sun is on our side. We find our way to the St Stephan and we have a look inside. The coffee on the platz was good. The weather is a bit chilly and after the warm days in Italy a thing to get used to. Especially the wind is still cold. But out of the wind and in the sun it is quite balmy.

The Karlskirche[29] was a big surprise. I always had my doubts about the front: the arrangement with the two columns and the dome. On photos the arrangement does not work; it looks fragmented with the two columns dominating the composition and the dome hardly interacting. In real life it is very impressive. The columns do interact

---

[28] I have a devastating message for the aesthetes: Old Vienna was New once.

[29] By J.B. Fisher von Erlach 1716-1729

with the huge dome and bring the dome more to the front. It is now a large-scale composition whereby the two columns are the entrance to the church, which is the dome. The real entrance in the form of a temple front is the second entrance framed by the first. The two side pavilions give the size of the complex and the necessary backdrop for the two columns. On entering one is not disappointed. The dome that is so dominant in the exterior is there and the size is as expected. There is an exciting contrast between the monochrome exterior and the colourful interior. The colours do support the structural articulation. The tall Corinthian order supports the main spatial definition. Between the columns is a second smaller order that opens up the wall in the main order; it forms the structure in all eight intercolumnia and the altar structures. The lighting of the high altar is lifted by additional windows, which allow it to work quite well as the main focus under the dome. It is an impressive work!

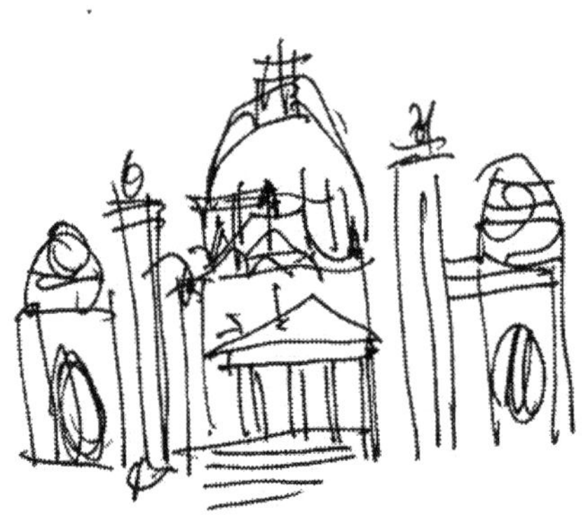

As the wind had died down we felt like enjoying the sun and decided to use our free urban transport and enjoy the sun and to have a look at Schönbrunn to see the gardens. The gardens are conceived in relation to the palace and terraced up around some waterworks. The scheme works on the relation between garden and building. Unfortunately the garden side of the palace is weak. There is too little emphasis on the central block to give the garden front scale and articulation necessary to be the base of the central axis of the symmetrical garden lay out. The terrace or balcony as an extension out of the belle etage is far to flimsy in its detailing to be convincing.

11 May.

Our second day in Wien. We saw the churches we had on the program; the Dominikaner Kirche, the Franciskaner Kirche, the Jesuiten Kirche. The Dominikaner is clearly based on the Il Gesu scheme, as is the Jesuiten Kirche. The Franziskaner Kirche is a Gothic refit with a not too successful integration. We felt that we had earned some refreshment and ad lunch somewhere on the Kohlmarket. The weather so far had been quite helpful but in the afternoon it started to rain. Museums are always good for shelter in such cases. I do not like museums very much. I feel that a museum is too much of a concentration of first class work to really appreciate the artistic merits of the individual pieces by lack of contrasts with work of the lesser masters. Furthermore you are tempted and often seduced to see too much, because there is so much that you would like to see. After an hour or so you are totally exhausted and no longer capable of taking in anything. This time we wanted only to see some of the own collection of the Museum. There was an El Greco exhibition on and for reasons of practicality entry to the own collection and the El Greco exhibition was covered by one ticket with a raised price. Luckily we found that tickets for senior citizens with an extremely healthy discount were available at a window opposite the normal. Armed with a little plan we started on the own collection. The collection of Dutch and Flemish paintings of the 15th, 16th and 17th century is extraordinary. There is too much quality there to really appreciate in one afternoon. There are hall full of Rubens big pieces. You cannot help to be impressed by Rubens talent to control a very large canvas and the control he must have had over his workshop. But in his

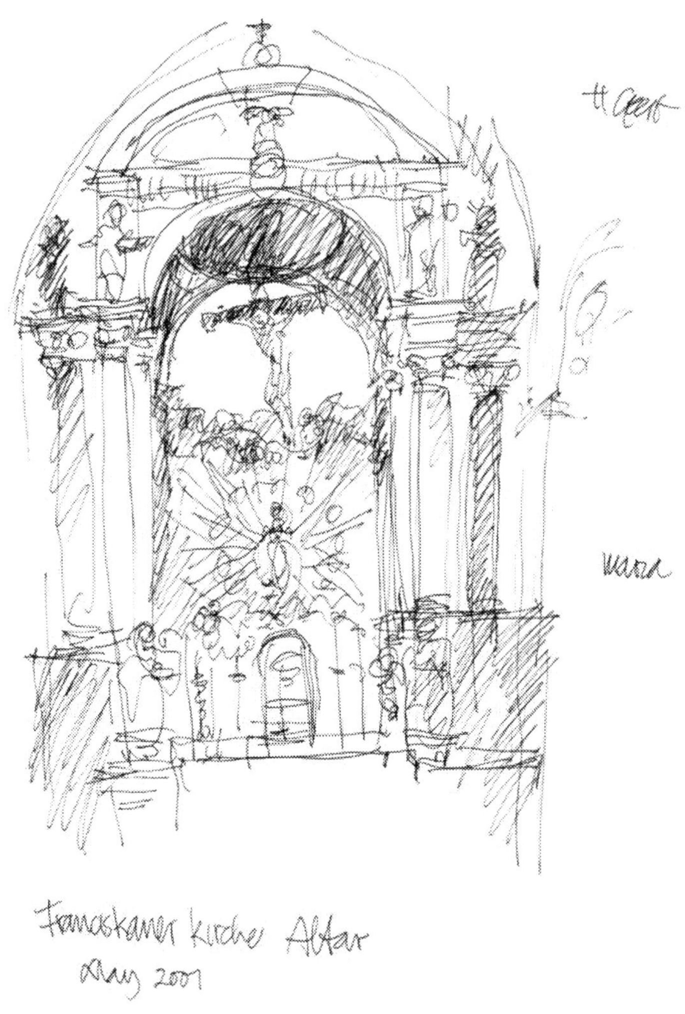

11. High Altar Franziskaner Kirche.

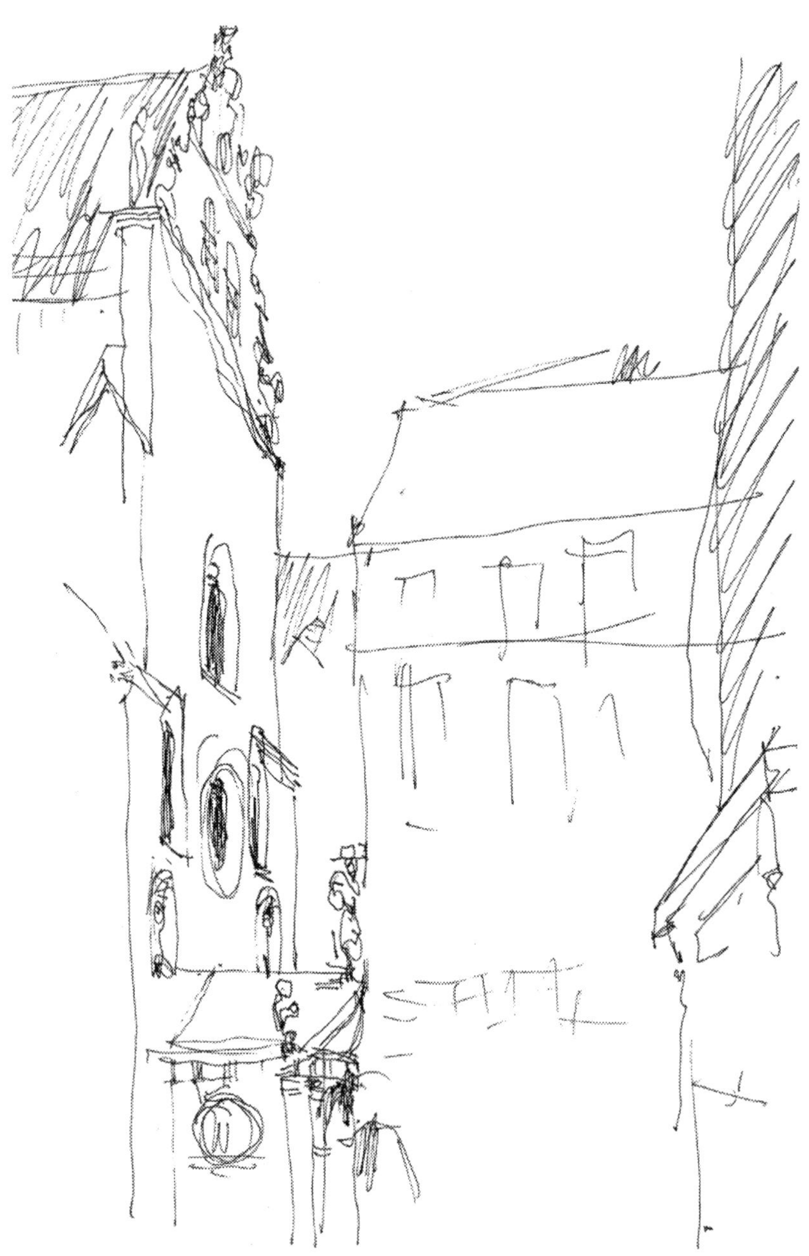

12. Exterior Franziskaner Kirche

portrait of Helen Fourmet you can see that he could also paint besides running a well organised and extremely profitable picture factory.

The museum is a real treasure and to see it all you need to really prepare yourself and have weeks of daily visits. I remember an odd six self-portraits of Rembrandt all famous or very well known. I believe they all need cleaning; they look green yellowy. From cleaning up the "Nachtwacht" we know that there is a lot of colour hiding under the varnish. The same goes for the Breughels. But they are still impressive paintings." Hunters in the snow" is an extraordinary beautiful painting and moved me deeply. Having lived for years in Brabant the region the Breughels lived and worked in, I recognised the landscape in its general texture. It looked so familiar and real; I mean so much the very essence of it that you recognise it, without knowing the precise location. There will probably never have been a precise location for his landscapes, but Breughel knew how it had to look to be real. I did spent some time with Avercamp, but we had to skip the rest. As it still rained we could not resist El Greco, we decided to have a look. It was again a surprise: the vibrancy of the colours and the way he paints. It looks to me that he was not overly interested in depicting visual reality, but focussed on creating rich textures of colours so bright and vibrant that it is a miracle that they stayed in the same plane of the canvas. The fire: one big, dominating splash of textured orange somehow dominating the canvas without destroying it. When we came out the rain had stopped.

12 May.

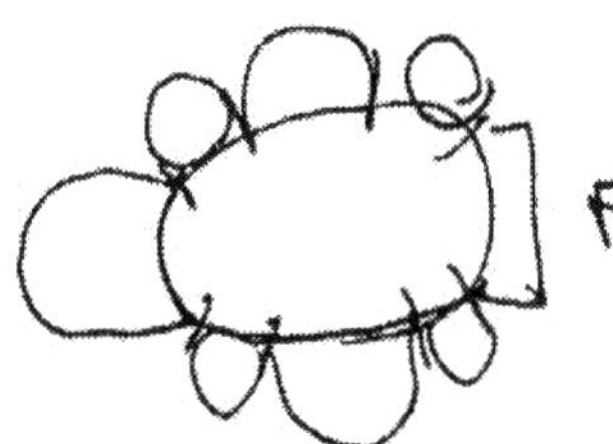

We had the St Peters Kirche[30], (fig 13) Schotten Kirche[31] on the program for the morning and the afternoon for the " Prater" But before we tried to find an Internet café. We had talked with some students near the Karlskirche and they believed that there was one near the Schwedentor. But there no one seemed to know. As a last resort we looked for a telephone box. When we found it we had the surprise of our life there were two directories there, in cardboard cover and all paper pages, both pristine condition. There is an Internet café on the Hoher Markt off the Stefanplatz.

And it was user-friendly bar a German keyboard with double strike to get the @. We then started to see that Wien is a remarkable city. Its urban lay out is still very much medieval with a 18th and 19th century definitions. There is a vast amount of outdoor seating related to restaurants and coffee shops. And similar to Italy it is easy to get a decent to good warm lunch for a very acceptable price. From what we saw people do take a warm meal at midday and a substantial for that matter. The lunch menu with the much more competitive prices is not available in the evening. Choices are fewer; prices are a lot higher. But Vienna did not strike me as a real international city like the others capitals of the European countries; it has a quiet, well-behaved population. There is no graphitti that I recall no litter, no hooning around in cars. From the telephone directories appearance it seems that public vandalism is no problem. I remembered that even a provincial town like Napier has for some time now abandoned the service of telephone directories in public phone booths.

[30] L.Hildebrandt.1702-1708

[31] Carlone 1638-1648

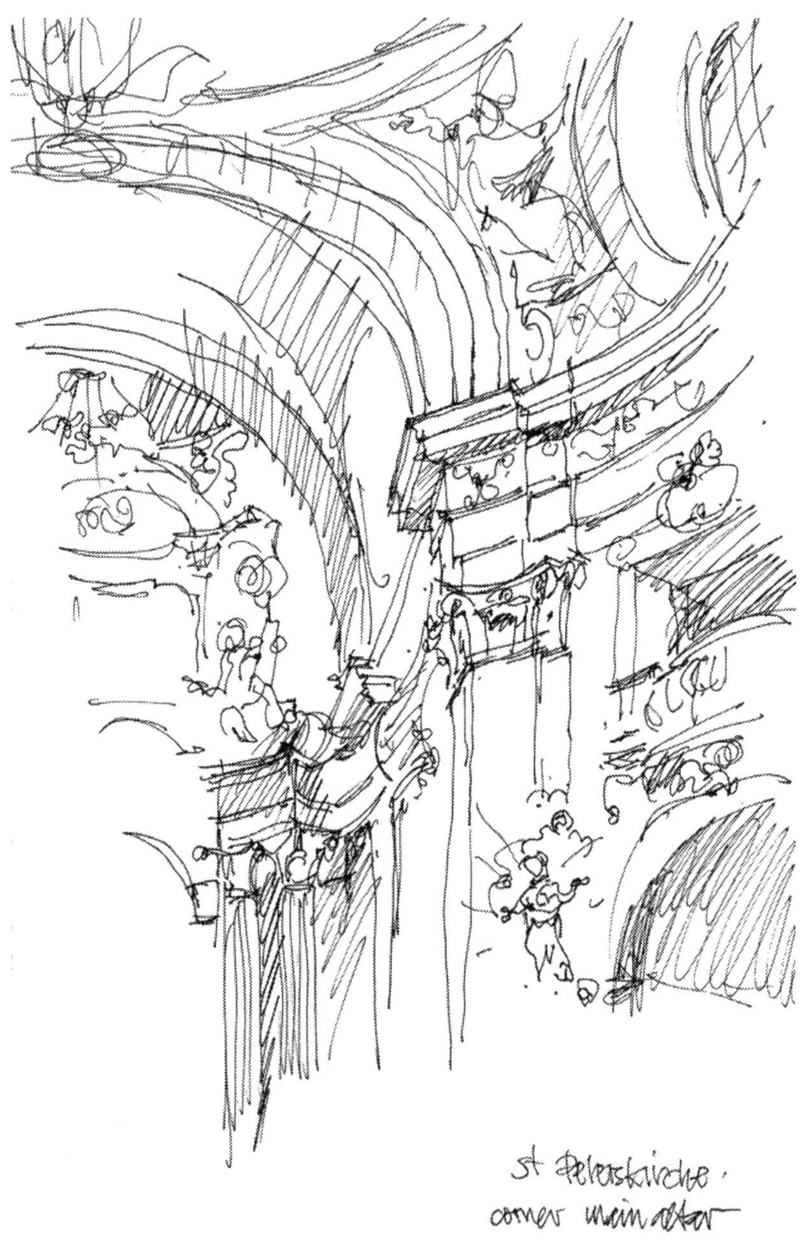

13. Corner of High Altar St Peterskirche

In Vienna near the Schwedentor they do exist, amazing! In the gardens of Schönbrunn we met a Japanese girl who told that she had gone for a walk through Vienna in the vicinity of her hotel at midnight and at other occasions had walked home trough town and had not encountered anything that could vaguely be regarded as frightening or risky. The traffic is unhurried, not aggressive. The language on the street is German there are hardly any tourists around. Vienna has more of an oversized provincial town than a centre of contacts between east and west and the gate to the Balkan. It is so tidy, well organised well behaved and polite. But you get used to it and it is a blessing to be able to walk around without having to be alert on all sorts of dangers lurking behind your back and the necessity of mistrusting everyone on the street.

The afternoon we walked through the Prater. It is a large permanent Fair that gradually runs into a large park. The chestnut trees were in bloom the sun was out it was spring again. The wind was still chilly but that was on account of the Eisheiligen the Ice Saints. From 10 to 15 may the Roman Catholic liturgical calendar celebrates Saint whose names all end on "ius" They were known in my youth as the Ice Saints. To my surprise they were still known here by that name. I found out that going to Austria brought me back to the devotional practice that I had known till early fifties in the Southern Provinces of Holland, but that had disappeared within a few years after the renewal of the Liturgy that had swept through the Dutch Roman Catholic Church. Here it was all very much every day practice and part of life as if time had not moved on.

13 May. Sunday, our last day near Wien, and we had planned on a walk through the Wiemerwald. We had three maps that did not quite fit together, so we had some difficulty in finding the walk through the Wienerwald we had planned for our last day. Road marking and signposting on the secondary and tertiary roads will undoubtedly be very logical and clear to all Austrians but we found it difficult. At last we found the starting point and were off. On our wanderings we strayed into some sort of round valley artificial it appeared. There was an explanatory sign stating that it was a zodiac circle with the tree species connected to that part of the zodiac planted in the particular location. The whole circle was divided in about 40 intervals. Each interval is about nine days; three intervals are 27 days. Each interval has its own tree species. As always you look up your own birthday to see what tree is your tree. A Salix Alba does not immediately bring up an image nor did the species tied to my wife the Acer Campester. The whole structure professed to be based upon old lore and could be beneficial for those who would know how to use the knowledge. How exactly we could not find out and we did not have enough time to study it in great detail.[32]The Wienerwald is a stretch of hill country west of Vienna. It is gently undulating with some little streams that have cut in very narrow valleys. It reminds me strongly of Luxemburg but there are some differences. Pine forests are not very prominent. There is beech as in Luxemburg but there are plenty of oak stands, very uncommon in Luxemburg. In the more urban areas there is a lot of horse chestnut. They were in bloom at the time it all is very pretty. It was a pleasant walk not exactly what we had planned, but a good walk with some splendid views on Vienna. But to enjoy the walk and the landscape in a relaxed walk you need better maps than we had. There seems to be a booklet with extensive information on walks in the Wienerwald that covers also the parts not within the city boundary of Wien.

---

[32] I have noted part of the full circle:9, 3-12 Salix Alba 13-22 Tilia Cordata,24-3?10 Corylus Colurna,10,4-13 Serbus Domestica, 14-23 Acer Pseudoplatanus and so on.

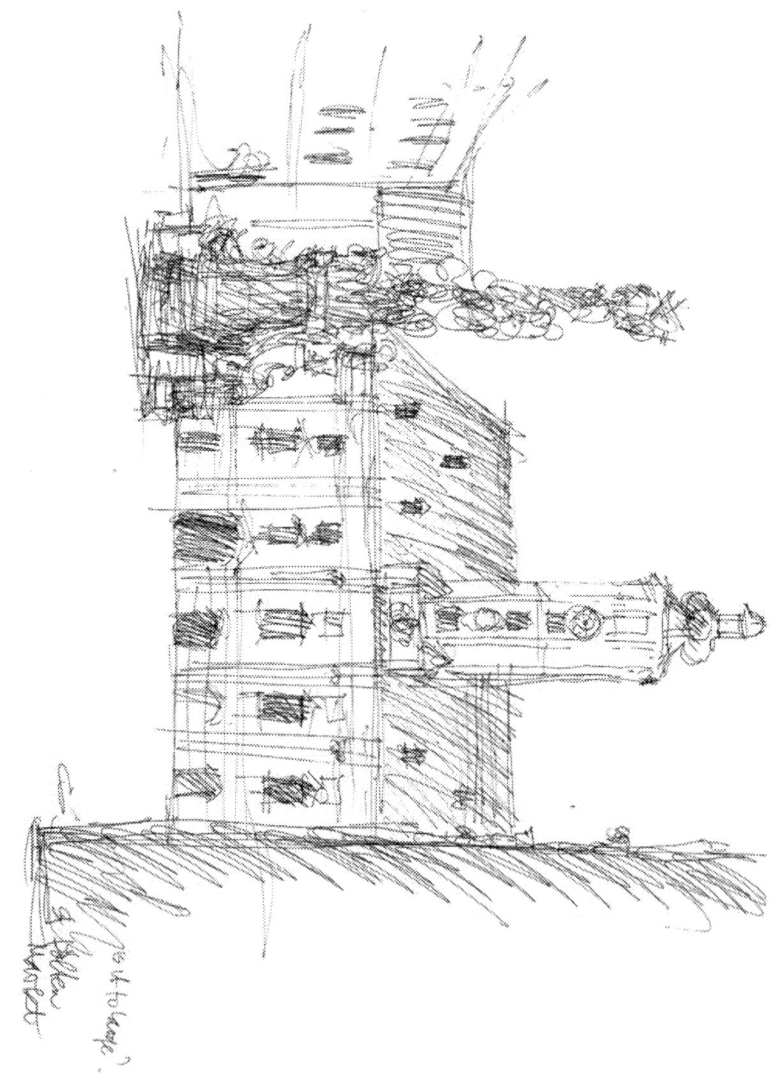

14. Marketplace St Pölten

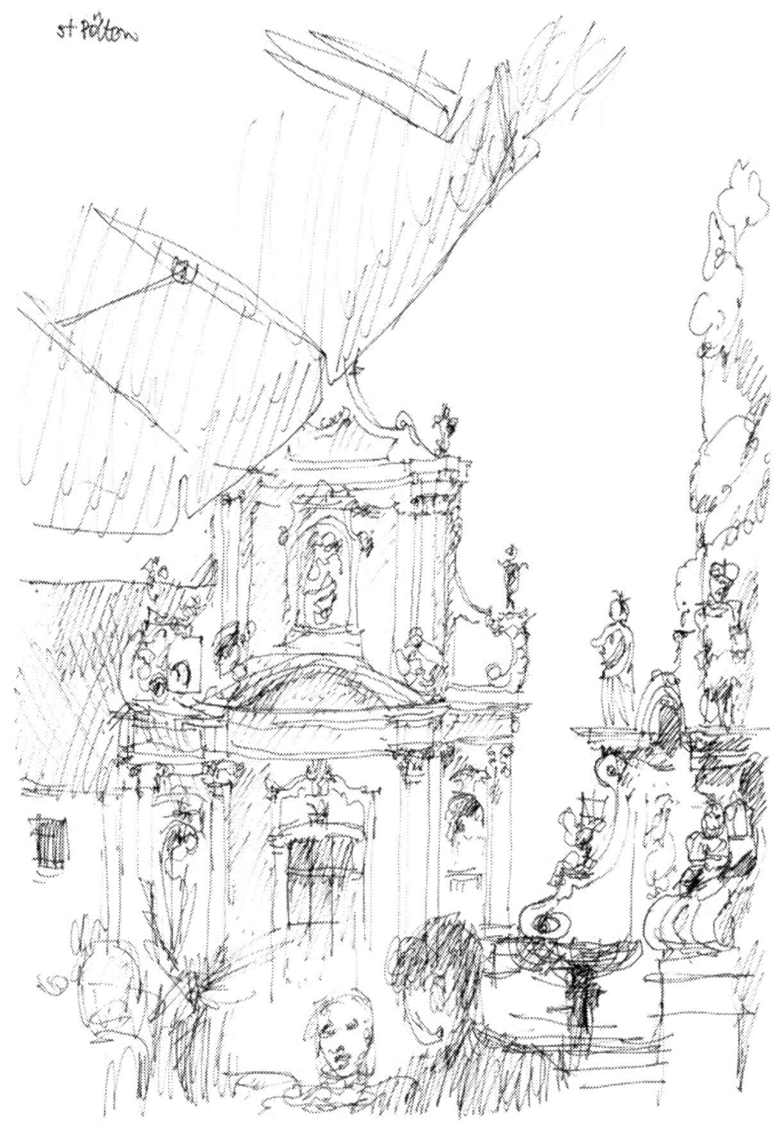

15. Coffee on the Market Place St Pölten

An ideal short holiday now could be a week or so in the Wienerwald. The place in Breitenfurt is quite suitable as the home base. Good connections with Vienna. The car trip to Liesing is about 15-20 minutes; parking is unlimited and free near the station. The railway connects up with the U-bahn and within the hour you are on the Stefanplatz in the centre of Wien. It is a bit far from New Zealand but living in one of the large conurbations in the North West of Europe for instance it would be a good spring holiday. We picked the right season. The weather was mild; the sun is warm without getting too hot. The green has not jet lost its freshness and there are not many tourists around. It is beautiful and Austria is clean relaxed, sleepy it sometimes seems. Very easy going for visitors. It looks like a very rural society with all the signs of strong social control and very traditional views. It might not be so good a place to live all your life if you want to have and proffer original and new ideas!

14 May.

We are off in the direction St Pölten and Krems to find residence for some time to visit the Rococo in Nieder Östereich. St Pölten as a first impression is a sugar town in pastel yellow and pink with white highlights on the structural decorations. The Rathausplatz is completely surrounded by Rococo buildings in pink and yellow. We are not certain about the pink it could be caramel with a dash of raspberry juice, but the yellow is definitely custard. The Rathausplatz is what every body expect an Austrian Rathausplatz to be: clean sauber without the rush and hustle and bustle of modern life. (fig 14) The platz is very large in fact too large for the height of the defining Buildings around it. It looks empty not only because there is hardly anybody there but also because of its size. The central area is well outside the influence of the surrounding buildings and feels very much outside and empty.

The Rathaus at one of the shorter sides and the Church on the other are not important enough to hold it together.

After a cup of coffee (fig 15) we decide to go to Krems on the bank of the Donau and Krems and leave St Pölten for a more extensive visit later.

Krems is a different town; in many ways more alive. Its location is interesting on a very steep bank of the Donau it follows the, for want of a better word, Plaka structure: main streets parallel to the contours and steep connecting streets sometimes with steps. It looked more interesting and with some assistance of the Fremdenverein we found a decent place to stay in Senftenberg a few km upstream along the Krems. It appears to be a Kurort for elderly people- we did not realize that we both over sixty and looked very much like the real patients. It is amazing how easy it is to forget ones age. But being "under roof" as the Dutch saying goes, we could quietly plan for the Rococo the next day starting with Altenburg.

Senftenberg.

15 May.
The program for the day was a visit the "Stift[33] Altenburg[34]", Maria Dreiechen[35], Wüllersdorf[36].

The trip to Altenburg leads us through the valley of the Kampf, a tributary of the Donau running north, quite enjoyable.

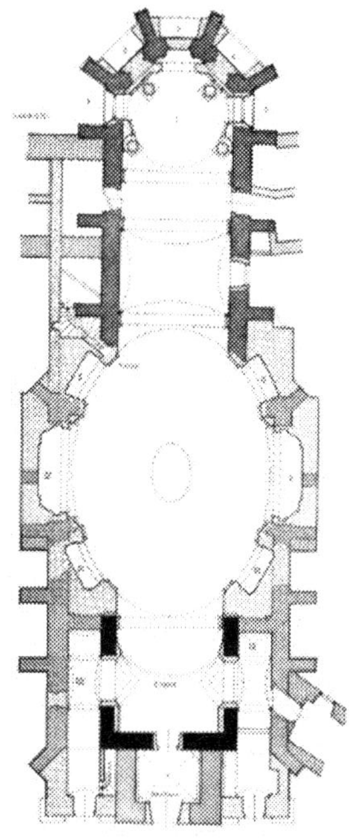

The Stift was our first in Austria. We were not really prepared for the sheer size of the monastery. We had no idea of the vastness of the post Trento [37] religious building program in Austria and Germany. The number of buildings, the size of the monastic complexes and the intricacy and extent of the decoration is something that gradually dawns on you. The building industry has not changed fundamentally as far as techniques and labour content goes. A rough estimate of the costs in today's terms is not too difficult to come up with. It is hard to understand how the vast sums of money needed to build these enormous and richly decorated complexes could have been extracted from the faithful. Most of the returns of the lands belonging to the Stift must have gone into it and being a farmer working the land belonging to the Stift must have been a life of poverty or very modest circumstances. To us in hindsight it has a feel of extreme feudalism and arrogance. I must admit that looking at the splendour created, I soon forgot about the poor farmers that had to pay for it al.

We decided not to visit all the buildings, there were going to be more monasteries so we had a good look at the church only. The rather flat and non-sculptural exterior (fig 16) does heighten the transition into the exuberant colour full and rich interior, dominated by an oval dome. The church is an extensive re building of a Gothic church with a long history of alterations and additions. The narrow chancel is in its dimensions the late 13th century chancel

---

[33] Stift: religious foundation, generally a monastery or bishopric

[34] Muggenast.1730-1733

[35] L. Wissengrill 1744-1750(attributed to)

[36] J. Prandtauer 17265- 1733

[37] Post reformation synod of the Roman Catholic Church (1545-1563) which in an effort to roll back the Reformation dramatically changed the Catholic Church.

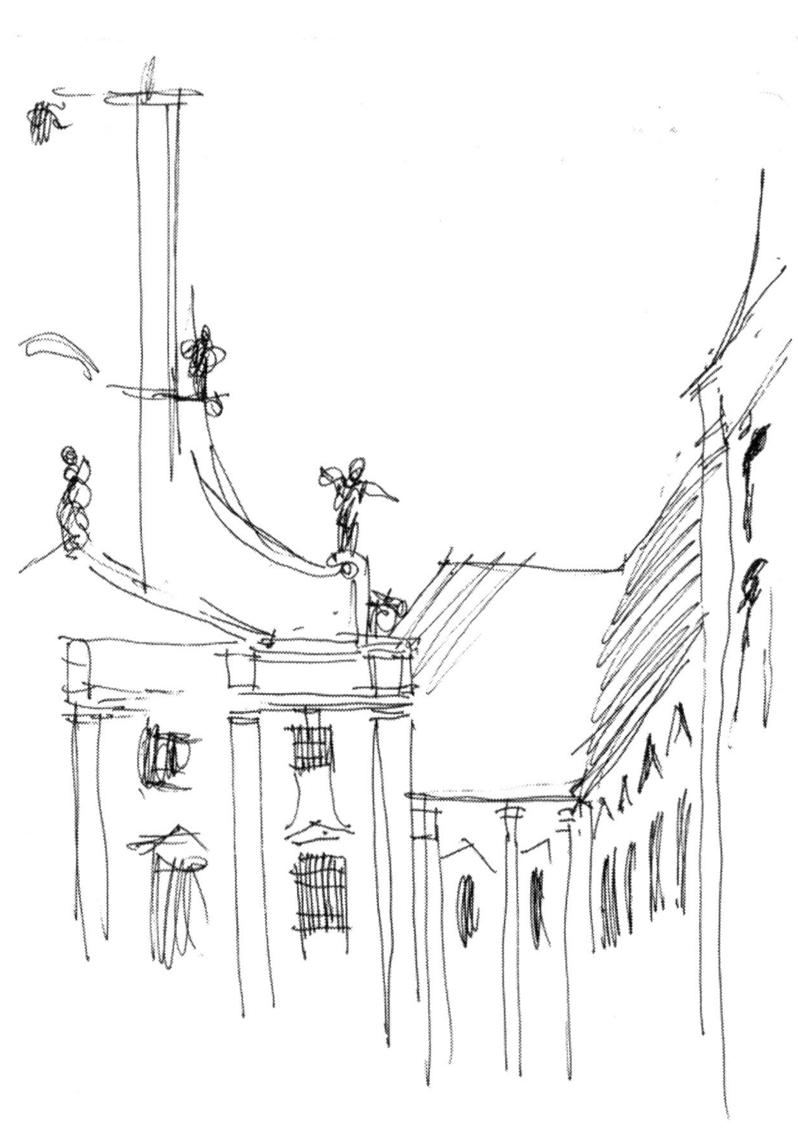

16. Stift Altenburg. Courtyard with entrance to the Church.

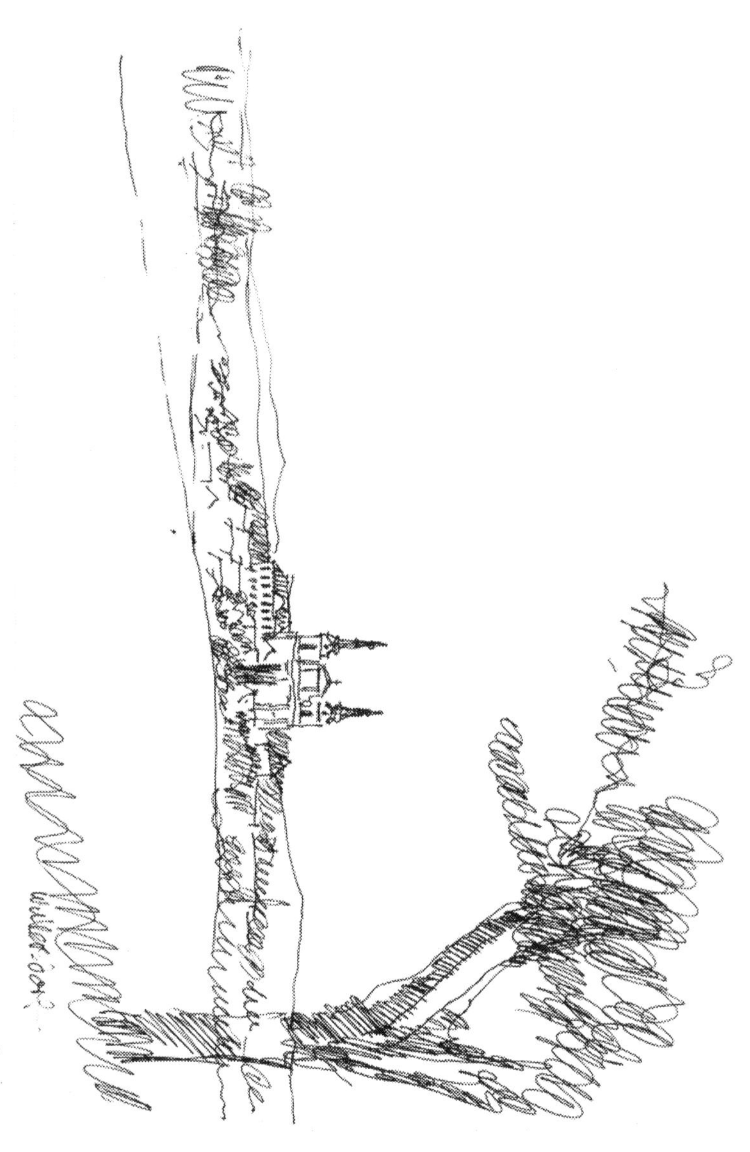

17. Approaching Wüllersdorf

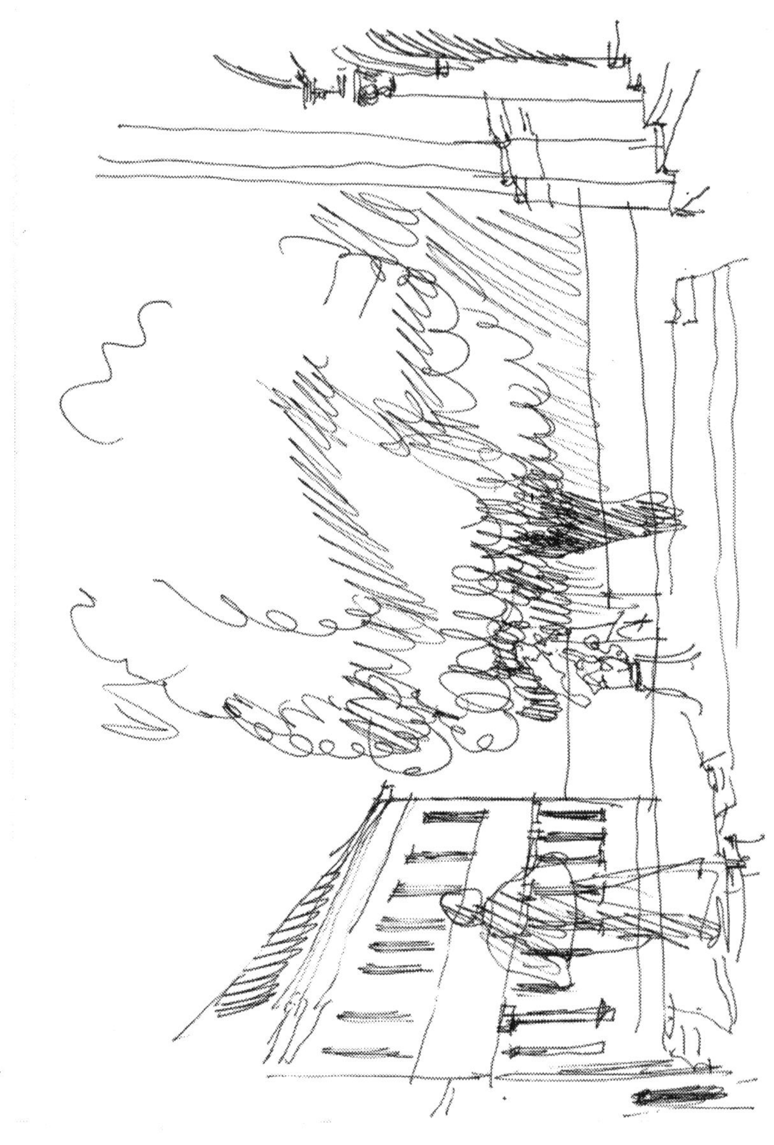

18. Wüllersdorf. Forecourt

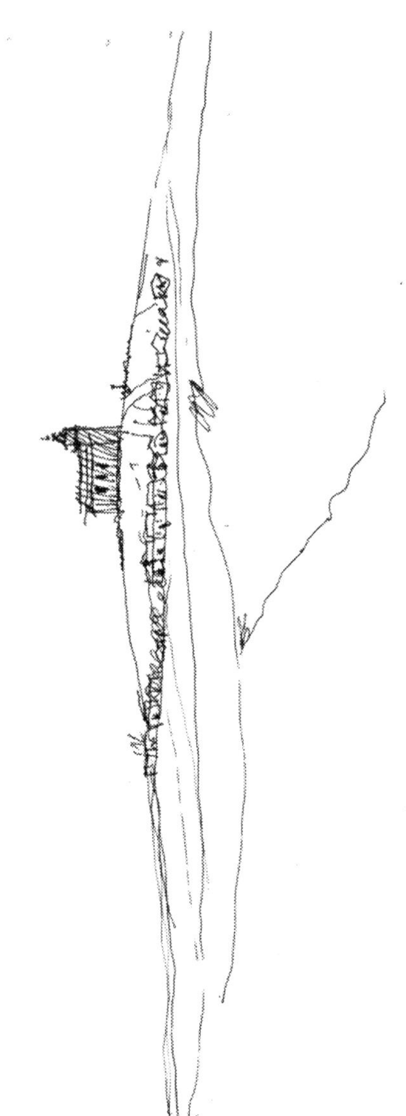

19. Wartberg .Along our way to Ravelsbach

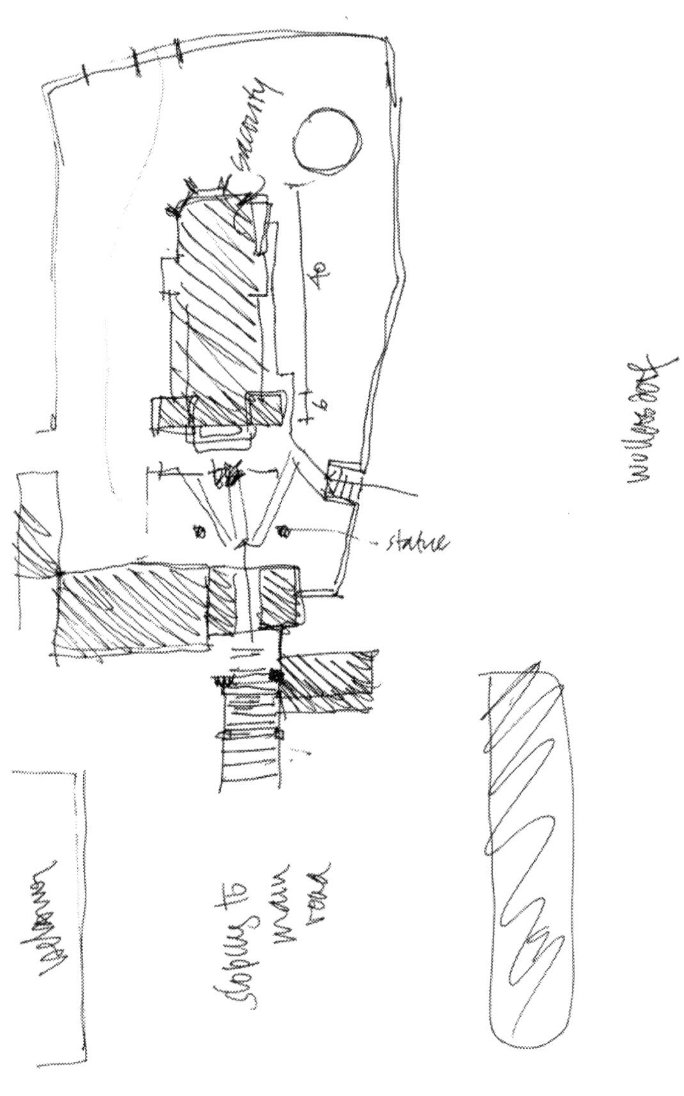

20. Site plan of Wüllersdorf

The dome uses the full width of the 15th century church, but no recognisable feature remains. The core of the tower, which is set back from the entrance, dates in its structure from before mid 12th century. The central dome is supported by pilasters with Corinthian capitals, which in turn rest on the entablature of a much larger structural colonnade of Corinthian pilasters that includes the chancel. Under the dome the spacing of this order is alternating: four main spacings and in between four much smaller spacings. In the chancel the order includes four full round columns round the high altar. The plan is in essence not different from die Wies Kirche, (see page 150) but the effect is quite different. There is a clear separation between structural and decorative with very little effort to dissolve the distinctions. The structural elements of the high altar are conceived as part of the structural order and although freestanding round columns they are in appearance very much part of the main structural frame. All in all a very attractive interior although one could maintain that the chancel is not fully integrated. As we were there at a relative early hour (10 a.m.) it was all very quiet and peaceful. We enjoyed the visit.

In planning the itinerary I had included a fair number of what are believed to be not very first rate churches. By having a trip that includes only the highlights you tend to loose perspective on quality; amongst the giants a slightly shorter is quickly regarded as a dwarf. I found later that even that is not enough to keep a reasonably perspective on the quality of the work so we included churches in little towns nowhere on any of my three-tiered lists.

From Altenburg we left the Kamp valley and turned east to Maria Dreieichen[38], which did show that there is difference in quality. The plan also shows a central dome and a similar alternation in the dome support. It is in the integration of the interior that this charming church was not so convincing. The same goes for Wüllersdorf (fig 17, 18, 20,). Here the impact is mainly in the situation. From far it dominates the landscape and the village and announces its presence miles around in the fairly flat only slightly undulating landscape. In the direct approach the raised position of the church is enriched with a sequence of entrances. The road opens up to a forecourt sloping up towards a set of steps. From the landing at the top of the steps a vaulted gate way leads through the Vicarage- also a large mansion-- into the precinct of the church, which is a large elevated platform. Walking round the church you have beautiful views out over the peaceful rural land. The Church itself is modest in its quality of the interior and furnishings. It suffers from a not fully coordinated concept of church and interior. This dominance of the church in the landscape showed itself in a somewhat frightening form in the arrangement of Wartberg (fig 19). The almost threatening towering church sits on top of an empty hill with the houses of the village huddled together at the foot. The contrast between the size of the church and the size of the individual houses and the village as a whole had something frightening and made us think.

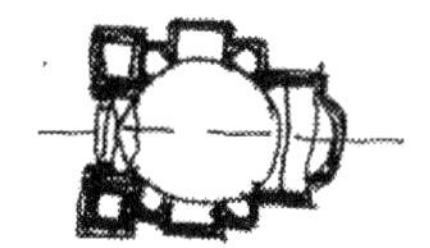

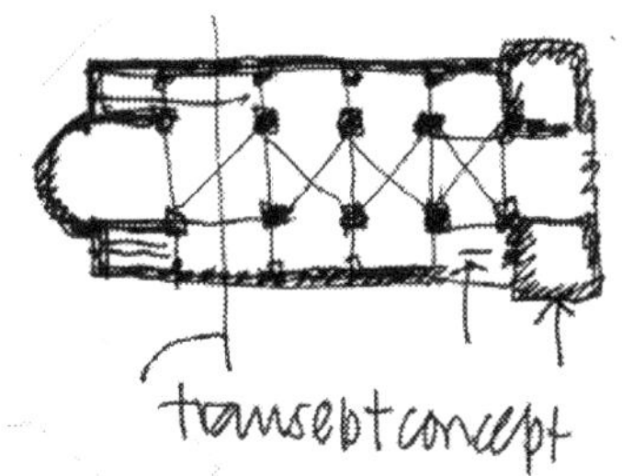

We ended the day with a visit to Ravelsbach

[38] I. Wissengrill(?) 1744-1750

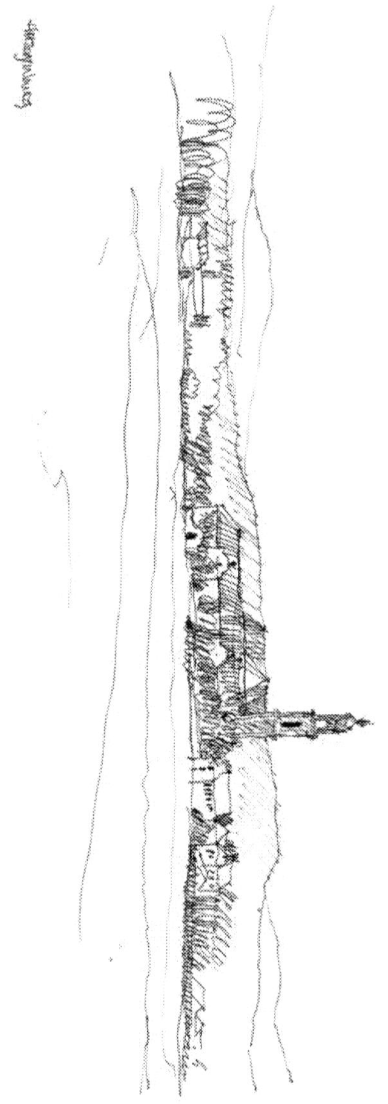

21. Approaching Herzogenburg

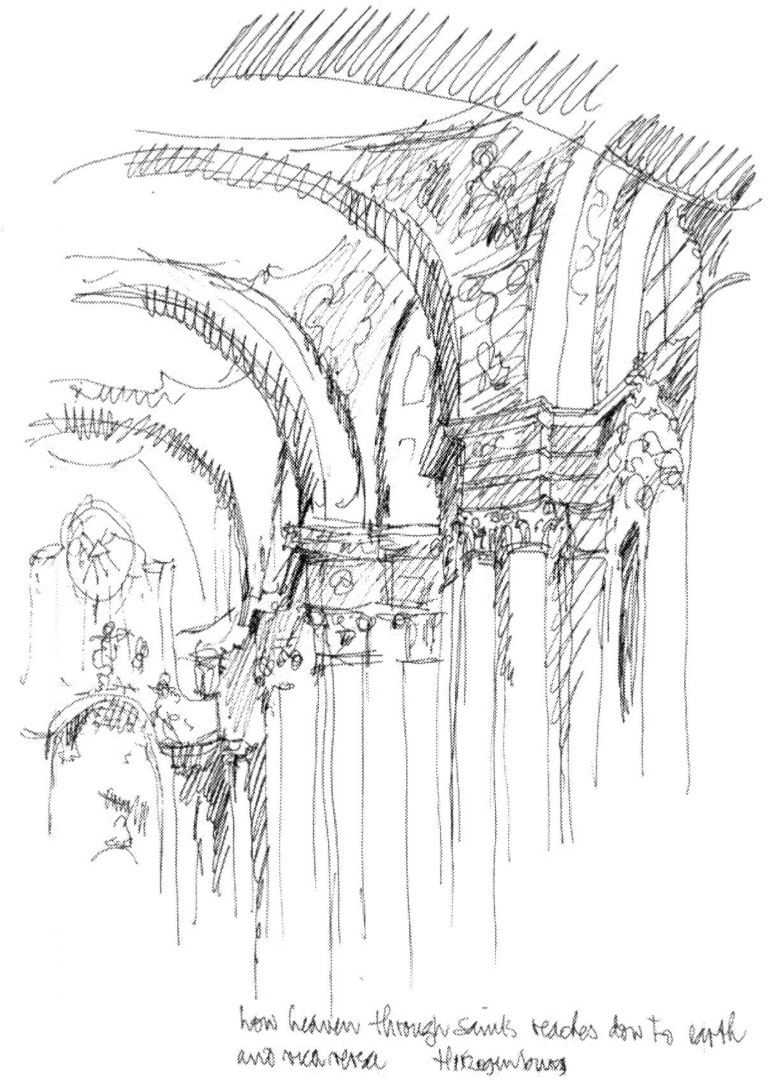

22. Herzogenburg. Nave and High Altar.

The church was closed; we had to satisfy ourselves with looking through the grilles The next day we had the Abbey in Herzogenburg[39] (fig 21, 22), St Andrä an der Traisen [40]for the morning and a look at the Prandtauer city St Pölten for the afternoon. Stift Herzogenburg turned out to be another of those gigantic structures in the usual decoration. Its situation is very attractive; it announces its presence from afar towering above the few houses around it.

St Pölten now the provincial capital of Niederöstenreich is much less of a lively city then Krems where we are staying. It can boast a large number of well preserved or restored 18th century treasures, many works of Prandtauer who has lived here. There is a Prandtauer house. The city is immaculately clean, no litter nothing out of the order but very empty. The market is large somewhat too large for the buildings. It measures 63x163 paces (approx 56 x 146m) and has as only object a Dreifaltigkeits Saule in the middle. (fig 14) It is a favourite object in many places but the very nervous small-scale texture of the structure and the modest height do not allow the monument to dominate the square and fill it. The buildings surrounding the square have not enough presence to claim the space. There is a large area that does not relate to the surrounding buildings and is no-man's land. The entrances and exits of the car park under the market suggest some relation but it is not clear what. The Rathaus which takes up one of the shorter sides of the square is too well behaved Rococo to really have sufficient grip on the open space. It looks somehow beyond the square. The Franziskaner Kirche[41] at the right-hand side of the opposite shorter side is not dominant enough; it just fits in the rest of the wall. The arrangement is not unlike the one in Delft with the Stadhuis and the Nieuwe Kerk. The size of the squares could be of the same order. But in Delft the Stadhuis is a highly decorated early Renaissance building free standing and bulky and sculptural enough to emanate sufficient presence to support the Nieuwe Kerk and take the square over between the two buildings. In St Pölten the very flat façade of the Rathaus with a decoration mainly in colour does not have the presence. The church on the other side does not have a vertical presence. So the longer sidewalls do ask for more attention and successfully compete with the Rathaus and Church. As a result the square breaks up in unrelated spaces without definition and form. The furnishing designed by the recent refurbishing (a car park under the square) has done very little to structure the square or to vitalise it as the heart of the city. But there is lot more to St Pölten. We enjoyed the walk through the city: there is quite a lot for who appreciate the delicate somewhat effeminate charm of Rococo facades. It is a treasure trove of Baroque and Rococo. We walked around; the sun was out in full glory and as the traffic was light we could wander around in leisure. We ended on the Market with a cup off coffee.

But coming back to Krems I believe it was the right choice to go for Krems as the home base it is just somewhat more alive.

17 May

Along the Donau today. Along the right bank to as far as Maria Taferl[42] (fig 23) and then back over Melk[43] and as last visit Dürnstein It was a glorious day sun little wind.

[39] J.Muggenast. 1745-1767
[40] Unknown. 1725-1729
[41] J. Prandtauer (?)
[42] J. Prandtauer.1660-1710
[43] J. Prandtauer.1702-1714

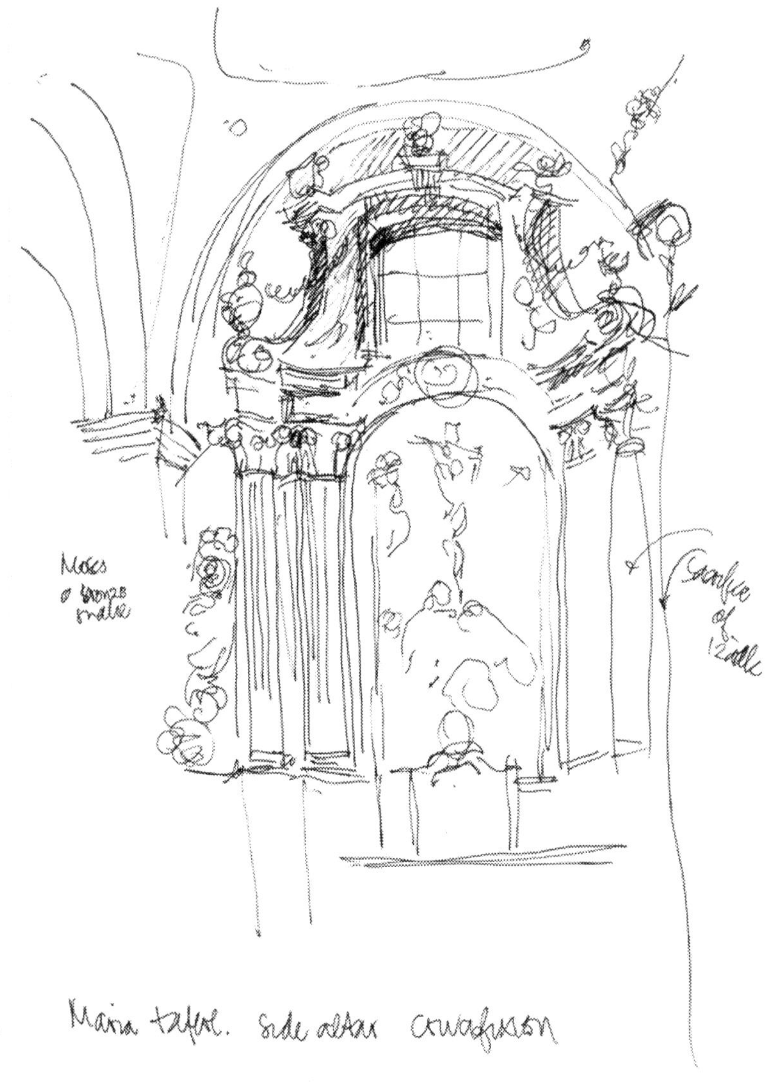

23. Maria Taferl. Side altar with Crucifixion.

and warm. It later appeared that we did see Dürnstein[44] but by error of map reading we believed it to be on the other bank and were looking for it on the way back. Anyhow, we cruised along the Donau had a cup of coffee near on of the stops of the ferries that go up and down the Donau carrying a lot of the local transport.

Maria Taferl is a charming and somewhat unusual church high up on a hill overlooking the Donau. From the forecourt of the church one has a fine view of the Donau valley. The church itself shows all signs of its 17th century concept. The structure is clearly expressed and all decorations confined to the passive areas between the structural elements. A hint towards integration is visible in the high altar where the lower half of the church starts to flow into the decorated vault zone symbolising heaven.

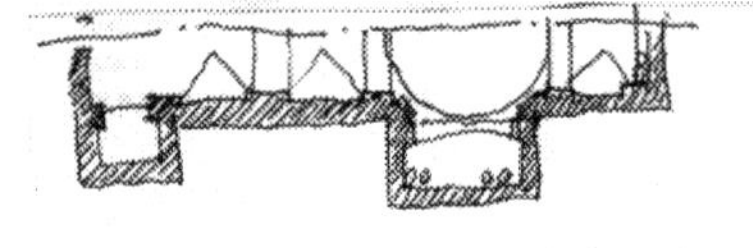

We had a relaxed lunch picnic in the woods around Maria Taferl on our way to Melk.

Melk is so well published that we did not see any surprises. The location is splendid; the church and abbey interiors are of the expected extravaganza. We had an unguided tour with the booklet we bought. I have not much interest in guided tours. Apparently they aim for the general market and provide a lot of anecdotal side information, not enough information on the more specialised things I want to know and generally spend too much time on places that are not of great interest to me and run past really interesting things. I can see that the things I am interested in are not generally of great interest so a guided tour has its difficulties. I hardly ever bother unless there is no option. But each time we see those gigantic complexes like Melk one wonders how the population felt about having to bring together all this money. It must have been a great time for artists, carvers, plasterers, painters and crafts men. With the amount of work there must have been plenty of opportunities and commissions even for the less talented. There is so much around apart from the well-documented first and second category monuments. Almost all even very little places have a church either built in the period or refurbished in the time. The amount of frescos, carvings, plaster sculpture is extraordinary. The number of artists and craftsmen supported by the rural population through church commissions must have been disproportionately large.

From Melk we had planned as our last stop before Krems the church of Dürnstein. Leaving Melk we had some difficulties finding the road on the other side of the Donau back to Krems. We found it in the end but what we could not find was Dürnstein. It is on the other bank and we did overlook it in the morning.

A change in plans; we crossed the Donau near Stein and went back along the way we had gone in the morning. Dürnstein is a curious place on a steep rock. The urban lay out is such that it has been made car

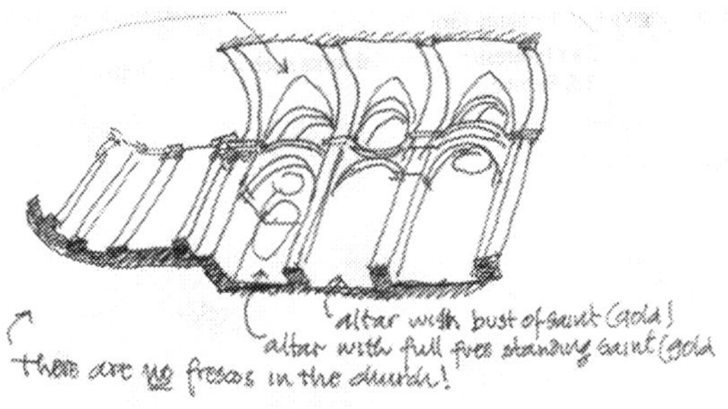

free except for residents. It is very much into the Arts and Crafts. The urban geography is the plaka[45] system, which accounts for the picturesque looks, alleyways and courtyards. The little town has a very cultivated Hansl und Gretl look designed to look like a "real old Town". The church is also different in many ways. It is located on a high terrace overlooking the Donau. The exterior is striking blue with white "structural" bands, very unusual. I do not recall having seen another one like it.

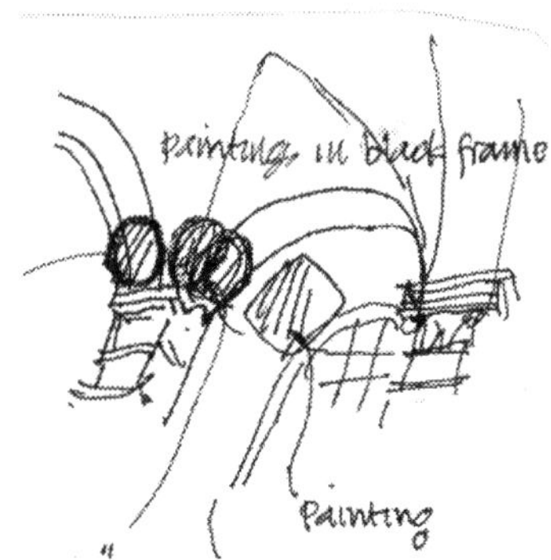

The interior is not fully integrated. The decoration is white stucco and isolated paintings hung on unusual places. The three bays of the nave have a concave or convex gallery. The side altars are more elaborate towards the main altar. Whereas the western most altars have only busts of saints in gold, the next set is fully equipped with life size saints also in gold. The climax is in the high altar in the one bay chancel with a semicircular closure.

We had a drink outside town overlooking the Donau. It was peaceful in the late sun, and we had decided to stay for diner but the menu was too limited even for the most modest taste. So we found our way back to Stein where we had diner almost on the banks of the Donau. In the mean time big dark clouds had built up and just when we had finished and paid the thunderstorm burst open. We ran to the car under the first droplets of what turned out to be a downpour. We had it all; lightening rain and an awful lot of hail on our way back to Senftenberg.

18 May.

We had the day planned as a day off to hang around in Krems, look at the shops, and sit in the sun with an ice coffee. The weather had not fully recovered from the thunderstorm of the day before, but it was dry. We drifted to Krems to do some shopping. We had a session in the E-mail café to read and answer mail. We were going to have asparagus and smoked ham and eggs with a bottle of rose. There was a kitchen facility in the house and we could use it. We found all the necessary ingredients and also a replacement for my 1980 army jacket, which by now did not keep out water anymore. I had found that out the other night when we went to town for dinner in the rain. Towards noon it looked as if the weather would clear so we decided to do one more stift; Göttweig[46].

Göttweig was in its design a lot bigger than even Melk but it was never finished. And good for the farming community one is inclined to think, but as a design it would have been magnificent. The abbey church isn't finished. The gothic chancel has not been replaced. All decorations look conservative given the building dates of 1719-1739. It could be that the fit out was intended to be replaced last. The decoration and furnishing lacks integration. The pulpit looks Mannerist rather than Baroque or Rococo, so does the high altar: a curiously frilly static concept with unusual green twisted columns. The quality of the sculpture itself is quite good as is the painting of the High Altar. When we left the church the weather had deteriorated, it had started

---

[45]Term coined by me to avoid long explanations. It is derived from the Plaka the old part of Athens on the slopes of the Acropolis. Streets follow generally the contours in a zigzag pattern. They are interconnected by steps and very steep alleys.

[46] Various architects. 1625-1750

to rain. The walk in the surrounding woods had to be called off. Not all can go according to plan. The home cooked diner of white asparagus with hard-boiled eggs and small potatoes with a bottle of rose was luxurious and a welcome change; the choice in simple Austrian restaurants is not that large and even well cooked Schnitzels every day is a bit much. There are luckily a fair number of Chinese and some Italian style restaurants so one is not condemned to have Austrian every day.

19 May.

The next day we were going to move close to Linz and had planned on Steyr as our base outside Linz to cover the region and have easy access to the secondary roads which we had to travel to get to our destinations.

The shift to the Linz region was not as straightforward as we had hoped. We had picked Steyr as it was close to Linz and had only two yellow roads leading to it. That appeared a mistake. Recently some large firms had shifted their operations away from Linz to Steyr and the city was on the move. The necessary adjustments to the roads and other infrastructure were still going on and made the surrounds of Steyr rather chaotic.

The decision to move on Saturday was also not too wise. We are used to everything being open seven days a week in New Zealand but that is not true in Europe. Our Italian experience should have warned us. Sundays and religious festive days are still observed with full closure of all activities other than first line hospitality like hotels and restaurants. They have in compensation for the missed free Saturday and Sunday one compulsory day of closure per week the so-called "Ruhetag". We had learned about that in Italy but also in Breitenfurth. We never dreamed that the tourist information would close on a weekend! When we arrived in Steyr it was just past 12, the Tourist Information office had closed and as it was Saturday it was not going to open until Monday. So there we were without any information. We first found us a map of Steyr and while discussing our situation with the staff in the bookshop a man introduced himself. He knew the girl who runs the Tourist Office and more he knew where she lived, which was a Gasthaus just of the main area or market. Steyr centre is a very long wide street or market on which all principal buildings are situated and also all of the most important shops and commercial activities. There are some parallel streets and secondary open spaces and the Gasthaus we were going to, was sitting on one of these secondary spaces. Our local man went inside and returned very quickly. Unfortunately the girl had gone out and nobody knew when or if she would be back. Our helpful local apologized profusely but there was nothing further he could do.

Back to the market we found some accommodation folders, nothing very helpful. So we had to organise ourselves. We had a look at some hotels; in the more expensive hotels there was room. The rooms were nice enough and we might have to take one if nothing more suitable turned up but for the time being they were way outside our budget. So we started the search by getting into every Gasthof and hotel that we saw. We ended up in Dittachdorf in the "Der Wirt im Feld". The room was nice and above budget but not too much. We had another walk through Steyr, had a meal in the Wirt im Feld also somewhat above budget but it was a nice meal. We had no plans to stay there for longer than Monday. That was a good decision; on Monday morning 6.30 we found out that the picturesque location of Der Wirt with one corner jutting into the natural course of the road forced traffic into gear changes with all the noises related to that. And also that the road was one of the two yellow roads that connect Linz with Steyr. There was a lot of heavy traffic. But Saturday night it was all peaceful and quiet and we slept well.

BAD HAL

20 May.
Sunday. As we had planned to move on Monday to get some assistance of the Visitor Information Centres we had the Sunday to get going on the program around Linz. For starters we decided on Kremsmunster[47] and Spital am Pyrn[48].
When we arrived at Kremsmunster around 11 a.m. the sun was out and it looked nice. Once out of the car the wind was very chilly. The fore court to the church as part of the Stift had the usual coffee shop and as it was Sunday locals were having coffee. But there were more than the usual number and there was a feeling of something special going on.
From the church came a constant trickle of parents with a child of about 10 or so.
The children boys and girls had a long white or cream coloured dress like an alb of a priest or a simple nuns dress. They all carried a decorated candle. They all wore a cross decorated in very strong enamel colours. It looked ceramic to me.
It appeared to be the celebration of the restating of the baptismal vows the celebration of reaching of adulthood for the Roman Catholic Church. It remembered me of a similar celebration in my youth in Southern Holland but now no longer of so visible a nature. Here it appeared to be one of the high points in the life of the community.
When we entered the church another Mass had started so we went out and first visited the fishponds. The Stift had been breeding fish, trout I believe, from early days and at the time of the construction of the abbey the same architect also designed a series of square holding ponds for fish surrounded by a gallery of rib less cross vaults. Walls and vaults are whitewashed which contributes to the feel of sober functionality of the set up. The ponds were and still are supplied fresh water from a nearby stream diverted to the abbey. Their utilitarian sober design is appealing. There is just enough decoration to give it the charm of the period and convincingly simple to look functional
When we finally got into the church we found a rather white interior apart from Flemish tapestry hangings at the pillars and the medallion frescos in the vaults. It clearly shows its date in the static and rather heavy stucco decorations.
The drive through the valley of the Pyrn up the mountain toward the Swiss border was very attractive. The church we came for was closed. This means that the main door is open but the grilles that close off the entry under the gallery for the choir is closed. You can see the interior but not walk around. The decoration is very much dominated by the fresco behind the high altar that suggests an opening in the architecture. It is one of the few churches that feature an exterior of cut stone and not the more usual plaster and paint exterior. It is possible that the climate so high up in the Alps is not very forgiving for plastered exterior surfaces.
21 May.
The early onset of the traffic between Linz and Steyr roaring just past the hotel strengthened our resolve to shift to quiet and more economical accommodation. We had picked Bad Hall as a starting point and it was in no time that we had a suitable room in a large farm in Adelwang, a little village a few km south of Bad Hall. The afternoon we had time to visit Schlierbach[49], again one of these gigantic monasteries. This time it was occupied by Cistercians monks who took up the

---

[47] C.A. Carlone, 1615-1712
[48] J.M. Prunner.1714-1736
[49] P.F. Carlone.1680-1713

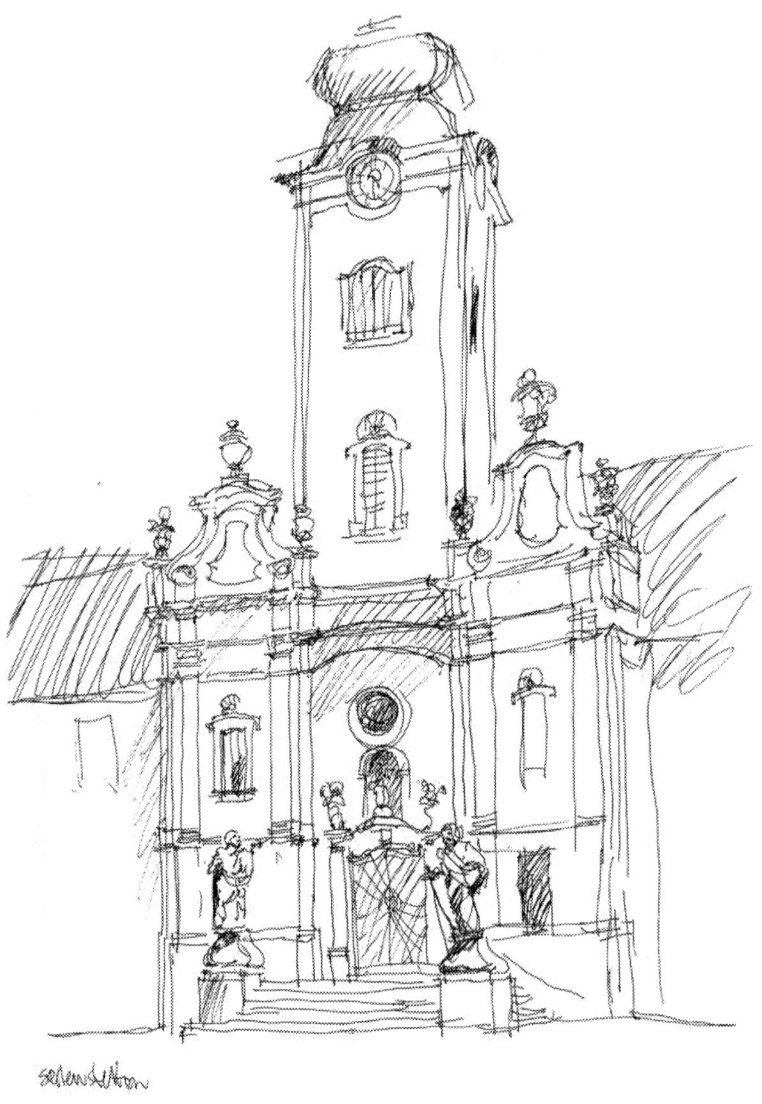

24. Seitenstetten

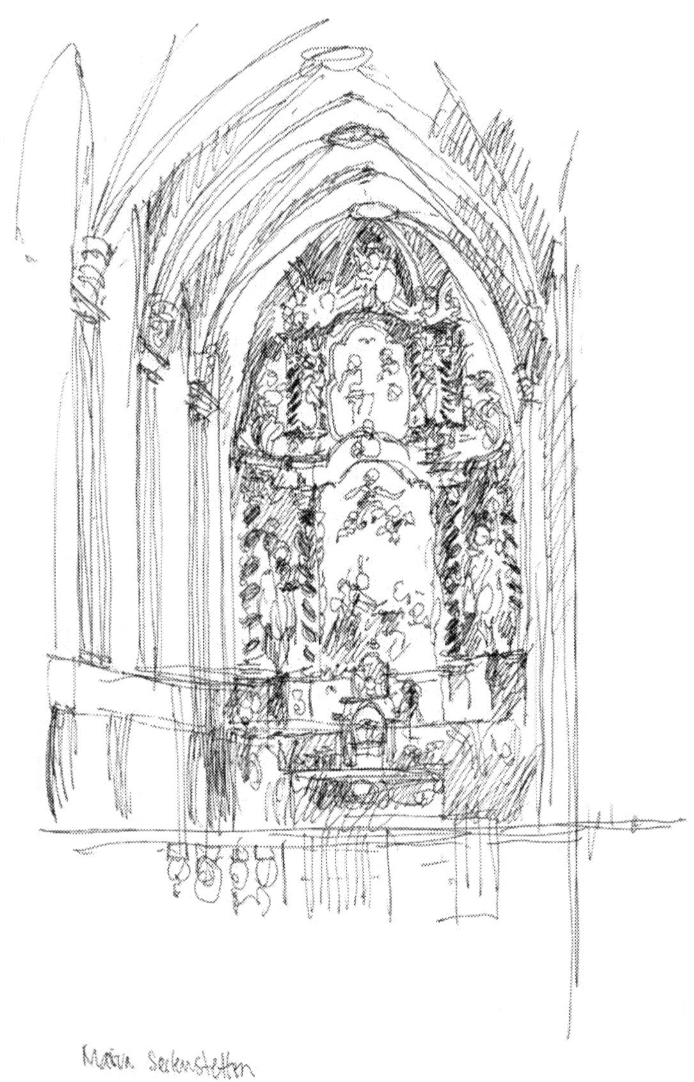

25. Seitenstetten. High Altar.

complex after the Reformation failed. It was formerly occupied by Benedictine nuns. The only way in was by guided tour, not my preferred way of seeing thing. But having no choice we had the guided tour, which included and started with the cheese factory and a glass workshop. Luckily by the time the tour through the buildings started there where only four left that wanted to see more than the cheese and the glass. So the tour worked out well. We had plenty of time and to ask for relevant information. The monastery has a curious cloister with frescos in heavy frames in gilded plaster to make them look like real wall hung paintings. The highlights are the library and the Benedictine hall. The church has an unusual decoration of the pillars; they are covered with gilded wooden frames around flowers painted on glass panels. The gold is too overwhelming and confuses the general impression of the church. It is an early Carlone with a conventional plan and section.

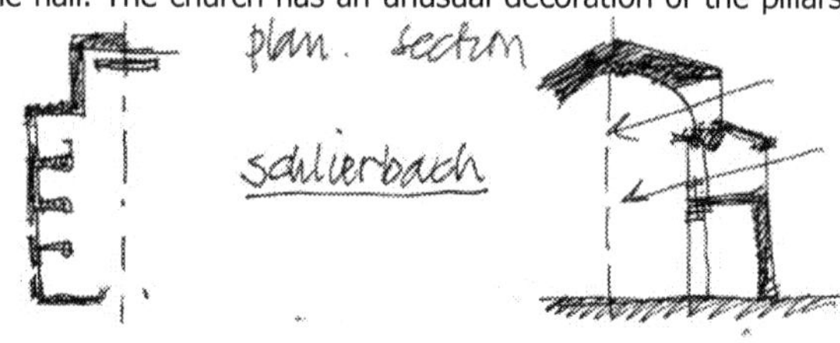

We had hoped to visit Garsten[50] and Christkindl[51] but the signposting of the area South of Steyr and the rapid change in the area of the past years made it very confusing. The maps that we had did not reflect the rapidly changing environment. We tried our best but one way or other the signposting all of a sudden stopped while the church was nowhere to be seen. We managed to get everywhere except in Garsten. In the end we decided to try our luck with Christkindl, which proved a bit easier to find. It sits in the middle of the open country at the end of a country lane together with the Pfarrhaus(vicarage) When we arrived at Christkindl at was already late in the afternoon, but we had a brief look anyway. It is a small church, not more than a central dome. The grilles kept us out and the Pfarrer wasn't home.

Back in Adlwang we were greeted by our hostess who enquired how the afternoon had been. It appeared that Frau Gastgeberin Maria had some connections that could get us in. We still had to go to Garsten and on our way back Christkindl would not be a problem.

The next day we spent the morning in Bad Hal for the necessary shopping and had a relaxed cup of coffee. The centre of Bad Hal is a very elongated open space or market a feature that is rather common in these parts (Krems) Parts of it have been closed to traffic and the outdoor seating for restaurants has taken over. It is a little place that derives its prosperity from the springs that gave it its name.

The afternoon we drove trough a varied countryside first to Seitenstetten, another Stift. We restricted the visit to the church. It is a refurbished Gothic church. The Baroque "overlay". The high Gothic space and the large high windows remain and work well with the modest decorations to produce a light and attractive interior. The ride on to Sonntagsberg[52] through the country gave us a very impressive view o f the location of the complex. And the location is spectacular. It dominates the approach from miles away. Once at the church the views are a reward for the climb up. The pilgrims really needed penitence they must have thought when the selected

---

[50] P.F. Carlone. 1677-1693

[51] C.A. Carlone and J. Prandtauer 1708-1709

[52] J. Prandtauer.1706-1717

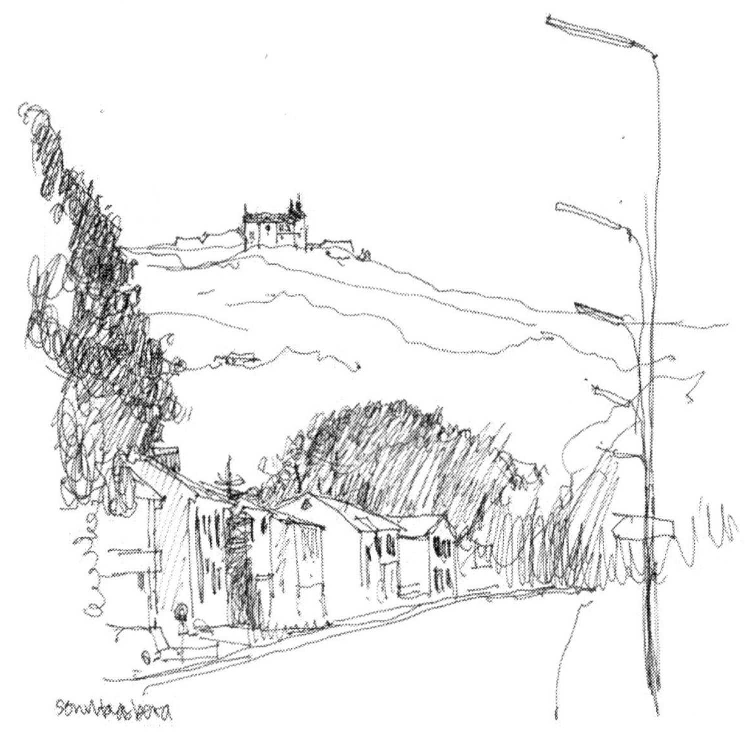

26. Sonntagsberg

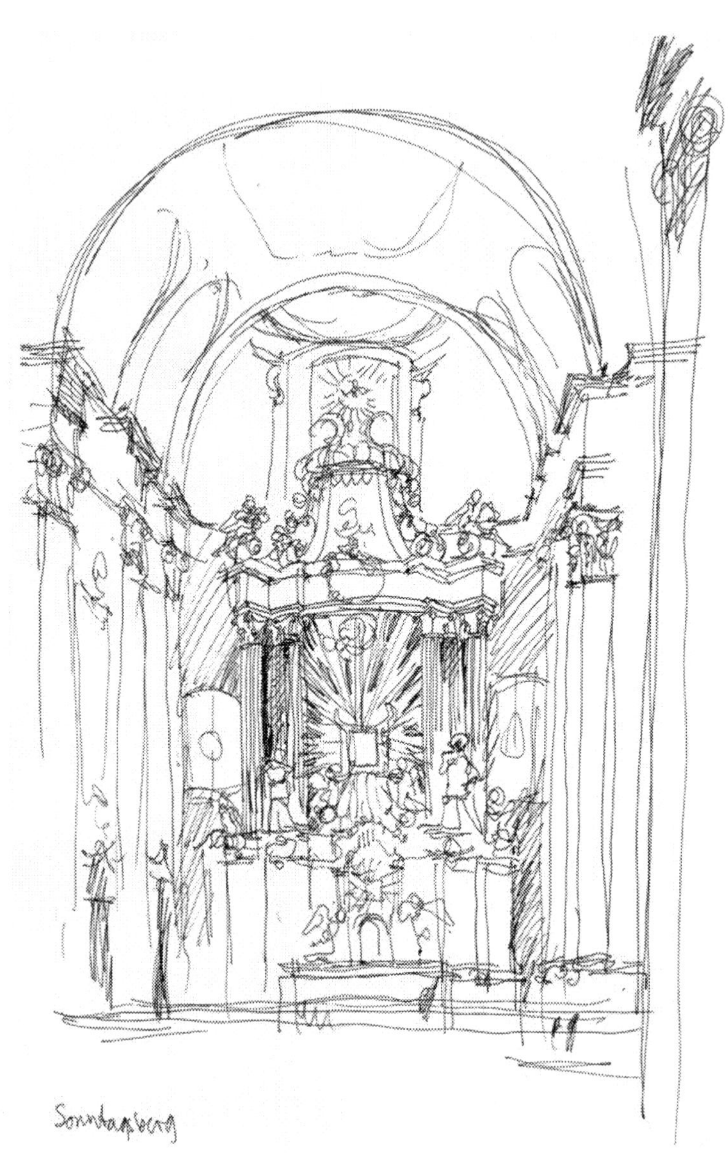

27.Sonntagsberg. High Altar

the spot. But in many ways the church is worth the climb. It shows the division in earth and heaven clearly. The earth is liver coloured marbled stucco while the heaven is represented in fresco and stucco decorations. The High Altar is very restrained but works well in the interior. The side altars in the transept and in the nave do in some way incorporate windows to enhance the effect of the design. A delightfully light and roomy church. The ride back again is a delight.

23 May. Linz.

Linz is not too far away from Adelwang and we entered the city midmorning along the Wienerstrasse and parked our Peugeot near the Goethe Strasse at the edge of the centre. Following the Landstrasse which appeared to be the main shopping street we found our way to the Hauptplatz (main square). The city centre did not impress us. Although located on the bank of the Donau the presence of the river is not felt in the city, even though the main square, the Hauptplatz, does over a rise connect with the Donau and a bridge over the Donau, both river and bridge are not really visible. The square itself is not an attractive space; it is to empty and the accentuation of the two tramlines that run through the square does nothing to address the overall emptiness. The structure of "whipped cream" officially named the "Dreifaltigkeits Saule" is not sufficient to take control of the space. There is a limited amount of outdoor seating where we had a cup of coffee. The square is not attractive.

The main street is fairly wide which would even if it had no tramlines running through it; make it difficult to act as a satisfactory shopping street. With two tramlines in the middle it is clearly divided into two separate pedestrian precincts. There are of course a few attractive and intimate urban details but on the whole we didn't like it. And what really finished it of was a retail experience that brought Elly to almost overt aggression. We had the car parked at the fringe of the inner city and on our way up Elly was tempted by an extremely good offer of a dressing gown. She did not buy but at the end of the day she changed her mind. Her size was not in the rack outside that contained the specials. No problem the woman said we have your size inside and produce the thing and also a price tag of double the price announced. The special offer was only for the gowns on the rack; and those turned out to be the more unusual sizes. After a heated discussion we left the shop and the woman to unpack the garment.

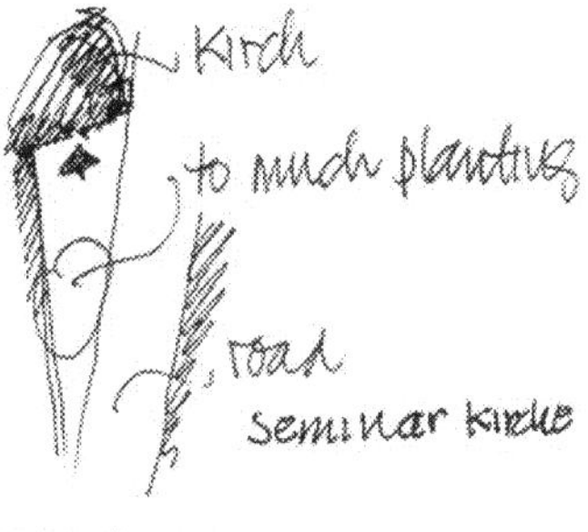

But we had visited the churches I wanted to see. The "Alter Dom[53],"is the church of Linz built for the Jesuits by Francesco Carleone. Given its date it is quite an attractive church with a rather standard cross section. The interior is restrained and strictly organised on structural principles. No decorations encroaching on structural members like columns and architraves. The Main altar in white and red dedicated to the Assumption of Virgin Mary features a very standard stucco sculpture. We had a look in the Urselinenkirche[54], and the Seminaristenkirche[55]. This has an interesting location just of the street. It could have developed a nice intimate forecourt but that has not happened.

---

[53] P.F Carleone 1669-1678

[54] J.M. Krinner. 1732-1772

[55] L.v. Hildebrandt 1725

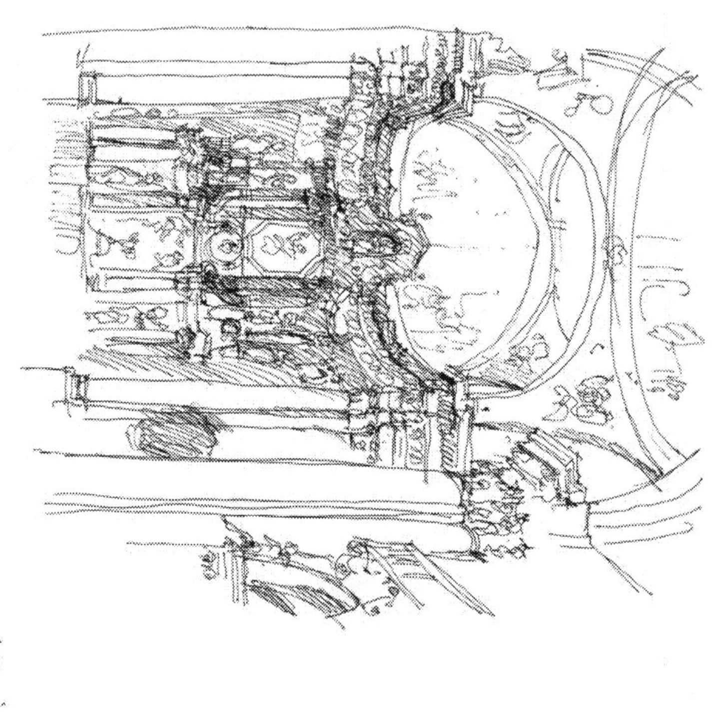

28. St Florian High Altar.

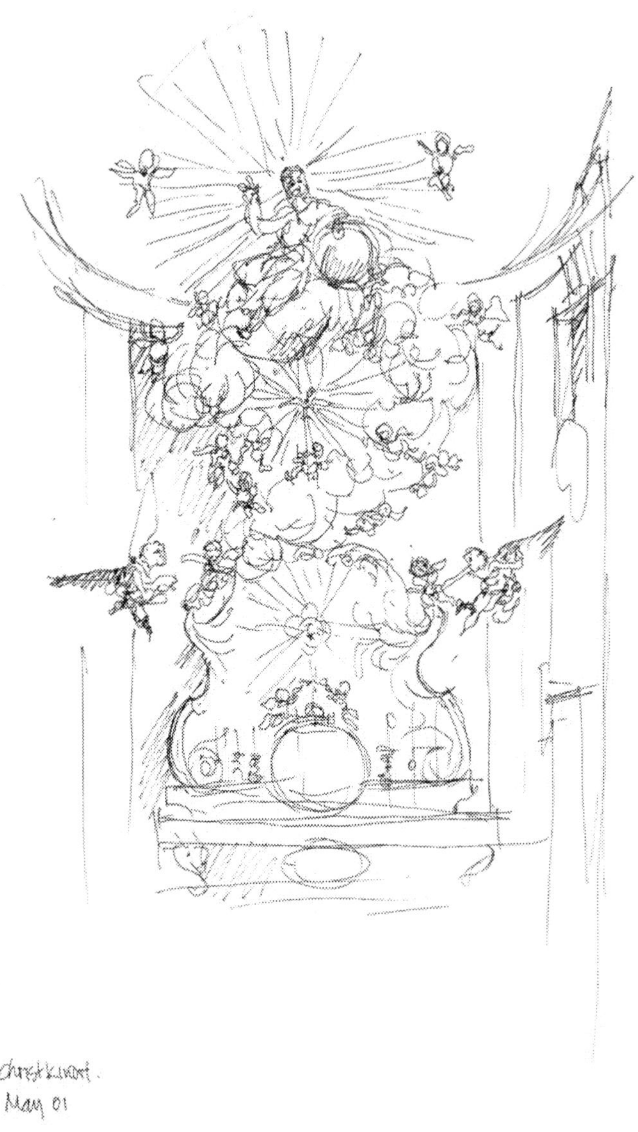

29. Christkindl. High Altar.

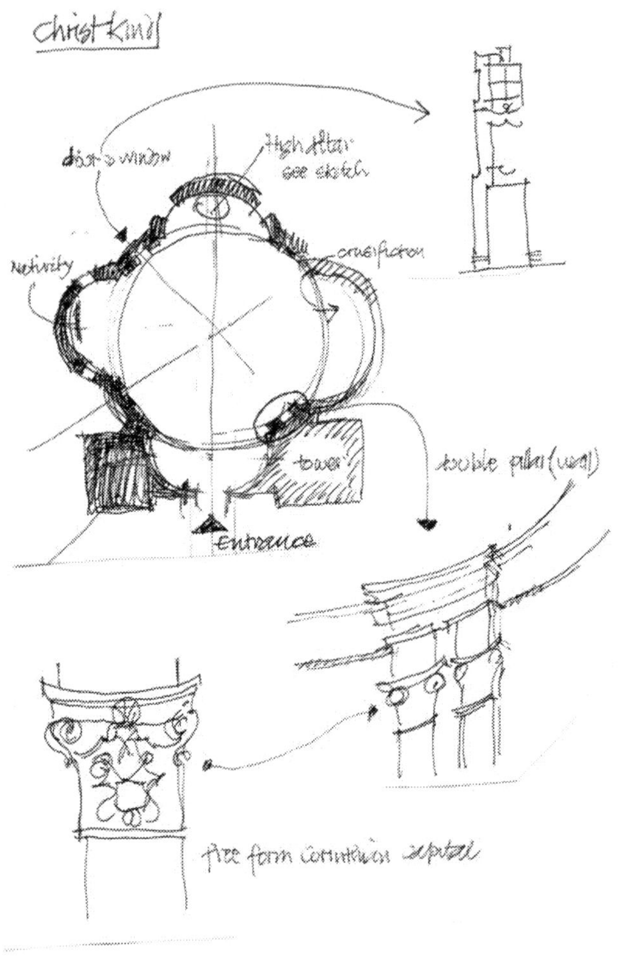

30. Christkindl. Plan and details of the interior

24 May.
Mauthausen

We had decided long ago that we would want to visit the concentration camp. We both have some memories of the War and the words related to the German program of slave labour and murdering of minorities and unwanted elements. It was not quite as we expected. It was more ordinary more banal and for that more harrowing. The display of documents from the administration and general correspondence makes it quite clear that the excuse "We did not know" does not wash. There are complaints of a farmer's wife, no doubt a respectable woman, out of the direct surroundings. The guards should do a proper job when shooting prisoners trying to escape. It was not on that dying people lay wailing all night and disturbing their sleep and peace of mind. They should have been shot properly and they should send out patrols to finish them off. The commandant of the camp on the other hand demanded that farmers controlled their dog; the animals strayed into the Kamp and devoured the corpses of dead prisoners.

The documents regarding the original setting up of the camp as a joint enterprise of the SS and others to give it respectability is equally cynical. The prisoners produced 100x100 x100 cubes of grey granite that are almost ubiquitous in Austria and Southern Germany. Seeing them I from time to time asked myself could these have come from Mauthausen. We stayed till the heat of the day before we left to have lunch somewhere. The thing that really hurts is that it has not been possible to build one memorial to all who were murdered here; you now have a muddle of monuments commemorating all the different nationalities. Those who died here were united in their suffering. Couldn't we the survivors respect that and forget national pride and build one monument?

The afternoon we went to Stift Florian[56] to look at the church and on our way up stopped at a little hunting lodge by Prandtauer (Hohenbrün). It was not open to the public but the exterior did not disappoint.

On the way back to Adelwang we stopped at the local church in Pfarrkirche[57]. We were lucky. While going into the church we met the Pfarrer who organised the restoration and raised the money for the work. We had a very interesting discussion on the merits of the church and at the end he presented us with a copy of the Church guide. He can justly be proud of it. Although the church does not figure in any of the literature it is a nice church and we will come back for a better look. The former is not quite right: the church is mentioned in the Michelin Guide for Austria under Bad Hal I found out later.

25 May

Friday. The idea was that we had Ruhetag so we were not going to do a long drive. This time we managed to find Garsten, which is just south of Steyr and not very far from Adelwang. We had not been able to get there the other day. The stift related to the Church is now part of a prison. The church itself is used by the local community and we could have a look.

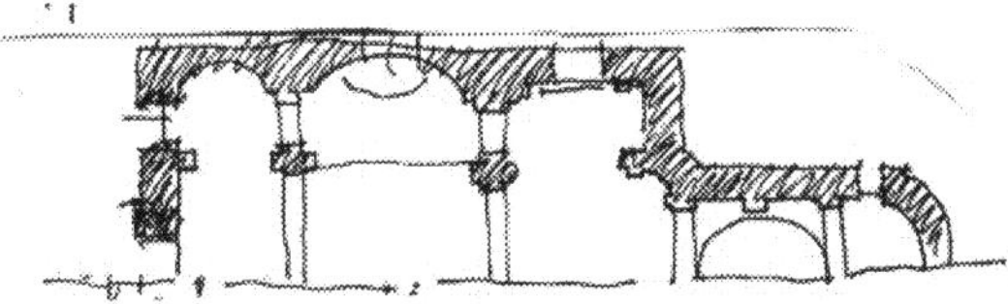

It is nothing revolutionary in plan. The decoration is very full. This is not unusual for a Rococo church but normally

[56] C Carlone and Prandtauer. 1686-1715

[57] H. Blut Kirche by S. Tempelman. 1744-1747

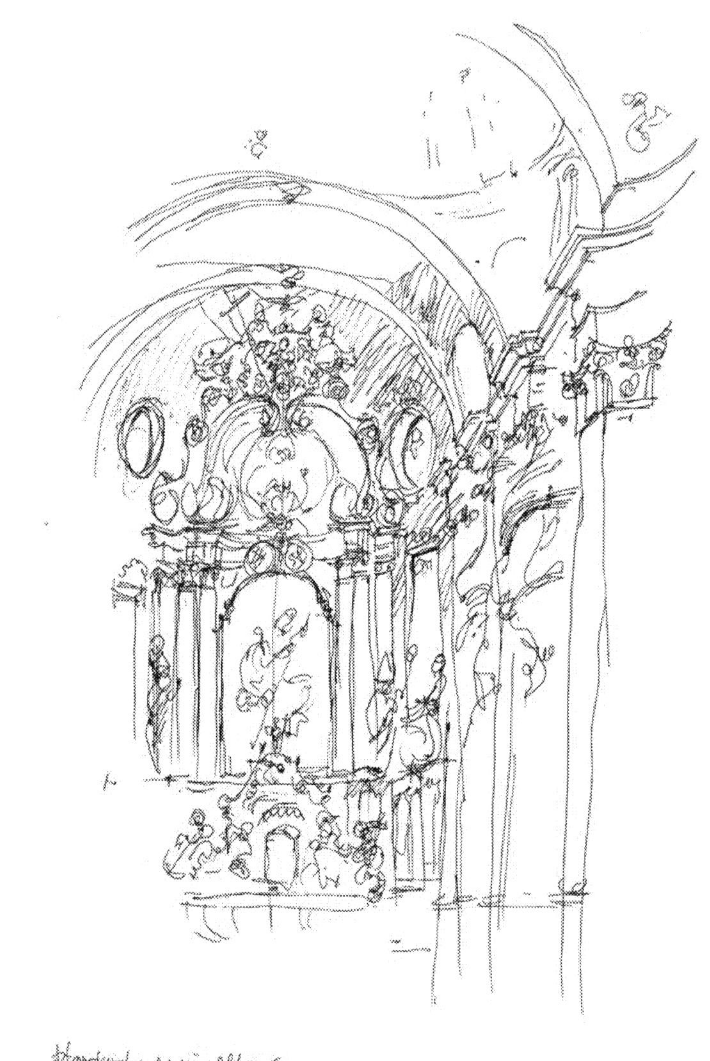

31. Pfarrkirche. Main Altar

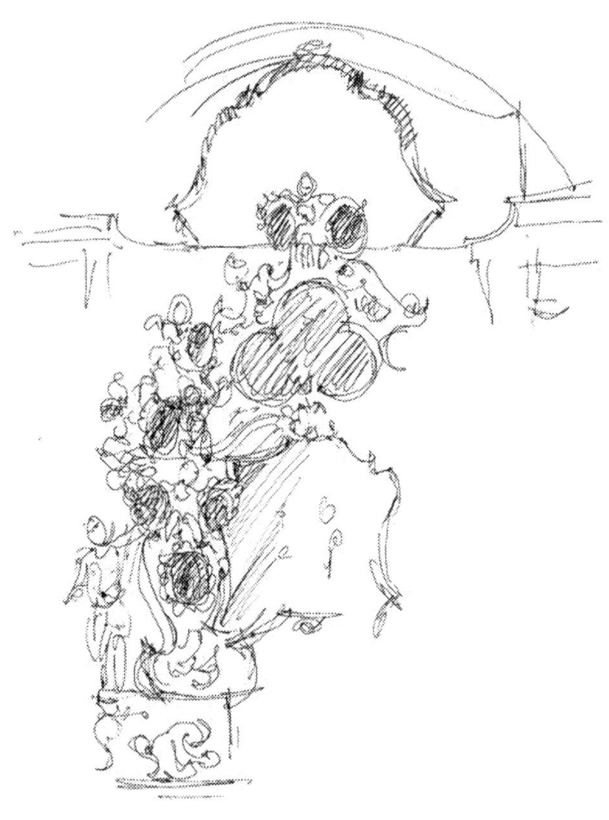

31. Pfarrkirche. Side Altar

one is not so aware because the decoration is well integrated. Not here; there are wall hangings of considerable dimensions and they do fragment the interior. The sculpture is flesh colour with gold for textile. Some of the life-size angels (what is a life-size angel anyway?) are downright clumsy. We on our way into Adelwang managed to see Christkindl

We had a brief talk with the Pfarrer who was just about to start a Führung. He left me in the church without shutting the decorative security grilles at the back. So I had a good look and could do some drawings of the interior. The little church is very restrained in its decorations, which works very well in the small interior. The sculptural decoration is monochrome gold, only the frescos have colour but very restrained. The whole interior is very focussed on Christmas and the Virgin and is in its entirety a very impressive (Prandtauer also built the Pfarrhaus next to it)

From Maria (Frau Gastgeberin) we heard that you have to have connections and book very early to get a seat for the Midnight Mass at Christmas night (Die Nacht messe). The church is in very high demand and given the size of the building there only a very limited number of seats available. The little church has a respectable income of the sale of postcards with the cancellation of the Christmas stamp reading Christkindl and date 25/12 200...

26 May. The visit planned was Wilhering[58]. We stopped at a little town Wels. It is like many Austrian towns: quiet, civilised, friendly, nice. The very elongated market square had recently been pedestrianised but the final result did not convince. It did not articulate the very long space in meaning full subdivisions relating to something. We had an "Eiskaffee" and went on to Paura[59].

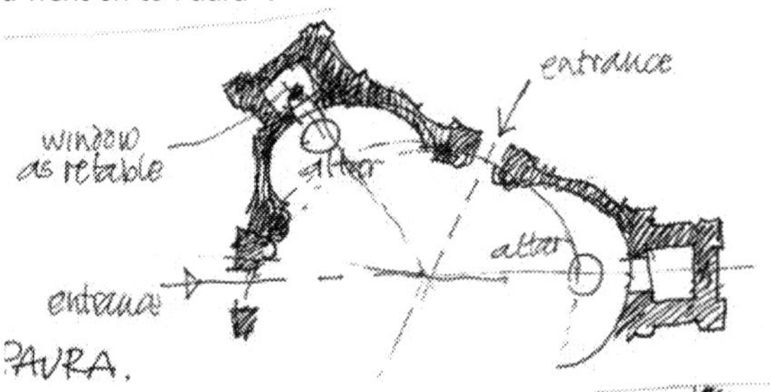

It is a little church dedicated to the Trinity. The church is a rotunda with three apses, each of them further emphasised by a tower in the axis and three entrances each opposing one of the apses. The arrangement is cleverly worked through in the exterior. Each of the three sides presents a traditional entrance façade with two flanking towers and does not show the triangular setup.(fig 37).It is in the interior that the composition becomes readable. The interior decorations of the three altars are dedicated to the three Persons of the Trinity. The Father is presented as the Creator, the Son as the Saviour, and the Holy Ghost as the Inspiration of the Apostles at Pentecost. The structure of the altars is identical, only the sculptural imagery differs with each altar. The altars have a curious spatial feature. As they are placed against the towers, the lower part of the tower contains as space used as Sacristy behind the Main Altar, as confessional behind the Son (the power to forgive sins is established through the Crucifixion) and behind the Holy Ghost a Chapel for the Virgin. The altars have no retable in the form of a painting. That place is taken up by an opening into the lower tower and shows a fresco painted against the wall of the tower interior. It does create an atmosphere of mystery and revelation. It is illustrative of what the church wants to do: reveal God's and the

[58] Haslinger and Goetz.1734-1750
[59] J.M. Prunner. 1714-1722

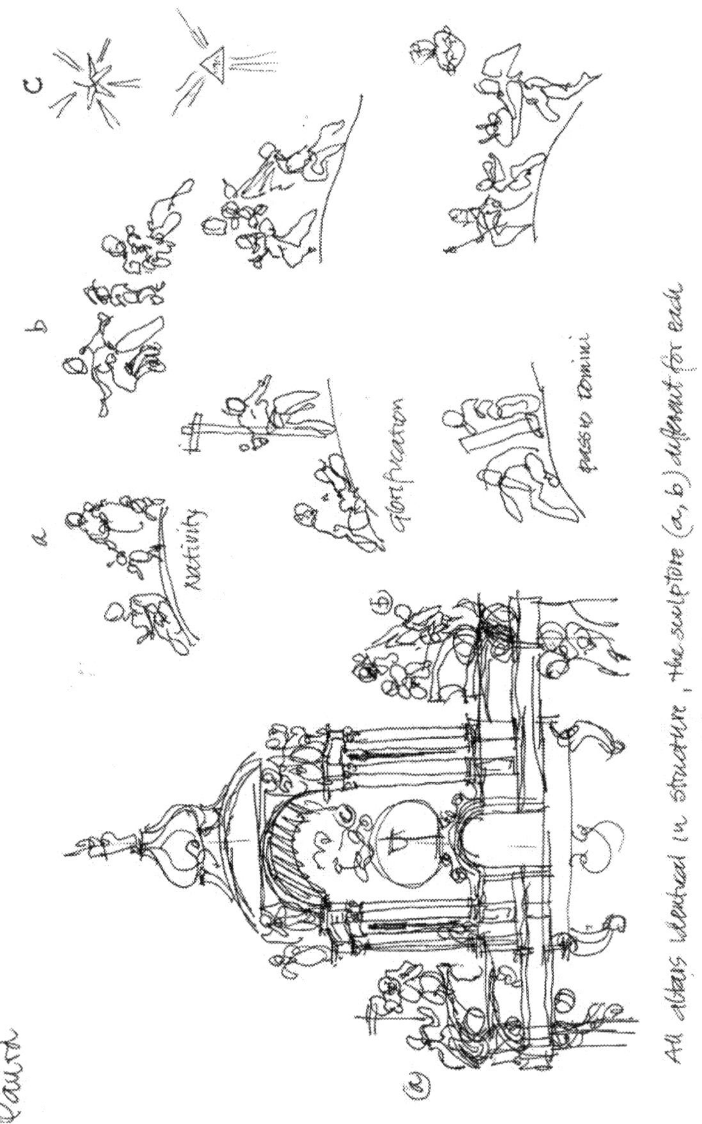

33. Details of the differentiation of the three altars.

34. Paura. The structure of the three altars

Church's efforts to save humanity from the effects of the original and individual sin and lead the souls to happiness in the eternal glory of God. It is quite an accomplished church with an admirable unity between form and decoration and theological teachings.
The difficulty that the seating has to be orientated to one of the three altars, which are in their decoration of equal weight and only in sculptural detail different, has not been resolved. So there is a slight dominance of one of the three axes. Well worth the visit.
As we had some time to spare we went back to Pfarrkirche and had an extensive look. It is over and over again amazing how much quality must be hidden in little known or entirely unnoticed churches in little villages. Pfarrkirche is one of them. It is an overall good quality, simple but effective design well decorated. Worth a visit just to remain aware of the enormous amount of artistic talent that must have been around.
This concluded our program here. We have another day which we will spend doing nothing. There after it is off to Innsbruck, that is somewhere in the valley of the Inn with the idea that we can see Innsbruck, Salzburg and the region between. It could be too much.
27 May: We spent the day in leisure. I had to write a contribution in the Visitors book (Gästebuch) I wrote something in English to stress that we came all way from New Zealand and produced a German translation. My wife had already given some free tutoring in English for one of the children. I updated my notes. We went to the village to see a parade of old-timers; tractors mostly of Steyr make. The host showed us around on the piggery. It is amazing coming from New Zealand and having seen some piggeries in Holland in the seventies how small these Austrian rural operations are. There must be an awful lot of subsidy on agricultural produce. Admittedly they also produced some cider but on the whole. We went to the village to eat and got ourselves organised for the shift to somewhere in the Inn valley to be able to visit Salzburg and Innsbruck and the localities in between. The initial choice was Kufstein.

Kufstein.

28 May
Monday. We handed in the Gästebuch, paid the bill and said goodbye. Waved out by the family we were on the road again. The most practical way to that part of Austria is the Autobahn to Salzburg and München through Germany and near Rosenheim take the autobahn south to Bolzano. We had to buy a ten-day vignette for the Austrian Autobahn; in Germany there is no charge. But as Innsbruck can be reached quickly from Kufstein along the Bolzano Autobahn we might get some benefit out of it. The Autobahn in Austria is not very busy but that is different in Germany. The bit on German soil was not ideal. There were quite a few Werkstellen and at some places stretches of single file. Being early in the season does bring you in the tail of the maintenance program. So we had our amount of stagnating traffic, trucks and diesel fumes. It was warm and very smelly, but we made it. After turning into the Autobahn to Bolzano there was markedly less traffic and Kufstein was Austria again; friendly quiet and well behaved and organised. Kufstein itself is somewhat chaotic in lay out, largely through the presence of a horrendous rock at the edge of the Inn fully occupied by a fortress or castel the" Stein". The town is organised around it. Combined with the very narrow valley of the Inn and a maze of one way streets and a pedestrian area it was not directly clear how to get somewhere.
The Fraulein at the tourist information was friendly, efficient, trim as always and in no time she had booked us in a rural hamlet Morsbach just on the other side of the motorway. We had not too much difficulty finding it and die Uhlie, our Frau Gastgeberin, appeared to be a blond young Austrian farmer's wife. She ran the farm stay facility. We found ourselves in a real Austrian postcard farm, a real" Heidi und Peter". A radio started the morning with Tiroler music and yodel. We had a balcony with red geraniums and petunias; we looked out over grassland up the Inn valley. The motorway that separated us from Kufstein was carefully enclosed to reduce the sound, and camouflaged by planting. The view was splendid. So was the weather, Tyrol as on the postcards. And Kufstein appeared to have sufficient restaurants to give us some choice other than the Austrian cuisine.
29 May.
The plan for the day was to leave early for Innsbruck but after breakfast downstairs it was later than intended when we turned on the motorway. Innsbruck was not that difficult. The parking place we had selected was near the University and going through a gate like underpass under a building brought us straight in the centre and close to the information office. We first saved an Austrian intellectual: he had noticed our French number plate and we saw him scraping together all his French when he approached us to explain something about parking restrictions. We reassured him in French that German would be all right for us if it suited him. And it did. We had the restrictions explained and thanked him profusely.
At the tourist office we got a map of the city and the address of an Internet café. They had Internet access there also but their system was down and very expensive. So we could give our daughter our first reaction and support. Why she wants to have car accidents when we are overseas neither she nor we probably will ever know. On an earlier occasion when we were in Europe she managed to be in the way of someone in a hurry who ignored the red light. She was unharmed the car lost. Now she had a truck driving unto the back of her car while waiting for the traffic lights. She also had a new job the job she always wanted. By than it was lunchtime, the Hofgarten was a pleasant place to have our picnic. We normally only have a very light meal at midday. We mostly carried with us a thermos flask with tea, bread, jam cheese and some fruit and some yoghurt. A little cool box for six cans of beer, readily

available in NZ for rugby fans served us well, just large enough to carry it all and keep it cool. We then had to shift the car and parked near Sankt Johan im Innrain[60], which was one on the list so I had a look inside. It has a very classical front; the interior is in the same manner static or classical. The blurring of definitions of separate elements is not there, the structure and decoration are still not connected. Given his date it is a conservative building. We left the car there and walked into Innsbruck for the Dom or Jacobi Kirche[61]and the Jesuiten Kirche[62] near the University, which we could have visited in the morning; we were parked almost in front. The Dom has an unusual feature that in the interior looks different from what one expects from the exterior. The church is a three bay wall pillar church the third bay somewhat extended and with circular closure. It is in many ways a transept. One would expect the dome to sit here but it is shifted into the first bay of the chancel. The last bay of the chancel is more a square apse. It does not go up to the height of the nave so it seems that the dome is the chancel ending in a square apse. In the exterior, the dome and the two towers rise to approximately the same level and the towers have on top of a dome like roof a lantern-like structure very similar to the lantern on the dome. Rather than leading into the dome the towers with the dome do seem to define the extent of the church. The interior is very light and pleasant. A red marble entablature structure, gold, pink and white stucco. The pulpit has some very nice sculpture. The faking of three domes in fresco in the first three bays is not quite convincing.

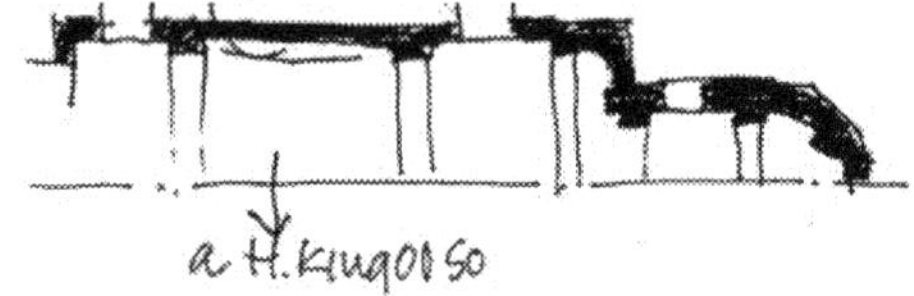

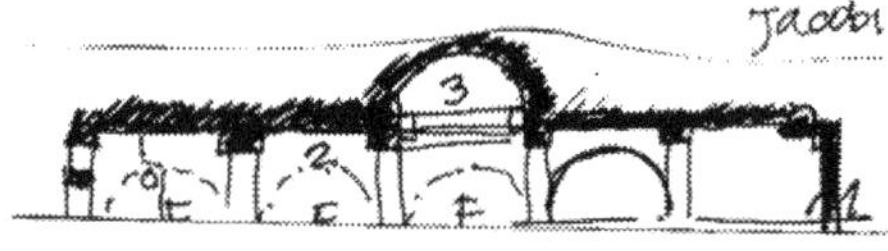

The Jesuitenkirche is a very early church following on the Il Gesu scheme. The church was badly damaged and most of its furnishing is lost.

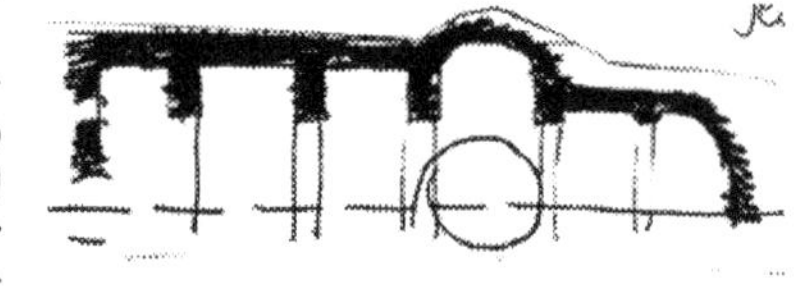

Back in Kufstein we faced the ever-returning question where are we going to eat. Generally the Gasthöfe and Wirtshäuser have not a very extended or imaginative menu. The do have Sauerkraut on it and liver with onions from time to time but the amount of vegetables against meat is not very much to our liking. Of course they serve the Austrian and Bavarian specialty referred to as "Knudeln". This has nothing to do with noodles although its pronunciation is not un-similar. "Knudeln" consist of flour and fat kneaded into balls and cooked. They are for the untrained virtually indigestible. I tried one in Breitenfurt; one wants to try the local specialties. It brought me a day or two of solid indigestion which convinced me that this was only for the locals. My wife never tried one! The universal alternative to MacDonald's is luckily now well established in

[60] A Gump 1729-35
[61] Herkommer and J G Fischer 1717-24
[62] K Fontaner 1627-40

Austria. We have found that almost everywhere there is a Chinese restaurant and like everywhere they supply acceptable food for a very competitive price if you do not want to venture into the local cooking.

What surprised us was that a not at all Chinese but more Malayan or Indonesian dish like Nasi Goring or Bami Goreng with some variants is invariably on the menu.

30 May.

Wednesday. It was going to be a light day. The first stop is Hopfgarten[63]. It is a fully "Heidi und Peter" village i.e. all traditional Tiroler farm buildings. We parked the car on the place in front of the church. Right opposite is a Gästhaus. We had a coffee there to start the work of the day and while we sat a class of primary schoolkids with teacher came to get their reward for some clean up they had done; ice cream and cola or some other fizzy delicacy. They all were very cheerful and polite and well behaved. Of course they all had to go to the toilet. My wife checked: they left it in immaculate state. That is how children behave in The Sound of Music and Heidi und Peter. It is real in Austria.

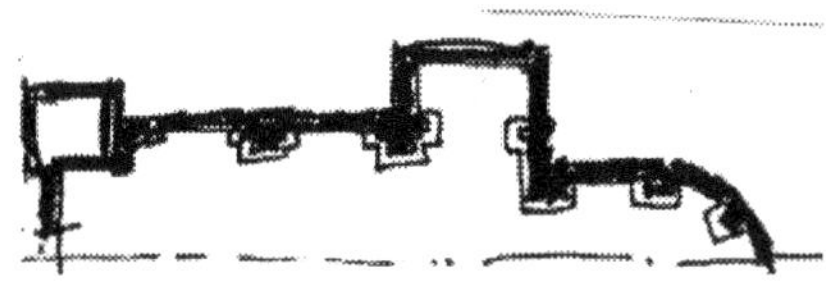

The church itself is on an elevated platform connected to the little square by a flight of steps and has the normal white and light yellow exterior, rather sober. The whole makes you think how romantic "Weinachten" would be here. Stay in the hotel opposite and of course there has been fresh snow. At the time for the midnight service the church bells ring, people find their way to the church over the snow-white immaculate street. That would by like a Christmas postcard. The inside of the church lives up to the expectations inspired by the Christmas fantasy: it is as it was intended a revelation of heavenly splendour in gold and light. The church clearly supports this heavenly dream. The separation of vault and wall is no longer continuous: the entablature is only crowning columns and pillars; the wall gradually changes into the ceiling or heaven. There is some very nice sculpture. The altars seem to be still somewhat isolated from the whole. Very attractive; it would be nice to book us in for next Christmas. But it is the beginning of Tirol's tourist (Ski) season. It could be very difficult to book and given the ski ambiance not such an attractive idea after all.

We took our time and ended up in Rattenburg[64]. It is a one street town like so many in the narrow valleys. The townscape is dominated by a very long wide space running from gate to gate and one or two parallel streets connected by narrow rather steep streets that sometimes turn into steps. The church is remarkable: it is a Rococo redecoration of a gothic double church (i.e. two parallel naves) The basic Gothic structure and window arrangement has not been altered and it is amazing to see how the light of the late Gothic church sits so well with the much later Rococo decoration and furnishing. The decoration is generally very attractive with good quality frescos on the vaults. One could have criticism on the crucifixion group which looks very disjointed, nor Mary nor St John appear to be interested in the crucified at all. But all in all a delightfully light remake of a late Gothic Church.

---

[63] K Singer and A Huber 1715-64

[64] D F Carlone 1707-09

We turned into the Ziller valley to go to Zell[65]. The main church was closed i.e. the grill in the entry was closed. The access to the church was very limited but it allowed still a very good view of the structure. It is an interesting plan. It consists of a central domed rotunda supported on 4 groups of two pillars. The spacing of the coupled pillars is such that space between the groups is larger than the total dimension of the group thus forming a cross arrangement of wider openings and narrower pillar groups (See Sketch) The 5 Western sides have a shielding wall as sides of an octagon. The West bay is extended out beyond the outline of the perimeter and forms the entrance portal. The Eastern arm leads into oval chancel and apse of the main altar.

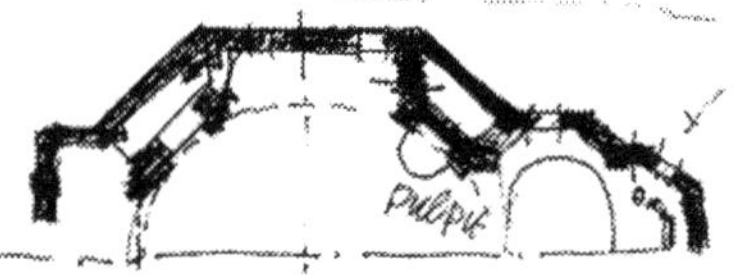

The decoration does not differentiate between structural support and the vaulting. All is in pale green and pink with some highlights in gold.

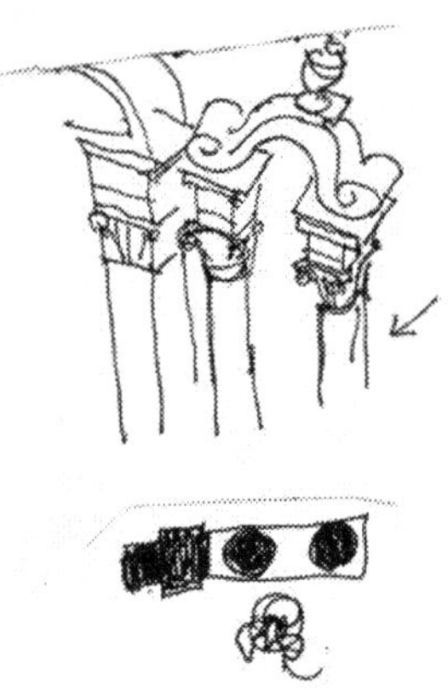

The fresco in the dome suggests trough a painted balustrade resting on the structural balustrade that the central space is in direct connection with heaven. This does not work quite as the dome is not as well lit as the lower half of the church. Some of the considerations that lead to the Wies Kirche are here visible. The central dome still is dominant and forms the church. Other then in Die Wies the chancel or sanctuary is not a natural continuation of the colonnade of the main church; the oval space placed across the main axis does create a separation between church and sanctuary which in die Wies is not there. The screen of pillars only covers the 5 western sides and still adheres to the strict linear geometry. There are attempts (not very convincing) to blur the real and make believe space of the painting: two angels are partly free sculpture and part painted (Würzburg Tiepolo's fresco shows a similar more successful effect)

The main altar sort of peters out in space and is effectively assisted by the side windows. The later addition of an altar for St Mary is unfortunate the red of the baldachino clashes with the rest of the decoration. A lovely little church but given its dating (later than Vierzehnheiligen and die Wies Kirche) not quite with it! The drive through the Ziller valley and back to Kufstein was interesting and very enjoyable.

[65] A Huber 1772-82

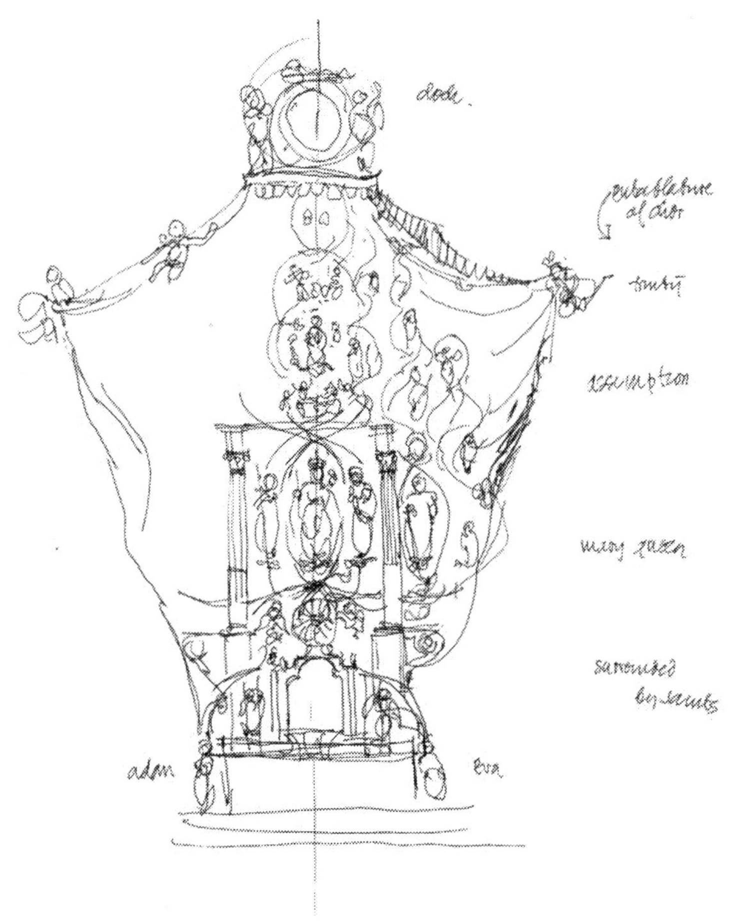

Stamms, main Altar

35.

Stamms. High Altar in the chancel of the part exclusive to the monks.

31 May

Thursday. We decided to visit the churches East of Innsbruck. But first we rearranged my wife's flight now to be on June 14 at 10.45 a.m. We had informed ourselves where to go in Innsbruck and that was not too difficult to find. It was not too much

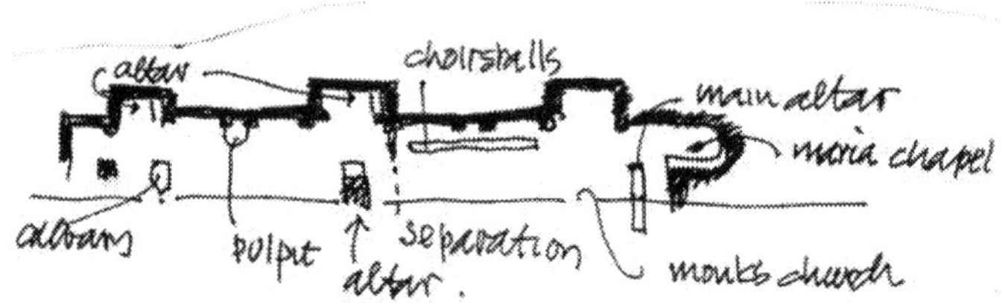

after planned time when we left for Stamms. The showers in the morning forecasted had developed into solid rain. We arrived round about noon. The stift[66] had closed and with it the church. The next guided tour would be at two and the church would be open then. We did not want a tour of the stift and the shop would open again at 12.30. We had lunch under the trees. After lunch I went to try to get into the Church by using the letter from the Goethe institute. The man in the shop was deeply impressed but it was outside his authority. So I tried the Abbey. A novice, who was having lunch alone, opened the door and after reading the letter went away and returned with a father. He decided that I could be trusted in the church on my own. For my wife it was a different matter.

They could on the Abbots authority lift the closure for me being a male and let me enter the monastery exclusively reserved for members of the community. But not even the Abbot could lift the closure for a female. So I went in on my own.

It is an extraordinary long church and divided into a public church and a church for the monastery only. It is a redecorated and partly original rococo building. The main decorations are as could be expected for a scheme from the time. It is the main altar that is a miracle[67]. The huge retable is a delicate frail network of sculpture representing the delicate tree of life or mankind. It springs from Adam and Eve, placed solidly on the earth alongside the altar and grows up in a filigree work of branches and leaves. The fruits of the tree are saints incorporated in the open foliage. In the centre of the tree is the bridge between god and humanity the Virgin Mary The backdrop is a rich drapery of blue and red opened by little putti floating and sitting on the entablature of the chancel. It is gigantic and the same time so light and open.

The whole of the church itself is a beautiful interior with tasteful quality sculpture, light and well controlled.

We left Stamms to go to Ranggen.[68]

The church is interesting. The most remarkable is the floor in timber in a chequered pattern.

The last on our list for that day was Götzen.

---

[66] Various 1729-34 main construction

[67] By B Steinle (1613)

[68] F Singer 1775

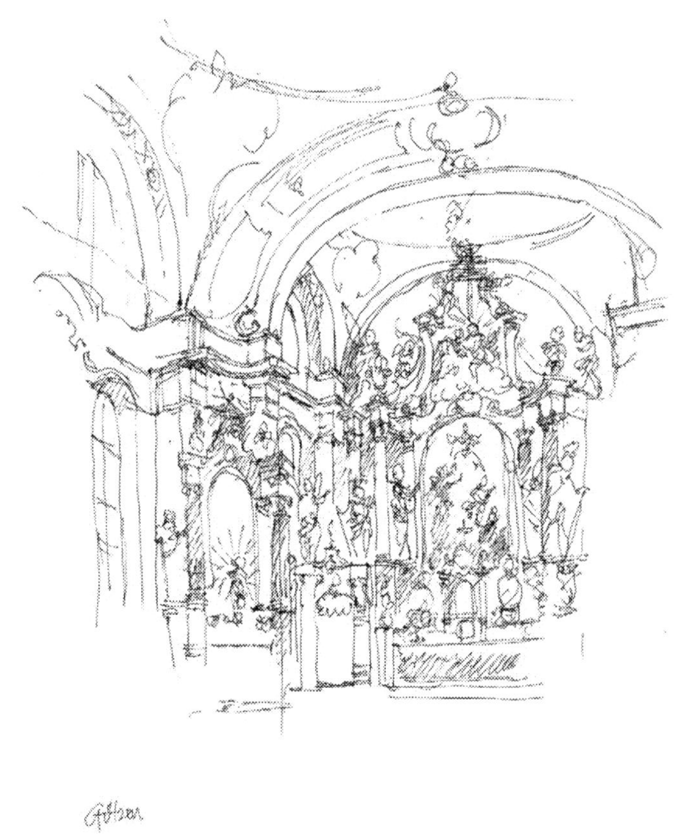

36. Götzen. High altar

Its is a brilliant design in its overall effect the way in which the four side altars are all visible on entry and climax in the main altar. It reminds of Rangen but much more unified. The décor is in pink, grey and gold.

The westernmost side altars are smallest. Upon entering they visually almost touch the second row of side altars. They are larger and again almost touch the main altar. The frescos are about St Peters miracles. If one wants to be critical: they are still somewhat unrelated like an add on. On the whole the boundary between structure and decoration begins to dissolve into one environment of unworldly splendour and beauty. The plain exterior helps to make entering the church into a transgression into another world hidden in our every day's life; the world of Gods involvement in our lives and the function that the Saints have in this plan. It visualises the message of the Roman Catholic Church: only in this church is God's splendour and his miraculous involvement in this world present. The High Altar is the connection and gate to heaven. Here the whole scene culminates and emphatically states it: only in the church heaven opens and comes down to incorporate us humans and with assistance of the saints we also can live in this splendour forever and ever.

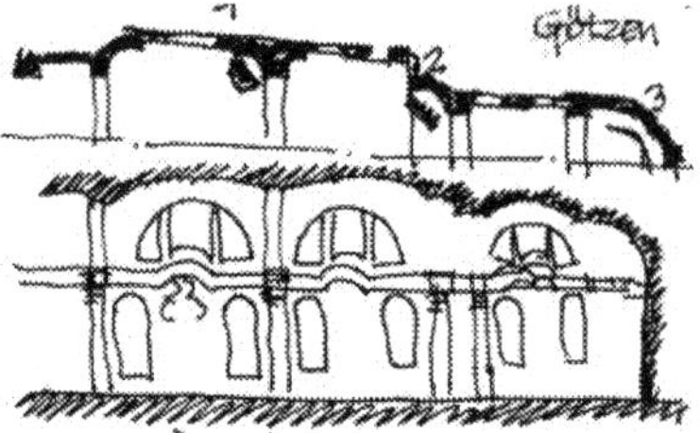

There were lots of fresh flowers in the church like in most churches we have visited. It makes the whole architecture more convincing to see that these works of art are not jet empty musea like many in Italy but still a place carried by a community and used as a place of worship. But given the cost of maintaining these treasure troves it will if not already does, require money from the State to keep them in good repair.

1 June.

The idea was to cover the Salzburg region from Kufstein. We decided to test the practicality of the idea and went on a trial run. We decided to take the route trough Austria rather than the Autobahn trough Germany It is a long drive trough valleys of small rivers south of the Kaiser Gebirge and a good climb up and a short stretch trough Germany near Berchtesgaden.On arrival we found that Salzburg is not the easiest city to get in to. The three hills around the old city force you to decide on the entry point early and once on the route it is difficult to change. We ended up in a rather expensive parking building under ground. When came out it had started to rain. We found the Tourist Information at the Mozart Platz quickly enough. They had a plan of the city and an address of an Internet Cafe, just around the corner. That was filled up with youngsters. There was a second near the other end of the old city. It really did rain by then. We hopped from shelter to shelter found the thing all right did our mail and hurried back to the other end to rescue our car and ourselves from financial disaster.

We had lunch in the car. The Peugeot 206 is roomier inside than its exterior suggests. After lunch, it still rained and kept on raining. We decided to see some of the minor churches north of Salzburg on the list. There were only a

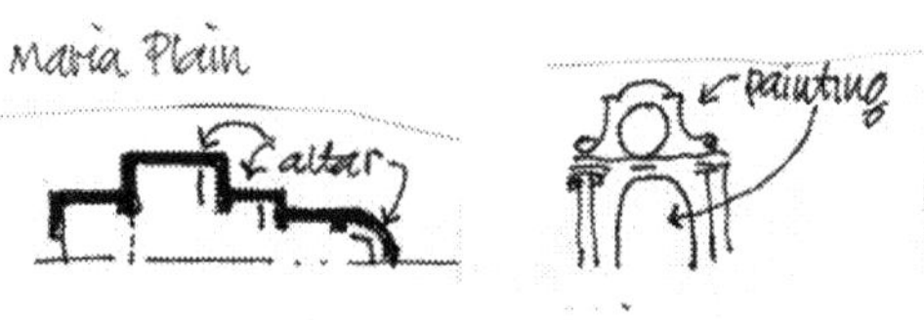

few, al North of Salzburg on the other side of the motorway or E 55.Maria Plain[69] we had some difficulty finding her. She has a bit of an unusual décor: dark blue and gold. It is a small but very attractive church. From the entrance, the five altars melt into one presentation. There was a wedding so we were somewhat limited in our walk around. We later found that it is quite fashionable to marry in Maria Plain. We stopped in Hallwang and it still rained when we went of to Kufstein. It also rained in Kufstein.

2 June.

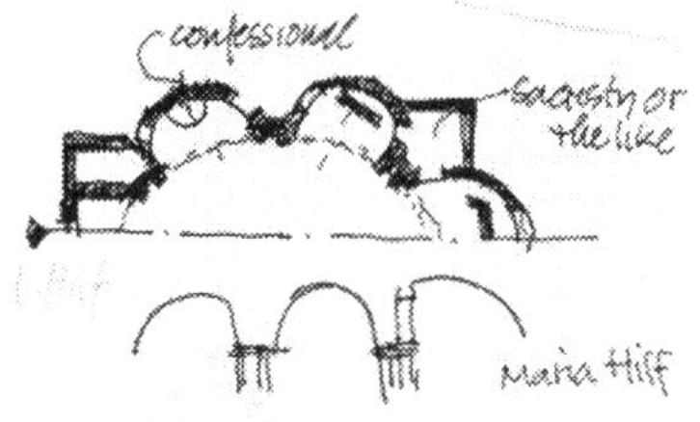

The program for today is a last visit to Innsbruck to see the last of the program. Innsbruck is very accessible. It is easy to get close to the centre and easy to shift from one parking place to another.

The program was Maria Hilf [70]on the other side of the Inn. The plan is based on a central dome supported on a hexagonal structure .One of the sides is the entrance porch, the other sides of the hexagon all are extended out in a half circular apsides except that the one containing the main altar is slight deeper. Upon entering the two side altars are visible. They are similar in structure to the high altar be it less elaborate. The dome is very dominant and decorated with frescos in medallions and is a bit much. A later addition of a vivid red baldachino over the main altar does not help the rest of the decoration and the full round statuary, which is in white, and gold. The exterior is very classical and would benefit from the removal of the wooden bell turret. After a visit to St Mary Conception,[71] we went to the Stift Wilten[72]. The interior is very nervous, white and the altars in black and gold. Having done what we came to do, we turned on the road back to Kufstein. There is only one alternative route if you do not want to take the Autobahn and that is we decided to do. We stopped in Hall famous for its old mint (Halle thaler) and had a look at the churches, just to keep in touch with the quality in the second and third tier works.

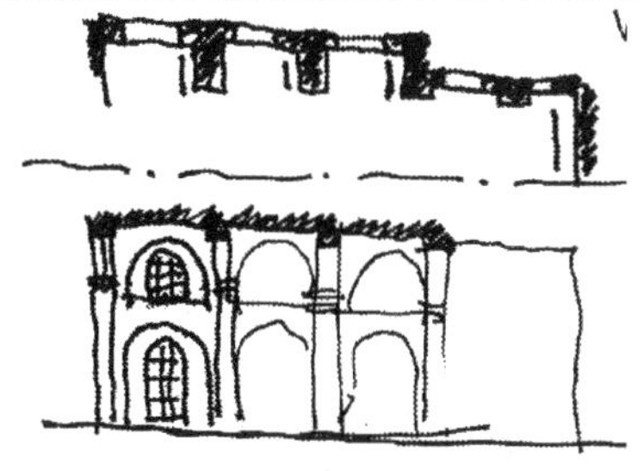

Like real tourist we had a look at the Mint with its display of minting practices and had silver thaler hammered by operating one of the old machines; quite interesting actually.

The last stop was the Karlskirche in Volders. On the way up to Innsbruck you cannot miss it with its unusual exterior. We had a brief look around and visited the inside. There was a wedding on, so you have to restrict yourself. A very interesting

[69] A Dario 1671-74
[70] Ch Gump 1647-89
[71] F X Feichtmayer refurbished with stucco decorations 1751-56
[72] Ch Gump 1651-57

building and in its exterior and in its interior. It rained again when we started out to Kufstein

3 June.

It rained and got rather cold. Snow levels came down to 1000m. As Kufstein is high up all hills had a good dusting of snow. The temperature felt like a Dutch summer day: Kufstein 11.45 a.m. 5 degrees; very cold indeed. Uhlie had the Kachel fired up. A Kachel in a traditional Tirol and Bavarian farm is large construction of brick covered with tiles. It sits between the two living spaces and is fed the about one meter long bits of wood one sees stacked up. The entry into the fire chamber is from the Diele the wide long corridor running through the middle of the house. The chimney runs trough the bedrooms in the roof space. When this whole mass of brick is heated up it is large heat reservoir that moderates temperature fluctuations. You can see these constructions also in Gästhöfe in the rooms for the public

We went to Ebbs and a flower show nearby to do something. It was as in New Zealand; lots of plants you have never seen and all manner of tools for the garden.

Tomorrow we will go to Salzburg to organise a shift. It is too far and the road takes so much time that visiting Salzburg and surroundings from Kufstein is not practical. We took the Autobahn and found the Tourist information closed. We had hoped that on a Sunday in a place like Salzburg they would have the service open. There was a collection of pamphlets on accommodation in the vicinity available outside in form of leaflets, so we picked what we thought useful and tried to have a further look at Salzburg. But the rain did not stop so we decided to go back to Kufstein, take it easy and return to Kufstein to get organised. We had diner on the Inn end of the Markt. They had heating on the outdoor place an elevated paved area shaded by horse chestnut trees in bloom, but everybody went inside in to the rooms where the Kachel was going. You had to put up with smoke and the smoking of the locals, but outside was no option. It was cold, very cold; just not funny!

Salzkammergut

5 June.

The day of the shift to Kopple for that was the place we had picked to try our luck. It is east of Salzburg just of the road to Bad Ischl. We thought it handy to town and away from it for a bit of peace and quiet. We decided to take the Autobahn to Salzburg and the north bypass and then near Thalgau turn into the country. It all worked as planned; the sun was out, but the wind remained chilly. The Tourist Verband was closed. The Wirtin of the Wirtshaus opposite the church was not very friendly. The outfit was in scaffolding and the room she had to offer had scaffolding in front of the window. To be woken by the arrival of the workforce was not a prospect that appealed to us. So we went out to knock at the door of the first of the farms that were listed as having rooms. The first we tried had given that part of his economic efforts away. He might have bought another cow and the subsidy might be more than they made on the bed and breakfast business. But he directed us to another farm. They were into it and we took the room. It was not quite finished but the view was nice. The farm was situated in the middle of meadows and on a bit of a rise. It was quiet very rural. We had a quick look at Thalgau the nearest centre with some facilities. There was very little open in the nature of restaurants. We ended up in the canteen of a camping nearby. The wind had died down a bit so we started outdoors but ended up inside as soon as the sun disappeared. The air temperature was still rather low.

6 June.

It rained and it was to rain later. We decided to go for a drive. To Thalgau and from there to Mondsee a.d Mondsee along the lake and to the Au and the west side of the Atersee and along the east side down and back to Koppl

7 June.

The weather did clear somewhat and we went of to Salzburg were we had more luck with the Kajetaner Kirche; this time it was open. The structural concept of an oval central space across the central axis does not work very well. The bits at the right and left tend to go it alone. The Kollegien Kirche is a very tall or narrow church. The wall pillar concept together with the small dome make it look smallish.

The main altar is integrated in the whole structure by the stucco decoration that continues on the structure of the apse.

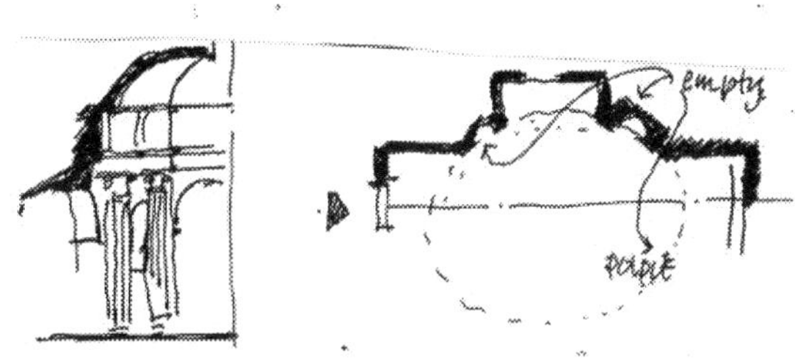

We had lunch on the other side of the river near the Residenz and its garden. The Residenz is known as Schloss Mirabell. The palace has been severely damaged in early 1800 and rebuilt in a much less exuberant form. The garden designed by Fischer von Erlach in 1690 is quite small for the Baroque period but quite delightful. The unsurpassed highlight of the day was the little Museum. The former Orangery is now a museum. It shows a collection of design and presentation sketches for large frescos, sculpture and the like for the interiors of churches and palaces. The artists are quite well known like Rubens, Tiepolo and many of the men that created the Rococo interiors of Austria and Bavaria. It shows first of all that those men who ran a factory of large-scale paintings could paint like no one. And secondly the freshness the directness and the concentration on the composition and concept rather than detail of the concept-drawings, paintings and clay sculpture make the display unforgettable. It is exiting to be able to almost see the masters at work. It is a place to go back to and a must for who wants to see how good these fellows really were.

We could have stayed longer but we wanted to see the Dreifaltigkeits Kirche [73]and the Urselinen Kirche[74]. From the Urselinen church, which is somewhat isolated at the less busy end of the old city to the car park lead us past the Stadt Pfarrkirche. The church has a curious situation. It sits high above the street. There is no room for an approach in the main axis. So you have to walk past the church coming from the bank of the Inn and with a double left turn enter the approach. It is quite a sizeable stair to a landing with a small chapel or more an aedicule for St John de Deo and another flight before reaching the entrance. It was worth the effort; quite a nice small church. There are some curious features; like windows interrupting the entablature. The main altar is an elaborate spatial structure in red and gold dedicated to Maria, Mother of God, Queen of the Earth. The side altars are nice with some good sculpture. As there was no Kirchenführer I do not know who designed it all. But well done. There is a lot of good stuff around that is not mentioned in any of the guides.

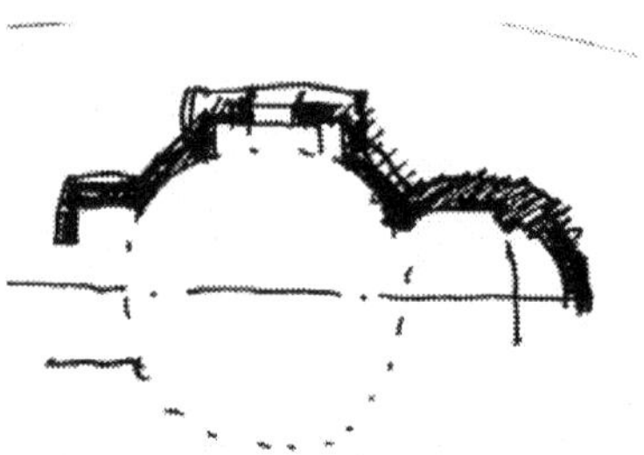

At the end of the Salzburg visit there need to be some comments on the City.

The Medieval City for so far it exists is as any other there are some openings to the river but not many. It has of course the charming twists in streets, differences in level, little squares. The City is very much dominated by the Burg that acts as a point of reference to have an idea whereabouts one is in the maze. The "grandiose" Baroque schemes are not completed and therefore very unsatisfactory. There is a sequence of open spaces that lacks unity because of their muddled relations and definition of the separate elements. Each of the elements on its own is not satisfactory. Together they are a formless sequence of open spaces.

The Mozart Platz; the north side is barely two story; the south side is 3 to 4 storeys high. The paving is convex which stresses the inadequacy of the north wall and gives more prominence to the Mozart Statue, which in itself is too heavy for the place.

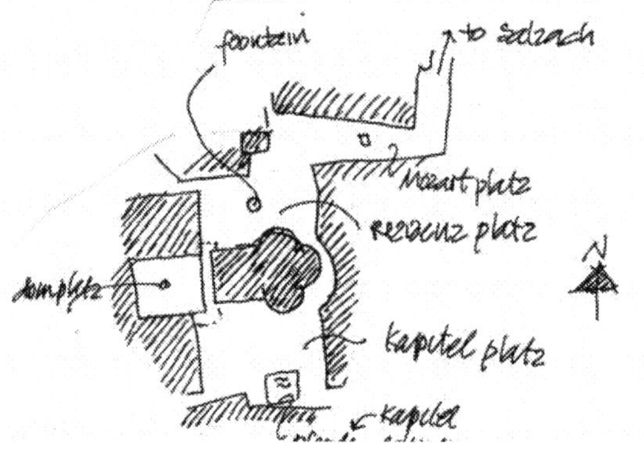

The ragged West side and the imbalance of the two main defining walls make the space drift into the Residenz Platz. This square is of enormous dimensions. The uninteresting façade of the Residenz on the west side, the monument in the middle

[73] J Fischer von Erlach 1694-1702
[74] J Fischer von Erlach 1699-1705

(too small) and the defensive and closed wall of the Dom create a sort desert, an empty desolate space that does not belong.. A clear definition towards the Mozart platz a more dominant centre piece or a screen of trees to reduce the size could help. The Dom platz in front of the Dom[75] which one can reach through a colonnade at the same time portico of the Dom is so formal and lacks interest.
The Kapittel Platz is again large and ill defined. The water work at the south side is not related to anything and looks somewhat lost.
Salzburg is not a baroque city. It is still medieval in character and damaged by the overambitious plans of Baroque princes, who lacked money, vision or will to create an urban Baroque Salzburg that is connected into the old fabric. But it has Baroque jewels like the gardens of Schloss Mirabel and the Baroque Museum

8 June.

We did not like the location of our farm near Kopple so we went out and found a new address in Oberdorf, very close to Thalgau. So we said good bye, packed our things and went for a trip. The weather had improved; we had sun in the morning.
We went for the St Wolfgang See and St Wolfgang of "Im weissen Rössl". It was the tourism industry on a Ruhe Tag. It is still early in the season, not really season. There are some people, oldies like us, in for a visit but the whole township sits ready for the herds to arrive. The souvenir shops with white horses in all sizes shapes and material are massed, shoulder to shoulder with the Wirtshauser, Gasthöfe, Pensions, Botvermieter, Reisefuhrer, Postcard sellers they are all there, arranging their tasteless stuff painting their blatantly sentimental lies.. But the herd will come, they are going to be the defenceless victims, they will be skinned. I am certain, we were skinned too, to some extend. The coffee was too expensive, the quality second rate, the service disinterested routine, not at all like Austria.
Anyway the See is majestic, also from any other point along its circumference. The little town St Wolfgang turned into a horrid Walt Disney exploitation of a sentimental operetta of doubtful quality.
Even the church was ghastly; a Baroque refurbishing of a Gothic church. But someone must have had taste. The Gothic altar is good and there are a few works from Guggenbichler[76] and he knew what he was doing.. We left and did some shopping in Gemunden. There it started to rain.
You can't have sun all day all the time.

9 June.

As the forecast had said, it did rain. We tried to visit a traditional farmhouse without much success; it was closed.
The alternative was the St Kolomon Church.
It is the oldest timber structure in Austria. As it is at 1114m, my wife did not manage the last steep climb through pine forest and volunteered to wait for me in the car. The little church is touching in its primitive form on this remote location. And it is a remote

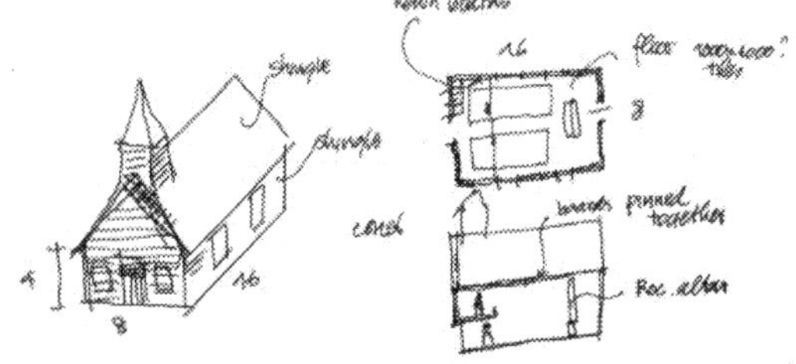

[75] S Solari 1614-28

[76] Johann Meinrad Gugenbichler 1649- 17 23. Woodcarver in the Schwanthaler tradition. From 1679 working in the Mondsee area

location near a well mentioned for the first time around 750 AD. The wooden structure has been maintained, parts have been replaced the whole restored numerous times. How accurate the present form reflects the first plan is every body's guess. To get there is quite an effort. On has to leave the car at the entrance of a pine forest and follow a forest road for a few hundred meters. Then the route to the church turns sharply left up a steep hill. There is no path just marking on the pine trees. The climb is probably a good fifty meters; it is difficult to estimate climbing a slope with an angle of 30 degrees or more. Then the last bit being formed steps you reaches a higher forest road. By then I was in the low hanging clouds we had seen this morning and it was cold. It is not rain it is stationary drizzle; it does not move it just floats. You get quite wet. The road to follow turns right and continues to go up. And past a recent military compound you reach the little sanctuary. It was dead still the drizzle fog did muffle all sound. There were no birds, a grey circle against which the motionless pines stood dark and waiting. I spent some time there and made some sketches of the structure.

Sunday 10 June.

Rain or no rain we had to get out. On an isolated farm the rain does seem to affect you more. It is more omnipresent and its effect on the landscape is so much more visible, noticeable. So we went in the car and guided by Lydia[77] we just went. The goal was Raitenhaslach on the west bank of the Salzach just in Germany.

We had to pass Oberndorf- and not many will know this- nor did we, Oberndorf is the "Stille Nacht "town or hamlet. Here lived the poet and the composer of the probably most widely known Christmas carol. There is the church of the "Uraufführung" There is a "Stille Nacht Museum" where they sell "Stille Nacht" in all varieties, colours and sizes. The also sell a photocopy in colour of the original manuscript, texts and music. But there is little else in Oberndorf. So we crossed into Germany into Laufen.

Through Laufen we went on to Tittmoning. The main church there is a three nave Gothic church with a Rococo refurbishing with some good quality sculpture.

The town itself is nothing out of the ordinary and very typical for the region.

11 June.

We continued our expeditions into Germany and assisted by Lydia we found some very interesting spots. The main visit Altöting, a little place with a long and colourful history. The most interesting place is then Kapellen Platz. It is a large open space very large indeed. In the middle is a square defined by hedges and trees. In this square cut out of the main open space sits the Pilgrim church. This in its oldest part, is a round building about 7 m diameter of which inside shows an eight conch. This structure goes back to the eighth century and was designed as a baptistery. It has been extended and surrounded by an ambulatory. The church and the ambulatory house an ever growing collection of votive offerings of those who came to seek help and found it in some form. There are quite a few very recent votives proving that the devotion is very much alive. The other churches (the place counts a further 4 churches) are of little or no interest. The central place in a way has the same structure as the square in Padova. Outside the central green area there is a similar feeling of nowhere ness. Very interesting. On our way back we stopped at St Oswald in Traunstein. It is an attractive little church, nothing out of the ordinary.

12 June.

The weather had improved and we ventured out into Germany again to Rupolding to visit the St Gregory church[78]. Its plan is very accomplished and achieves a good unity.

---

[77] Lydia L Dewiel; Oberbayern. Dumont Kunst und Reiseführer

[78] J B Gunetzhaine 1738

The altars do work together and the pulpit (the eternal problem) is nicely balanced with a more elaborate Crucifixion group this time with St Peter and S Magdalena the two famous repenting saints. The frescos are not integrated in the structure and look more like applied tapestry. The quality of the sculpture is good and the much earlier Madonna is quite good. The day was filled with an interesting drive and a prolonged stay. A relaxing day.

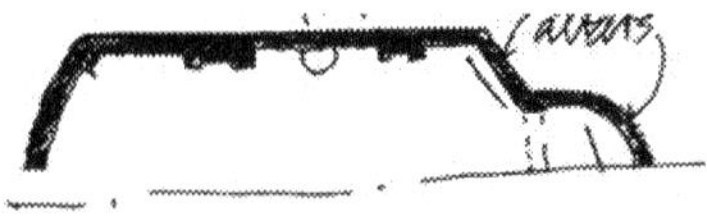

13 June.

We had booked ourselves in accommodation near the Salzburg airport and packed our things. We had said good-bye to Thalgau the night before and had a bottle of wine with our hosting couple the same evening. So we were free to go. We were a bit introverted both, to morrow my wife would fly back to Holland and I would be going on into Germany to visit the Rococo in Southern Germany. We went into Germany to the Chiemsee and Fraueninsel.

It was interesting but not of the quality that we had expected. And there were quite a number of tourists around. We went to Salzburg in time to inspect the accommodation and get prepared for to morrow. We had a quiet diner down the road in a Chinese restaurant, in the courtyard. The evening was beautiful and quiet. After diner we walked a bit around. It amazed us that the built up area along the main road is only 5o meters or so wide, once out of it we were in rural land.

14 June.

I saw my wife off at the Airport. It was overcast and we both did not say much. A very nice trip had ended when the last call for boarding sounded. I did not wait to see the plane take of.

Somewhat concerned how I would cope with doing and the driving and the way finding and having none to unload the tension and frustration on I got in the car. It was "Froleichnams Tag" and a holiday in Germany and Austria. All Tourist Information Offices would be closed. It might be now that the camping gear in the back of the car would come in handy. So from here it will be part two. But a preliminary conclusion or remark:

A church building is a part of the teaching and indoctrination. It has to convey the message of the Roman Catholic Church. This means that the theological background is important. Most churches appear to have a theological concept of what the Church as a whole and the interior of this church, dedicated to a Saint more in particular wants to put forward. I have no idea who created this concept, how important it is in the artistic concept and how prescriptive it is in detailing the interior.

The development from an Italianate Church type (Il Gesu or other plans like central ovals) to a fully integrated environment is very gradual. In the seventeenth and early eighteenth century the interior still is a structural skeleton and the decoration attached to the structure.

There are many indications where the development will lead. We have not seen a fully integrated church jet. Some do come close. Many of the churches in Bavaria and Baden Württemberg are later and could be close to the end of the development. But we will see.

Viechtach

14 June.
I found the way to Oberndorf easy enough and from there to Osterhofen was not a problem. Bavaria is deserted on Frohleichnam day; you have the secondary roads to yourself.
When I arrived in Osterhofen, the sun was trying to get through and it was at least dry. All I could find was an insignificant parish church with absolutely no features of any interest. I walked around a bit to stretch my legs when I detected a town plan. It soon explained the whole situation. The church I was after was in Altomarkt[79], Gemeinde Osterhofen. So assisted by the map I found the church and it was well worth the effort. It is a really nicely coordinated interior. The side altars visible from the entrance do lead into and work well with the main altar. The structural building starts to work with and answer the decoration. The structure and furnishing flow together in one space defining interior and the distinction between structure and decoration is fading into irrelevance.

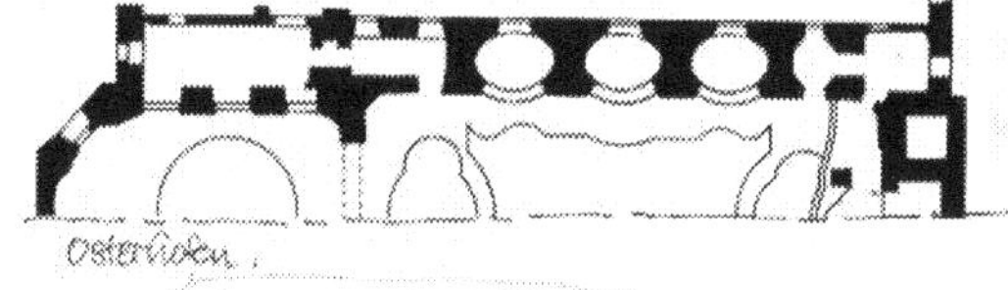

When I left the church I sat down over a cup of coffee to work out what to do. Bavaria was deserted. On the way up I had seen the decorations for the Frohleichnam festivities. Frohleichnam translates as Corpus Christi day a celebration of the holy Sacrament and more particular the post Trente emphasis on the actual presence of God in the sacrament. The celebration climaxes in an elaborate procession through the village or township. Traditionally the houses are adorned with displays of flowers around a sculpture or image of Sacred Heart or the Virgin Mary, elaborate flower carpets with religious symbols and display of yellow white flags and banners. I remember them from the forties and fifties in my home village Best. Flower carpets, white-yellow banners and decorations; the decorations of the houses along the route of the Frohleichnam procession it all was there. It seemed not a good idea to rely on any Tourist information office for accommodation, especially not in the rural centres. They all would be closed.
The weather forecast had been optimistic: sun in the afternoon and Friday would be sunny. So it would be possible to camp. I looked at the map to find an area with a few campings and suitably located in view of the program for the next days. I decided to go in the direction of Cham through the valley of the Schwarzer Regen.
Just past four in the afternoon, I saw a sign from far enough away to be able to make up my mind and turn of without creating a major traffic incident, and turned into the road to Viechtach. Following the signs, which did not stop somewhere in the middle of nowhere leaving you at an intersection with no further directions, they continued right up to the entrance. So this time I arrived at a many stars camping; Knaus and ANWB recommended. The man in the office was helpful, the price reasonable and he had plenty of room; so I booked a campsite. The sanitary was excellent: good clean showers, a drying room, and laundry. There was at the entrance a little shop and a restaurant with a modest card and prices. So you did not have to go to Viechtach, which was the nearby town, a few kilometres away.

---

79 J.M. Fischer.1726-1740

The whole set up is German: "ordentlich organisiert" and for 60-70% filled with permanent campers, complete with front garden properly fenced and maintained, gnomes not forgotten. All with a TV disk etc," so gut als wie zu Hause!"[80]
I found myself a quiet spot away from the caravans not to far from the sanitation and started camp. It was not a problem; all was there and the tent was up in no time. I organised the tent, sorted out the breakfast stuff. I still had some bread and put the little Camping Gaz together for tea. By then it was time to see what the restaurant was like. I had a beer and a decent very simple meal for an acceptable price. I could have cooked an emergency ration of the cans we had bought in Austria but it was best to save them for a real occasion. I listened to the radio in the car prepared a route for the following day and turned in early.
15 June.
I was up and about at 6. There wasn't very much entertainment so I went to sleep early the night before. I made tea, had a shower and breakfast and then set about to fill in the road details for the program of the day. Being on your own in the car without the assistance of a map and sign reader the route needs an organised set of details to give directions at crucial points. You have to go over the route at least to the first goal or stop, noting road numbers, place names along the route and other towns or places that could be of importance in road finding. You write that out on a piece of paper so that you do not have to unfold it and fits into the alcove of the speedo without blocking the speed indication. The Peugeot had enough room there and you could flip it up with one hand to see where you should be going or looking for. It has worked well on the normal secondary routes with limited traffic but not so well in cities. There it is relying on the main route indications and instinct and good luck, lots of it. If you get lost it is in cities and more particular when there are detours for road works.
With the route set out I went to the office to inquire about the 'Fremdenzimmer" I had seen a notice somewhere mentioning fremden zimmer. They have a facility for visitors to the camping to hire a room for the price more or less of a campsite and car and of course I could have one. I decided to go on using the tent but if the weather turned nasty I had a fall back position and I could stick to the plan to stay and move headquarters early next week, Monday or Tuesday turning west again, away from the Czech border where Viechtach is.
Nothing holding me there I was off to Schönthal. Finding the place was no problem, but the S.Michaelkirche was clearly not the one John Bourke[81] had in mind. There are more Schönthals (the name translates as beautiful valley) in Germany. I'll have another look in the book. I obviously must have made a mistake in my preparations. These were quite elaborate; I had a photocopy of the maps of Austria and Southern Germany pinned against the wall of the spare bedroom and used coloured pins to indicate location and importance of the site. I on reading through John Bourke I had the sites classified in " must see" or category I," should see" or category II, " could see when time permits" or category III. And the sites grouped in regions and looked at possible central locations from where visiting the churches was practical. In this way you would not have to go through the hassles of finding a place to stay each day and most of the time you would not travel with all luggage. It had worked well in Italy and extremely well in Austria. The Church in Schönthal was definitely category I, this church was certainly not Category I, rather empty, war damage and rebuild without décor. I must have made a mistake when plotting.

---

[80] " Just like at home"
[81] John Bourke: Baroque Churches of Central Europe

I had a coffee and on the road again to Weltenburg[82], a former monastery on the bank of the Donau.

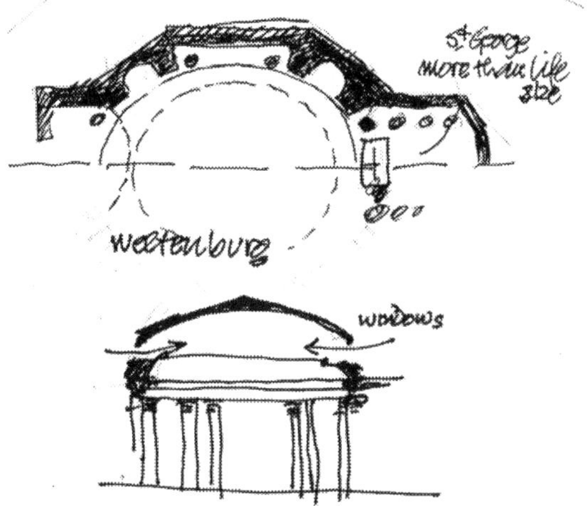

The former monastery is situated in an alcove in the steep bank of the Donau. There is only one road in very tightly fitted between the steep cliff and the Donau. There is apparently not enough parking in the monastery so a few miles before you have to leave the car and walk. At a point where the cliff comes close to the river a wall cuts across the road with a large gate, a little courtyard and another gate. Behind it is the former monastery. Now it is all geared up to "serve "the visitors. The church is a miracle; but luck was not with me. The high point of the experience, St George more than life-size riding out of the light to kill the dragon and rescue the girl was replaced by a photo of the right scale. St George was being restored. The compensation is a detailed exhibition about the finer aspects of restoring a sculpture like that, which was very instructive. It is easy to see still that the whole church is designed as one environment with the drama of St George riding out as the central high point. The plan is a central oval space covered by a dome with very shallow niches or recesses between the supports, the long axis running from entrance to the east or high altar. The retable of the high altar is a highly lit space from which emerges the figure of St George on horseback riding out towards the main space to kill the dragon and save the princess. The symbolic meaning again is clear: the intervention of St George trough the church can save you for damnation or being dragged away by the devil in the same manner he once saved the damsel.
The lower zone of the church is kept rather dark to heighten the contrasts. The dome is in itself a miracle of illusion. It is very well lit by a concealed window zone. It really looks like heaven opening with the Virgin Mary descending to receive Saint Georges into heaven under the approving supervision of the Trinity. The decorations are of good quality, but the quality of each individual piece is unimportant as long as they are not in any way detracting from the overall scheme. An extremely impressive experience of what can be achieved by merging structure an décor; the structural elements no longer look like necessary supports, questions what is structural and what is wall and what is decorations are not relevant. The contrast between outside and inside, the reality of the outside and of the interior not of this world is the architectural statement. It is the sudden exploding of the earthly reality revealing the divine reality immanent in this world and accessible through the Church as institution and in a way in each church as a building.

---

[82] Asam brothers. 1717-1721

It is nice to have to concentrate on finding the next location. You can purge your mind and heart of the last experience and go into the next with a fresh and open mind. The next was Rohr[83].

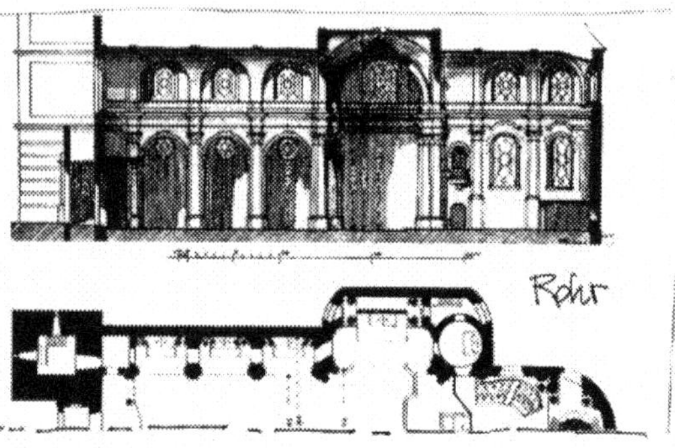

Entering the church you are immediately drawn into the spatial representation of the Assumption of The Virgin. All leads to the elaborate mise en scene behind the high altar. The décor in the church is sober if not austere for a Rococo church: white and gold and pink, no frescos, no saints no side altars visible upon entry, all is filled with the dramatic moment when the Apostles discover the empty sarcophagus. This scene receives an abundance of light from the windows in the apse. Above the life size (more than) group of Apostles against the backdrop of a large blue drapery (plaster), the Virgin is carried upwards by two angels. She together with the two angels form a life-size plaster sculpture supported in mid air on the end of a cleverly concealed steel structure. Gold light streams down from the Trinity awaiting her arrival. It is amazing what has been achieved. The effect in Weltenburg is intense in its richness of colour and contrast and dramatic light effects; the effect in Rohr is the serene contemplation of the miracle. You stand in awe really and that was what the designers wanted you to be. I reached home i.e. Viechtach after five. I cleaned up and had a beer and diner in the restaurant and turned in early. The forecast is for rain and more rain increasing till Sunday. I will have to look seriously at having one of the rooms.

16 June

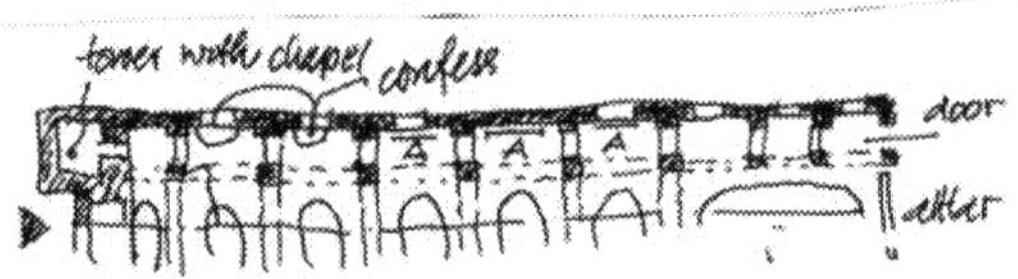

It did rain overnight but I slept well the tent kept me dry and warm. I was out at six. There is little or no entertainment and the days driving and taking in the essence of the churches ask a lot from ones concentration. The weather forecasts were even more pessimistic - the car radio helps-so I decided to take the tent down and go for one of the rooms. Before the tent was really dry it started to rain and this time a steady pour. So I took off to the office booked the room and began the transfer of my belongings. There was a dry spell and with some toilet paper and the wind I managed to get the tent dry and packed in the little Peugeot Al that organised I drove to the entrance to make good an omission. On my way up I had overlooked Niederalteich and making this good

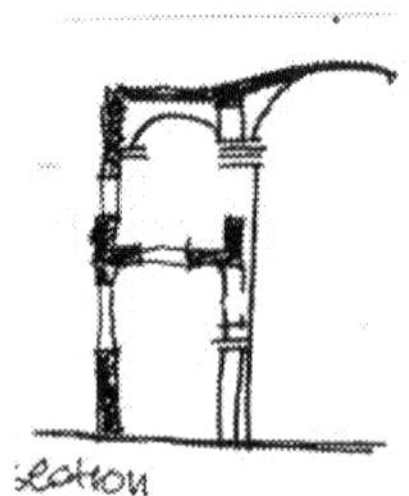

[83] J. Bader and E. Asam. 1717-1725

now I could at the same time visit Aufhausen. But the gate is locked between 1 and 3 to give the campers some rest or Ruhe. I managed to see Niederalteich[84] but Aufhausen has to wait. Back on the camping it started to pour. In the restaurant I met a Dutch couple on their way back from a caravan trip to the Balkan. We had a chat about relativity of anonymity in a smaller community and how that complicates life and also banking in a relatively small community (he was the loan manager).

17 June

I have a program for today as I could not make Aufhausen[85] the day before, I'll start there. Rural Bavaria is empty on Sunday, the roads through the undulating plane of green farmland and villages look deserted.. I reminded me of the absolute boredom of Sundays of my younger days when most activities were judged unsuitable for Sundays. You just hung around waiting for Monday. I saw Aufhausen and from there I went on to Rinchnach.

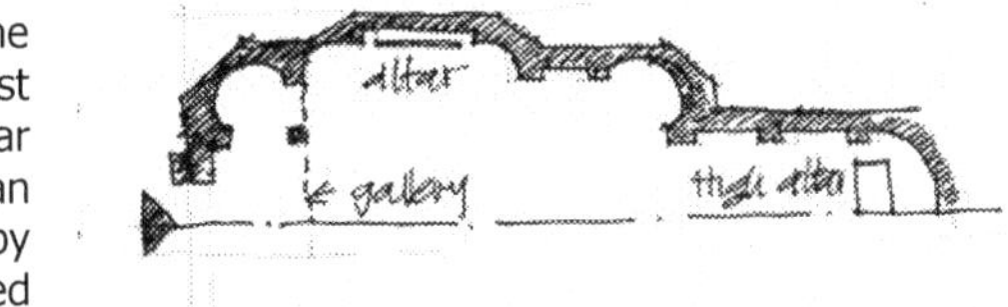

On the way up, the sun came through reluctantly; the forecast could be right: it would clear they said. Rinchnach[86] is an attractive little church by Zimmerman. I became engaged in a discussion with the only two other visitors a German couple about the only thing not right: the straight outline of the gallery for the choir over the entrance. In the middle of the discussion the Man stopped, looked at me and asked the untranslatable sentence" Was machen Sie denn eigentlich beruflich?"[87] We both appeared to be architect in public service, he recently retired. That gave us more common ground from which we ventured some appreciation of what the Rococo architects tried to achieve and the measure to which they had been successful. He had seen churches I still had on my list and I had been to many he had not seen yet. So we could give each other some previews and hints. So I was later then expected when I reached the camping.

18 June.

The weather was not much better, and now being in a room and far away from the car with my only time indication, it was rather difficult to organise oneself. So I had decided to buy a little alarm in addition to the only time device I had the clock in the car- I never wear a wristwatch; I don't have one- which had shown not to be very practical, even when in the tent with the car close by. To find a thing like that you have to ask a woman, I discovered. I had tried the man in the restaurant; he had no idea nor had the man in the office. Somewhere in town they thought a jeweller they supposed. To me that did not seem to be the place for a cheap no frills alarm. When I was about to wander of into Viechtach I remembered that women always know more about shops and shopping; so you should ask a woman. That was easy; the Tourist information always has practical women so I walked in and after finding something out about my next stop I began with some hesitation "I like to put to you a question that only a woman can answer". What happened was exactly as I expected; the office froze; I was the only client at the moment. I could almost hear them think who is going to ring the police. "It is a simple question, "I said "but I have tried a few men at the camping, but they have no clue where I can find a cheap but

[84] A.O. J.M. Fischer. 1724

[85] J.M. Fischer. 1736-1751

[86] D. Zimmerman. 1727-1729

[87] [May I ask what you do for a living]

reliable alarm". The tension fell away, general laughter and abundance of advice, good advice it turned out. The first address had a Braun alarm inclusive of battery for four mark fifty, about four and a half New Zealand dollars; a very good buy and a very reliable alarm. After some further shopping and a visit to the local Rococo it was time to prepare for the shift tomorrow: to Gössweinstein. In the restaurant I had again the company of the Dutch couple. They were leaving tomorrow morning early; they hoped to make it back to Holland and home in one long day. After they had left- they wanted an early start- I found out that the" wirt"did speak more than one word of Greek and knows Holland well and not because he was there in 40-45, for he was a bit too young for that, being younger than me.

Gössweinstein

19 June

I left Viechtach almost as planned at 8.45 and apart from confusion in Cham it all went like clockwork but for the weather. The sun was supposed to come through especially in North Bavaria but did not show. As Gössweinstein is not too far I had a few churches further North in the route the first being Wladsassen above Weiden against the Czech border.

I arrived in Waldsassen[88] after a relaxing ride. The church is nothing out of the ordinary but for the tabernacle in the shape of a golden globe. A similar tabernacle I saw in Christkindl. A very ornate church.

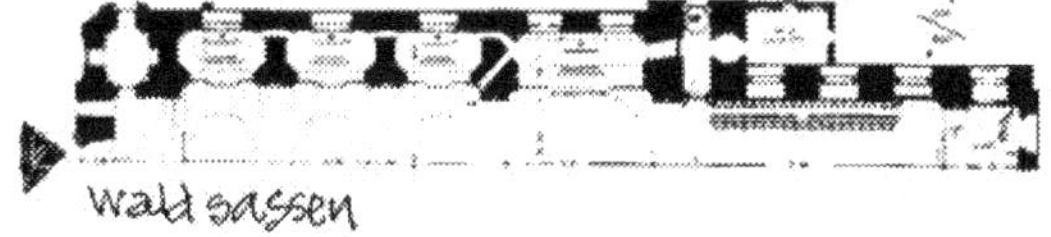

Kappel[89] had a very good rating in the guide. It is dedicated to the H Trinity and like Paura is based on the concept of three axes of the equal importance. The problem of three equal axes emerges when you put in fixed seating; the seats have to face something and be put in on one of the three axes. That immediately creates uncomfortably empty spaces at the sides of the seating area and puts the whole triangular scheme out. The entrance in Paura could be on any of the axes; there was enough room inside. In Kappel the church is smaller and not conceived as a central dome enriched with three apses but as a three conch with a triangular central space. Towers are placed on the three corners of the triangle. The body of the church is surrounded by an ambulatory that allows an entrance not related to any of the axis in the interior and close by you cannot judge how the interior relates to the exterior. The two entrances to the church itself are a bit problematical. You are sneaking in behind the back of the altar for the Son or the Holy Ghost as the niches on both sides of all altars are used as Confessionals. The Father has the sacristy behind it in a bit cut off from the ambulatory. This arrangement chooses for the Father as the first of the H Trinity, a proposition, which could be regarded as heretical. The hidden entrances do separate the outside from the interior; in the church you cannot see a way out; it is a closed interior static without progression from east to west, which you find so carefully orchestrated in most Rococo churches. The whole scheme reminded me of the Church for the Trinity and St John Nepomuk somewhere just over the German

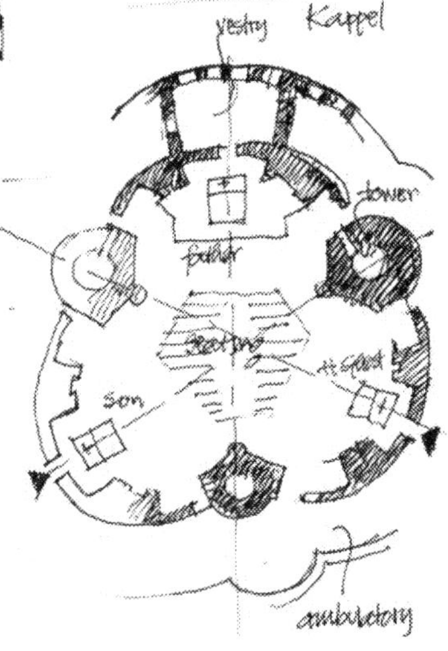

[88] Dietzenhofer. 1681-1704

[89] G. Dietzenhofer. 1685-1689

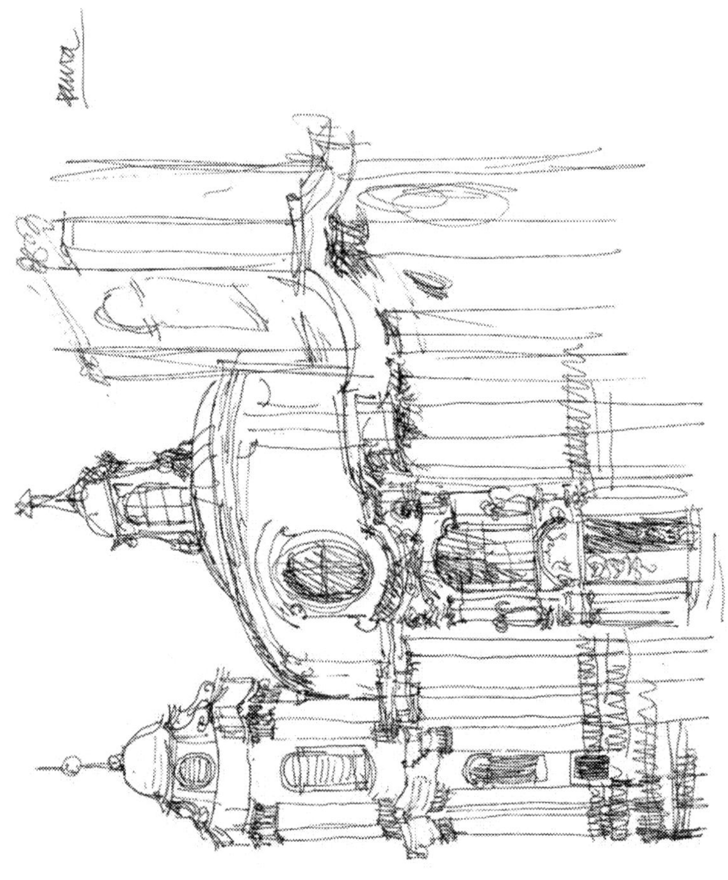

37. Paura, as Kappel based on a tri axial concept. A more convincing realisation.

border in Czechia. This sort of spatial games seems to have been popular in this region even in earlier times. My next stop for the day was the former Stift Speinshart. Here in Speinshart[90] you find a small community living in what in former times was a monastery or Stift. The church now serves the community and only recently some monks have returned. The whole is under restoration. It appeared to me that the restoration accepted the present occupation and alterations and was restricted to the church and consolidation the current use. Restoration could have been dogmatic and gone back to the pre secularisation and destroyed the very interesting conversion in to a little village of the former large Stift complex.

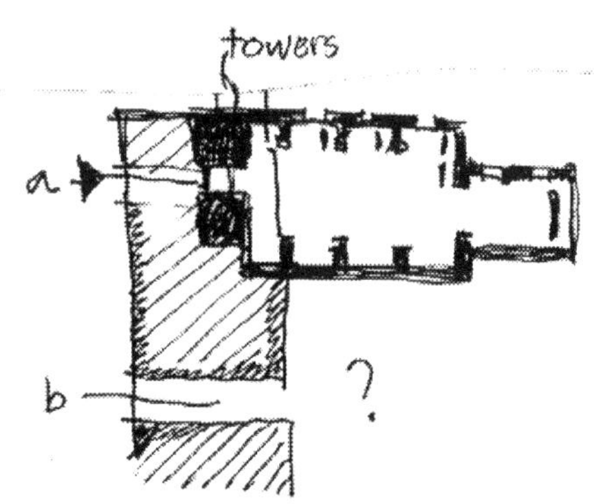

I arrived at Gössweinstein[91] just after three. I parked the car just in front of what later appeared to be the Tourist office. That I found out later when I was about to walk the little town for the second time looking for it. I soon had a room with shower toilet and breakfast for thirty-two marks, quite a good room and almost next to the tourist office. I had seen the sign "Zimmer frei", but thought it would be best to get a room through the Tourist Information. To make the day the sun came through and I had a quick look the Church by Balthasar Neumann. But I will have a better and more detailed look after to morrow, when I have been to Banz and Vierzehn Heiligen: the program for to morrow.

20 June.

The trip trough the valley of the Wiesent was very attractive. It is one of the many little Schwitzerlands that you find in Europe. It usually is an old undulating hill country with young erosion valleys. The Ardennes in Belgium and Luxemburg are sometimes given the same name; it is a similar landscape. It provides intimate valleys and larger vistas on the hills. The sun was out; the wind was still cool. The whole trip over Hollfield, Ebensfeld and Staffelstein went without a glitz. I had decided first to see Banz[92]. I had high expectations of Vierzehn Heiligen and if the church lived up to the expectation it would be difficult to see Banz in its own right. I am glad I did. Banz is certainly a very accomplished creation, though clearly earlier than Vierzehnheiligen. The decoration works well to create one overall experience. The individual sculpture is good; it is perhaps a bit heavy in the stucco decoration. I enjoyed it. And there was someone playing the appropriate music on the organ.

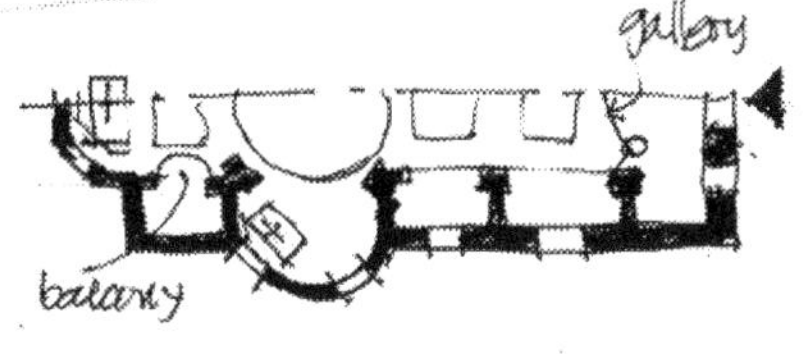

90 Dietzenhofers.1691-1706

91 B. Neumann. 1730-1739

92 J. Dietzenhofer. 1710-1719

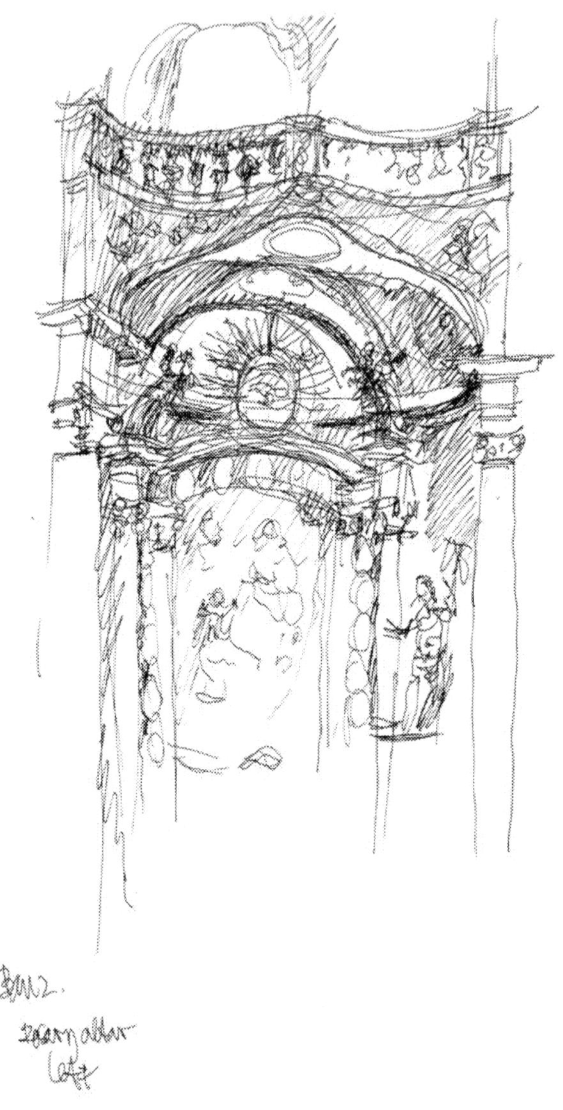

38. Banz. Rosary altar (left side altar)

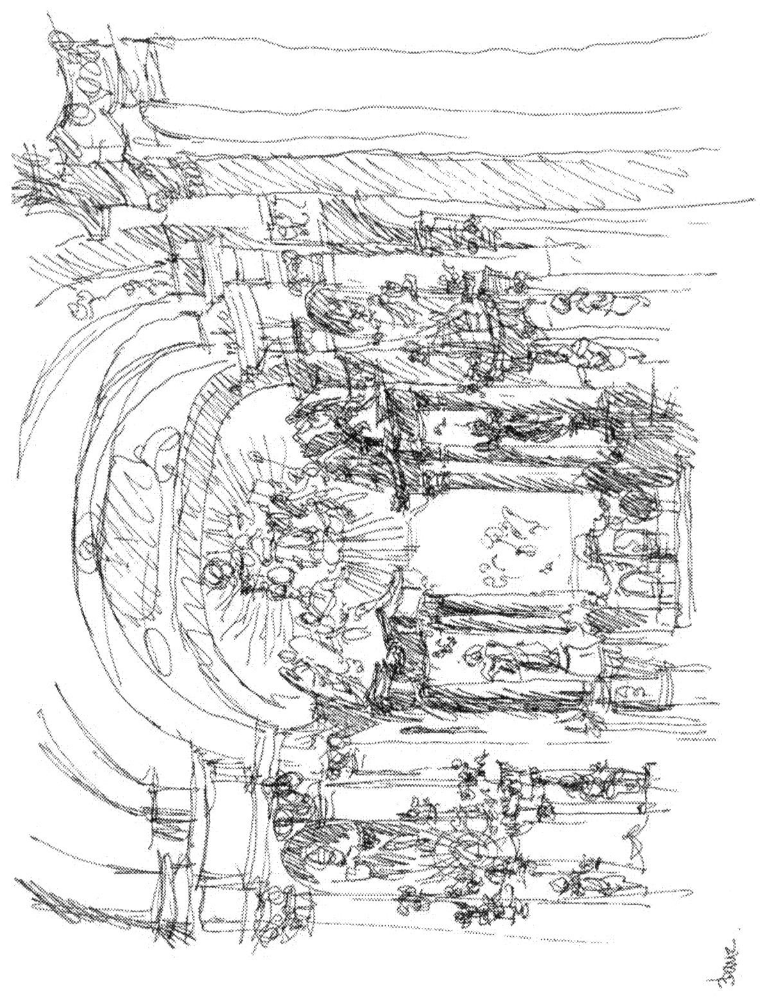

39. Banz. Nave to the East with High Altar.

To create some distance I stopped for a bit of lunch Coffee with Apfelstrudel mit Zahne and then to Vierzehn Heiligen. Coming from Banz you can see it sitting on its high location and there is along stretch where you can see and Banz, which has an equally high location, and Vierzehn Heiligen[93]. You have to approach the church on foot climbing the hill. I liked that; it gave me a chance to prepare myself. I know the church quite well from plans and publications. You form an opinion on what it is going to be like. And that sometimes is a disappointment. I must say I was a bit tense; I had been looking forward to this experience.

The main entrance under the two towers is closed; the entrance is through the transepts.

On entering I knew it. The real thing is better than I could have hoped for. It is one of those rare buildings where one sees space as the active formative entity in the design and the solids are there to make it visible and support it. I have experienced it only at a few occasions: Beauvais, Amiens, Vezelay and now Vierzehn Heiligen. It is all so right, so exactly as it should be! The texture the colours the frenzy of the sculptural decoration at all points to and supports the calm elegance of the spatial complexity. And what I had thought to be the high points all turned out to be as imagined but more so; amazing! I spent more then two hours there and I could go back again and not be bored.

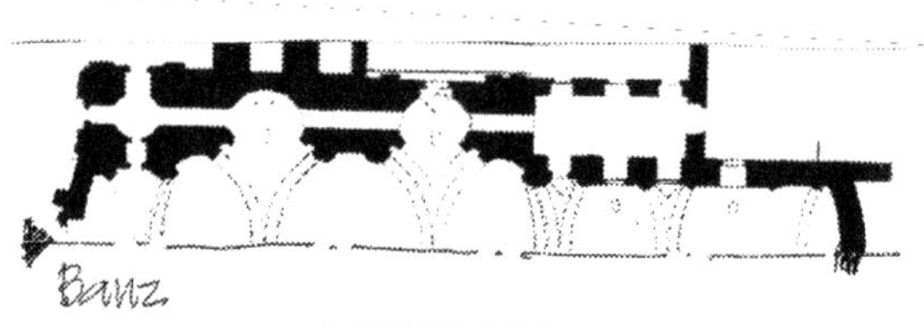

It is a miracle to conceive and a miracle to control the abundance of detail so that it all works towards the total concept. The way the space changes intensity with different height levels: great.(plan on page 159)

How the altar of the Vierzehn Heiligen gains in importance in the heaven and becomes the center of the composition! The earthly division in five oval and circular spaces on the main axis at ground level has the 14 Saints altar in the third of the spaces solidly in the nave. Rising up to the vaulting the second and fourth space are squeezed out by the expanding oval of entrance, the oval with the altar of the Vierzehnheiligen and the oval of the chancel space. The altar of the Vierzehn Heiligen is now the central moment. Entering the church from the west it is the vault that first demands attention where the space dedicated to the Fourteen Saints is the centre of the composition.. It is only at second observation that the position of the main monument in plan is noted. It is then that the two side altars immediately after the entrance connect and show the second space. In the third space or articulation it is amazing to see how simple and gracefully the galleries connect the round columns to define the shape of the space for the Saints altar. The spatial definition is just strong enough and at the same time open enough to show the second skin of the outer definition to make it into a real double skin definition or a fuzzy wall to the interior. The crossing gets just enough support from the four pillars with their entablature to be clearly there. It is all so extraordinarily accomplished. It all looks so natural so self-explanatory, so "that is how you do this" that I could sit there for

[93] B. Neumann. 1744-1772

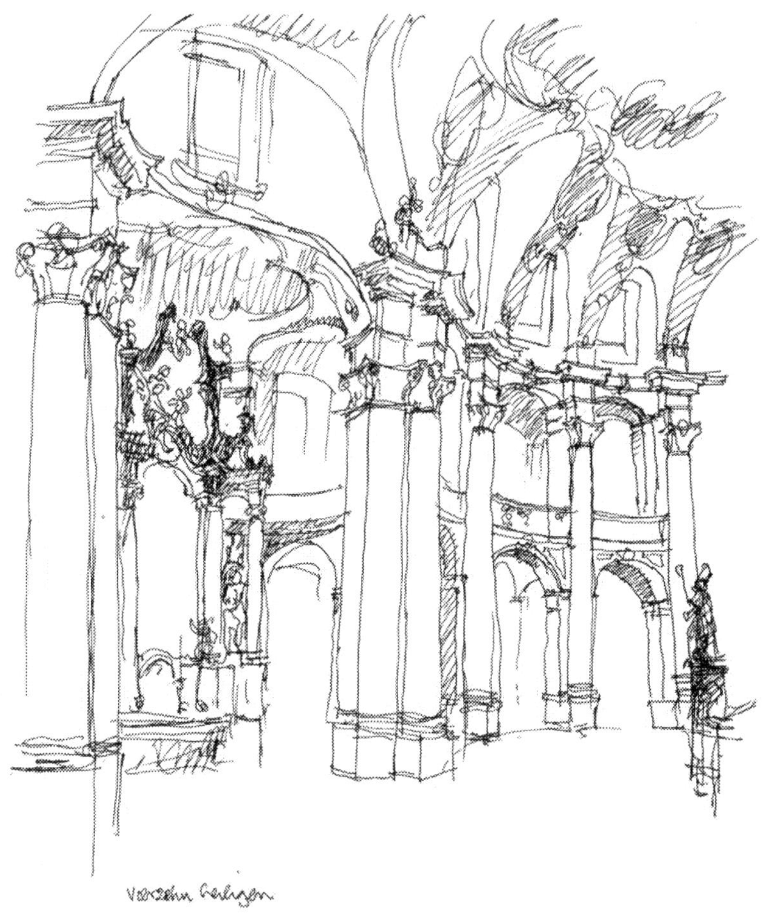

40. Vierzehnheiligen the third bay in plan, containing the altar for the Fourteen Saints.

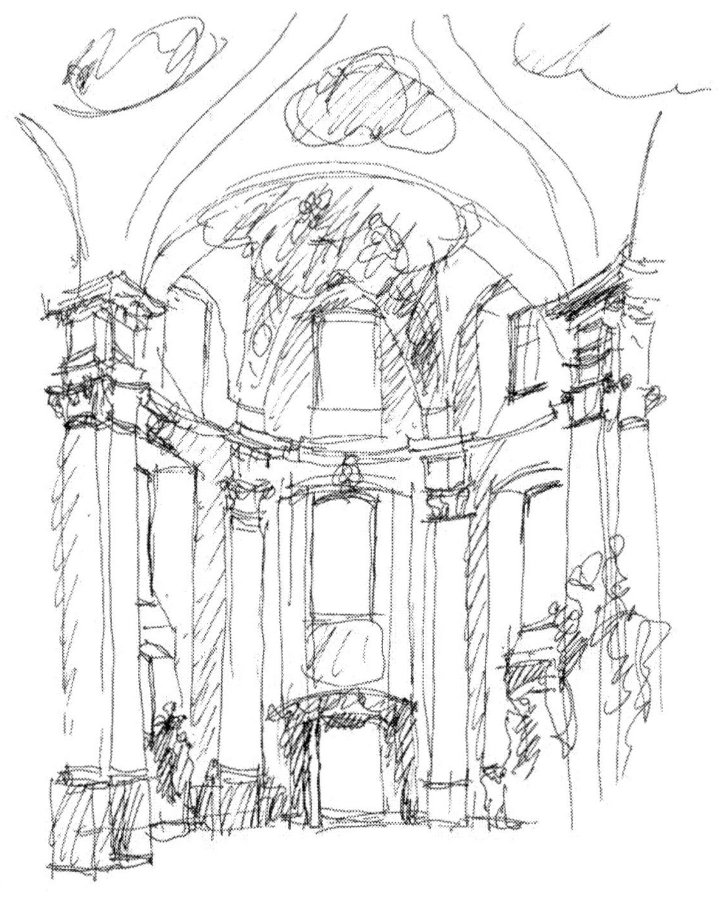

41. Vierzehnheiligen. Transept and crossing with entrance.

hours and enjoy the excitement of recreating. The complexity of the space is astounding. At ground level there is an increased drive towards the chancel. The second bay at ground level has small secondary spaces or niches in which the side Altars are placed. The third ground level bay is central nave only, the side aisles compressed to the space necessary to have a fuzzy wall. The fourth bay the side aisle are and at ground level and in heaven a space with a proper opening to heaven in a saucer dome with fresco, stronger than the second bay. Therefore, at ground level there is a steady progression or expanding towards the High Altar. At ceiling level, in heaven the side aisles are disconnected from the main line and it is now a perfect central composition a central oval with the two subordinate ovals of the entrance with the gallery for the choir and the oval of the High Altar. It is perfect; but if one has to say something: the west gallery, does it cut too far in over the entrance oval? Under some angles, it seems to do and from other viewpoints it looks convincing.
I tried some drawings to record how it seems to work. With great reluctance I left. I was given a lift to the car park at the foot of the hill by a German couple I had undoubtedly bored with a technical explanation of the difficulties Balthasar Neumann faced when he was called upon to rescue his original design that had been altered by his successor.
On my way back along the same route I decided to stop in Hollfeld to get the feel again of the ordinary Rococo. Out of luck; the church was filled with scaffolding it was under restoration.
Arriving in Gössweinstein I went to have a look again at the church also by Neumann. The sun was out, it was a glorious day and the church did not disappoint, but even Balthasar Neumann does not always make a masterpiece. But it is a good church: a strong solid exterior in cut stone like Vierzehn Heiligen and a fleeting and frail interior. The Church needs cleaning; the grey paint borders on black at places. Coming in the experience is the high altar; the altars in the transept are angled to the entrance and seem to connect with the main; the two little balconies in the choir lead the eye naturally from the side altars onto the main moment of the high altar. The pulpit though again is a pain; it disturbs the balance and is to dominant to be on the second plane of attention. It is beautiful with its life-size evangelists but in the whole again the unresolved item. With sunlight brightening the colours it looked convincing; a rewarding well-proportioned church.
After diner I rang Hans, my wife's cousin. We used to have regular contact before I emigrated to New Zealand but he is not much of writing person and we had not seen each other for quite some time. He had plans to come out and spent a week with me in Germany. We made some provisional arrangements. I will firm them up on Saturday when I know where I am and can give directions where to meet.

Sommerhausen

21 June.
I am on my way again to settle somewhere near Würzburg. I had my eyes set on Ochsenfurt some twenty km south of Würzburg on the bank of the Main. I left round eight and it all went like clockwork. I left the Autobahn just before Würzburg to turn south along the Main. Arriving in Ochsenfurt I found the Tourist Office easy enough and the man there was quite helpful. When I had explained what I was after he said he needed half an hour or so. As the trip had been without problems I was not in a hurry it was still early in the morning. I had a walk through the little town. Ochsenfurt has its medieval wall almost completely intact and has all the charms of a medieval town: a compact and easy to grasp structure and a lot of charming and unexpected corners and twists. When I sat down for a beer in the main street I got involved in a conversation with a group of retired men touring their Germany by bike. They were concentrating on Rococo churches. I could not help myself and had to give them some advice on which churches to see. In the end I got myself an offer to be their guide. They would provide a bike and so on. It was of course a flattering offer but for practical reasons I had to decline. I was somewhat late at the tourist office. All was arranged. Frau Furke in Sommerhausen would be pleased to have me. He rang to confirm gave me a map how to find my accommodation and a copy of the agreement and a copy to hand to Frau Furke. The original stayed in the office, probably for taxation - what else? - purposes. The house was a very new house in a small development just outside the little town's ramparts and gate. Frau Furke was in her fifties and her husband had early retirement. They had built the house for their retirement in this region and added a basement with one double one single bedroom and ablutions and an Aufenthaltszimmer which is a living area with T.V. Breakfast is served there at the time arranged; all very convenient and well presented. The quality of this B&B service in Germany as I have experienced it is very good and the prices are more than attractive. I was shown into the double room. It gave me some more space she said and it was still early in the season. I settled in and decided to have a look around in Würzburg. Sommerhausen sits on the right-hand bank of the Main a ten or so km south of Würzburg. The local road along the Main used to lead straight in to Würzburg but on approaching Würzburg you are now diverted into a ring road around the centre. I had a map of the city and decided to follow the ring road which would lead me to the Main again and use the parking on the bank of the Main shown on my map. It worked and the city was close by, the tourist information not too far. I did find the Internet café easily enough and checked for mail and send some letters. I had picked up from the information office that there was some work of Riemenschneider[94] around in the churches in and around Würzburg. Riemenschneider is not strictly on the program as he is a late Gothic woodcarver. His reputation however is such that I allowed myself the sidetrack. He has a larger exhibition in the Fortress that overlooks the town. I have put it on the program.
Without any hurry I wandered through the town and went back late in the afternoon. The weather was better than expected, quite warm and sunny. For diner I went to Sommerhausen. Outdoors, I had forgotten the luxuriously long warm summer nights of Europe at that latitude. It did not cool down you can sit out till midnight without any hint of chill. I have missed that in Napier. Although at a latitude of 38 degrees which is the same as Athens, Rome and Madrid, the summer evenings are not as warm. The proximity of the sea and the absence of large landmasses make the

[94] Tilman Riemenschneider c.1460-1531

summer in Napier not as hot as Athens and Rome and the evening much cooler. The presence of the vast oceans around a small landmass as New Zealand restricts the temperature fluctuations. The warm lingering of the light in a slow twilight sitting at the bank of the Main filled me with memories of my youth.

That part of Germany Frankenland is outside the mainstream and in itself time has bypassed it. Most little towns along the Main below Würzburg have not felt the need to demolish their medieval walls and lay out. Sommerhausen is no exception. It is situated in the Main valley which is relatively narrow against a sharp rise to the higher more undulating hills mostly farmland. The steeper banks of the Main are planted with vines and they have produced wines that were locally known. They have started to push their wines and to raise the standard of their produce. At the same time the little towns have been discovered by the 'craft crowd". It could save the little townscapes, but it will make them in the long rung very arty and artificial. I have seen that in many little towns in France well preserved or restored and filled with shops selling pretentious arts and craft ware. The dirt and roughness of everyday rural use carefully removed and the quaintness and little quirks carefully polished up and maintained. At present it was not to "arty" or tourist oriented as jet. But it will come! I did have I decent meal for a decent price and a good glass of wine. It is quite an attractive region.

22 June.

Today it is going to Würzburg to have a good look. The inner city has all the charm of a medieval town in its lay out. The townscape looks harder than e.g. Salzburg. I can think of two reasons. First the ridges of the roofs are parallel to the street. The street definition is more defensive as there is no axis connecting the definition to the street other than the secondary derived from the openings. Second the townscape lacks the common structuring in white and pastels, which is so characteristic in Austria and Southern Bavaria. The mono coloured skin is more defensive. Further as in Linz there is a double tramline running through the main street in the pedestrian area. Again this has not been resolved; people are conscious of it and the street works as two shop fronts with only limited people crossing the street at leisure. There are plenty of charming little corners and squares but on the whole it is much harder. The bombardment by the Allied Forces in 1945 just before the capitulation has almost wiped out the old town. What we see now is a rebuild that lacks the patina of ages. This of course is reflected in the new frontage. There was immeasurable damage to the historic treasures of the city. Most churches were not spared and lost a lot of their furnishings and interiors. The Residenz by Balthasar Neumann was also extensively damaged but has been painstakingly restored. There is an exhibition on the restoration, which is quite interesting as it shows how some of the gilding and painting of sculpture was done. It is a pity most of the churches of my list looked bare and one could only imagine what the full interior looked like.

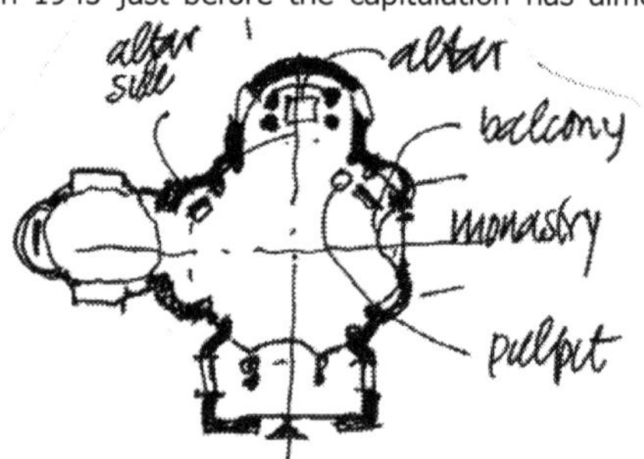

A visit to the Kapelle[95] by Balthasar Neumann, which had been spared, was interesting but the interior is desperately in need of a good cleaning.

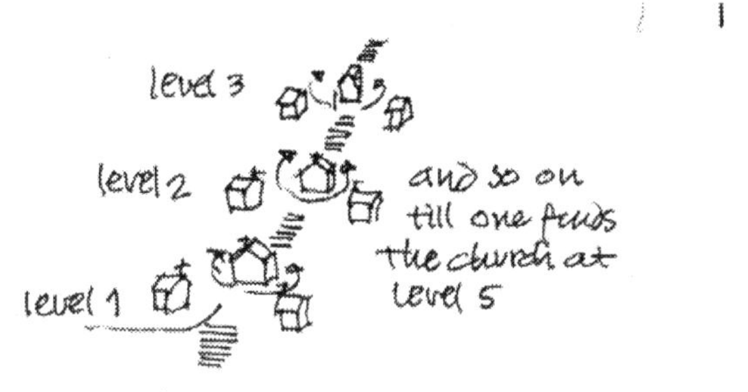

The Residenz[96] was on the list of "must see" and it lived quite up to the expectations. The main stair is grand. The ceiling by Tiepolo shows that the whole aim of the exercise is a merger of reality and representation, to destroy the definitions as separations and restrictions of space. It aims at connecting the space we are in with large spaces imagined by the artist. It is done by astonishing perspective and transitions from the make believe 3 d space into the real 3 d space we move in. Some of the figures in the fresco have a full-scale limb in plaster sticking out into the non-painted space. I have seen it before in some churches but not as accomplished as Tiepolo's efforts.

The Chapel by Neumann is exciting a bit busy of overdone partly because the interior is somewhat strong in colour for the size of the space. I quite enjoyed the free walk through the interiors. It is worth coming back to. The gardens I did not like as much as the Salzburg one.

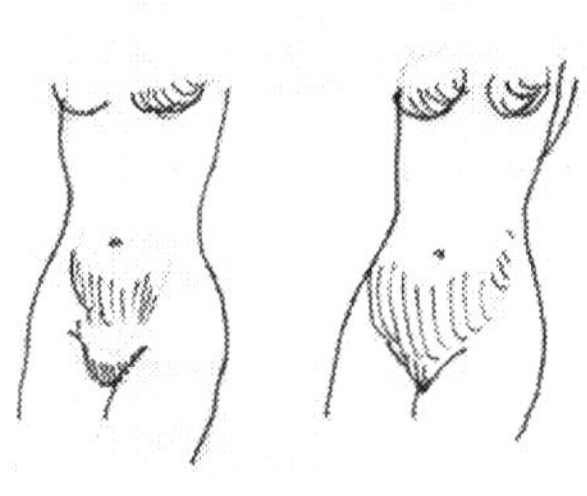

From there to the fort for Riemenschneider. The not too large exhibition- most work of Riemenschneider is still in the churches that commissioned his work- I thought quite exciting and instructive. To be able to have a close up look of carvings like that is very helpful. I saw that the master also puts hands and such easily damaged parts on later as separate bits of wood. You can have the best direction of the grain to carve the detail and the log does not have to be that big. Further and quite practical: sculpture intended to be only viewed fro the front 270 degrees or so gets hollowed out in the centre from the back to prevent or reduce the risk of cracking. In case of full round sculpture with a secondary view from the back, the work is still hollowed out and the resulting hole closed with a bit of matching timber. When the work is painted or Fasiert as it is referred to in German, the assemblage is covered and there is a lot of scope for this assemblage technique. For the natural finished sculpture careful selection of matching timber can make additions almost invisible for the untrained eye. It does help in technically very difficult to reach areas.

Riemenschneider I thought is superb. I really am impressed by the quality of his carvings in particular hands and faces. His technical skills and his control of

---

95 B. Neumann. 1747-1752

96 B. Neumann. 1732-1738

proportion and stance: that is something special. There was an Eve with the so characteristic late Gothic round lower abdomen, not quite as I like it but superb and her small girlish breast are feminine and enticing. Coming out of the exhibition I strayed from the straight and narrow or the recommended route and landed myself somehow into and Antique market. Most of the items on display were of German origin. There were a number of stands specialising in Rococo sculpture and furniture. It is amazing to see the quality of the items on offer. I did not ask for prices! I had a long talk with one of the exhibiting dealers. He gave me an interesting view on the sometimes obscene spending of the church and bishops on art. It did more for the country and the population than the princes and bishops who involved themselves in the great political wrangles of the time the sport of Kings and Princes. They had the countryside and towns ransacked repeatedly. The areas particularly rich in Rococo had rulers that had the good sense to stay out of war. They did not have to upkeep a large defence and offence force and were not ransacked at regular intervals and could afford to have the population involved in the building and furbishing of their architectural efforts. This goes to prove there is always a bright side, even to very high taxes. And we both agreed: there is still an awful lot of good quality work out there in the second and third tier churches and stately homes that has not been catalogued and identified. His collection of Rococo sculpture had some very good pieces of moderate size for prices a bit beyond my budget. It was time to return to Sommerhausen after a very rewarding day.

I still had to resolve how to organise to meet with Hans coming Sunday. If I was to leave before Sunday, I had to find a new station and then give Hans clear directions how to get there. As it was already Friday I would have to leave tomorrow i.e. Saturday with all the restrictions of closures to find a place to stay where they can also take a visitor for one night or where we can stay for the rest of next week. It could prove difficult to arrange an easy to implement plan to meet up. Having considered many options I decided to stay in Sommerhausen. I quite like the little town with its counterpart Winterhausen on the other side the West side of the Main. They used to be connected by a bridge running from the centre to the centre: die Alte Brücke. It was destroyed during the war and never rebuild. The abutments are still there as a no exit street in Winterhausen and a no exit road just north of Sommerhausen. There are enough restaurants to have a meal and the ambience is of a leisurely, rural pace and charm. So I booked him a single room with Frau Furke and decided on a Ruhetag for Saturday.

23 June.

Ruhetag. I had a quiet drive around the villages in the region and stepped of at some village churches. Luck can't always be with you so Ingolstadt was closed and Sommerhausen under restoration. The little church in Eibelstadt is a Rococo redo of an original Gothic hall church with a rather long chancel. Much of the 15th and 16th quality furnishing has been included in the refurbishing and the net vault has been retained. The roomy late Gothic space with the Rococo furnishing works well. I have noted before that especially the roomy German hall churches do work well with a Rococo refurbishing. The little church in Gaukönighofen is a pleasant church. The restrained decoration is just enough to pull it all together with the three –rather static early- altars. Here again as in Eibelstadt and I have never seen them else where, is an arranged in a diamond pattern around the Virgin Mary medallions with the effigies of the "14 Nothelfer" the fourteen Saints of Vierzehn Heiligen. They do occur with a slight variation in the saints included I know. The quality of the paintings and frescoes is dubious but a Rococo scheme does not rely in first instance on the quality of the individual pieces. It is the overall impression, the interior as one concept, which

is the important effect. In a detailed look the effect of the individual pieces comes into play.
When I came home Frau Furke suggested that I try the Alte Brücke in Winterhausen for a meal. It was run by two Dutch males one cooked the other served. She smiled while she said all this. Was she trying to evoke an opinion or just showing of her tolerance? I had the impression that she thought a man alone could be homosexual. There was also a "Johannis Feuer", she added, which traditionally was quite good.
In the end, I found the "Alte Brücke" after having walked past it a few times. As could be expected it was on the abutments of the former bridge and now a quiet part of the township.
After my meal I had a look at the Festplatz; a beer tent a marquis for the "Blaskapelle" and lots of long wooded tables with fixed seats, all at the flatter parts of the banks of the Main. I did not want to drink beer as I still had to drive back to Sommerhausen on the other side of the Main and to join the crowd on "Mineralwasser" was not an attractive option. I followed the example of the older and the teenage population and walked along the banks of the Main. Returning I decided to have a coffee and a brandy outside the Hotel" Dass Schiff" .It is located on the higher level of the town but also operates an outdoor area on the lower bank of the Main adjacent to the main outdoor area higher up. The fire would not start until after sunset which is very late. The waiter did not or feigned not to know what cognac was but in the end with some intervention of a gentlemen who stayed in the hotel and was about to dine on an more elevated outside area with a large company- I assume family- When I had my coffee and brandy a conversation developed in French which became somewhat awkward, I was sitting about 1.5 to 2 meters lower and facing up and he looking down over the railing of his elevated terrace. We both decided that it would be better to continue the conversation at equal footing i.e. on the same level. So I joined them at their table and while they enjoyed their entrée's and I my brandy, we continued our exchange about the merits of Rococo and its relation to Baroque and the apparent differences with the architecture in northern Europe at the same time. As some of the company were not that fluent in French we halfway switched to German. They must have been Schwiss to have mastered and French and German. It was an interesting evening and it gave me a project for the next day: "Schloss Weisenstein"[97] in Pommersfelden, just downs the road the motor way that is and about a 70 to 100 km. I knew about it but had not realised that it was fairly close by. They had visited it just this afternoon and thought it quite good. When their mains started to arrive I felt that I should leave them to their meal and took my leave.

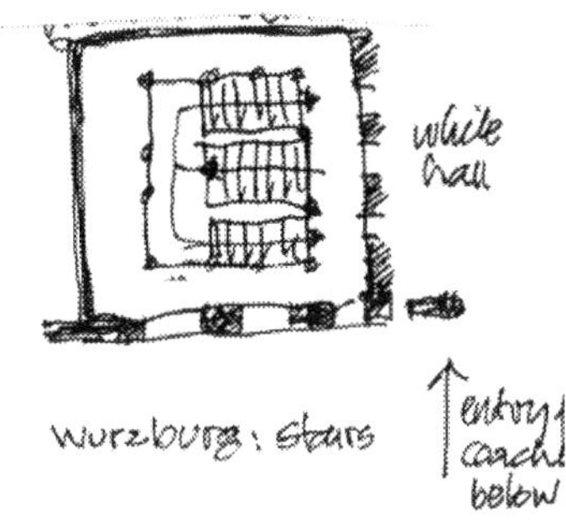

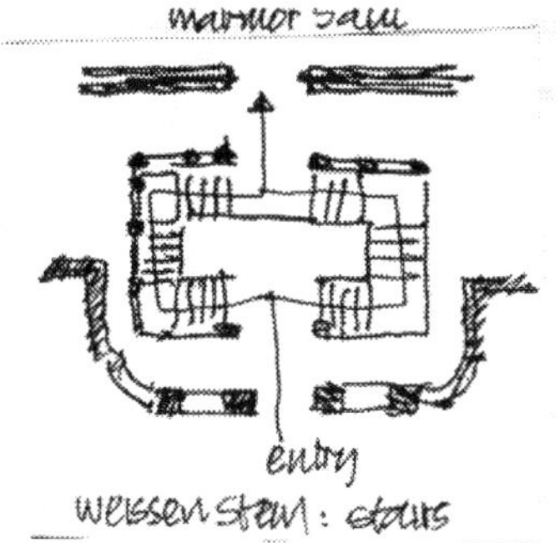

[97] J. Dietzenhofer. 1711-1718

It was a very good "Johannis Feuer", large and lingering.

24 June.

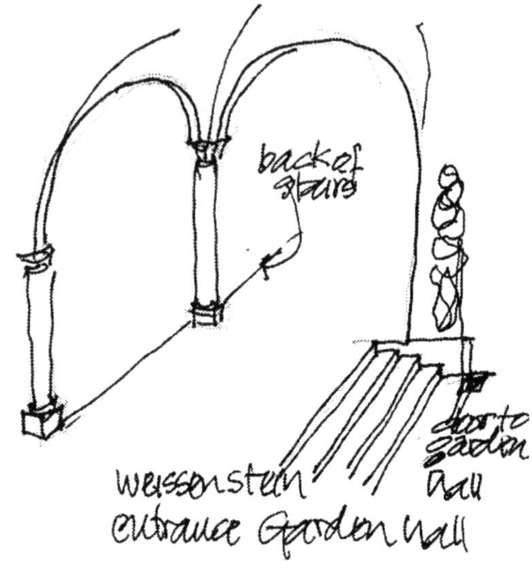

In making the final arrangements with Hans, we had worked out that he was to arrive around 1.30 p.m. I had directed him to "Zum Torturm" the Gasthof on the Northern end of town, just inside the gate. By taking the first turn off into Sommerhausen he could not miss it. So I had plenty of time. Originally the plan was to visit a little Neumann church but the meeting of the evening before had suggested an n interesting alternative. So I speeded down the motorway to Pommersfelden. When I arrived the first guided tour had just left and visits were only guided. At this moment I realized I had left my letter of Introduction of the Goethe institute at home. I am sure it would have worked and allowed me a free walk. So I walked around a bit. The grounds were not very inspiring. The weather was fine. The population of the nearby village (Pommersfelden?) uses the chapel as parish church and were trickling in for Mass. I almost joined them to have a look at the chapel. As I expected to be able to have a look at it later, I did not. A mistake; the chapel was not part of the bits that were open to the public. Again I regretted that I did not have the introduction with me.

The guided tour again proved that they talk about things I do not want to hear and run past the things I want to have a look at. This time it was embarrassing also. When we were guided through the rooms there was a rather frequent mention of paintings by Breughel. There happened to be a man amongst the group who knew something about Breughel and tried to correct the guide- are rather innocent young woman probably reciting what she had been given to learn. He carefully pointed out that all known Breughels were present and accounted for in musea and there nowhere was a mention of Weissenstein. So the paintings here could only be copies- and Breughel was frequently copied by amongst others his son- and she should say so. The young woman got a bit bitchy in German- the tour had been in English. Unfortunately and he and his wife were fluent in German so that did not really do very much to clear the air. The must have been Swiss as I later on heard the couple speak French amongst them.

The collection of paintings was interesting. But the spiritual leader collector had a penchant for biblical scenes with female nudes, which became rather obvious in the end. It does give you an interesting insight in the Bible and draws your attention to passages that you hardly ever think of.

But the building is interesting. Having just been through the Residenz in Würzburg you cannot avoid comparing the two grand staircases.

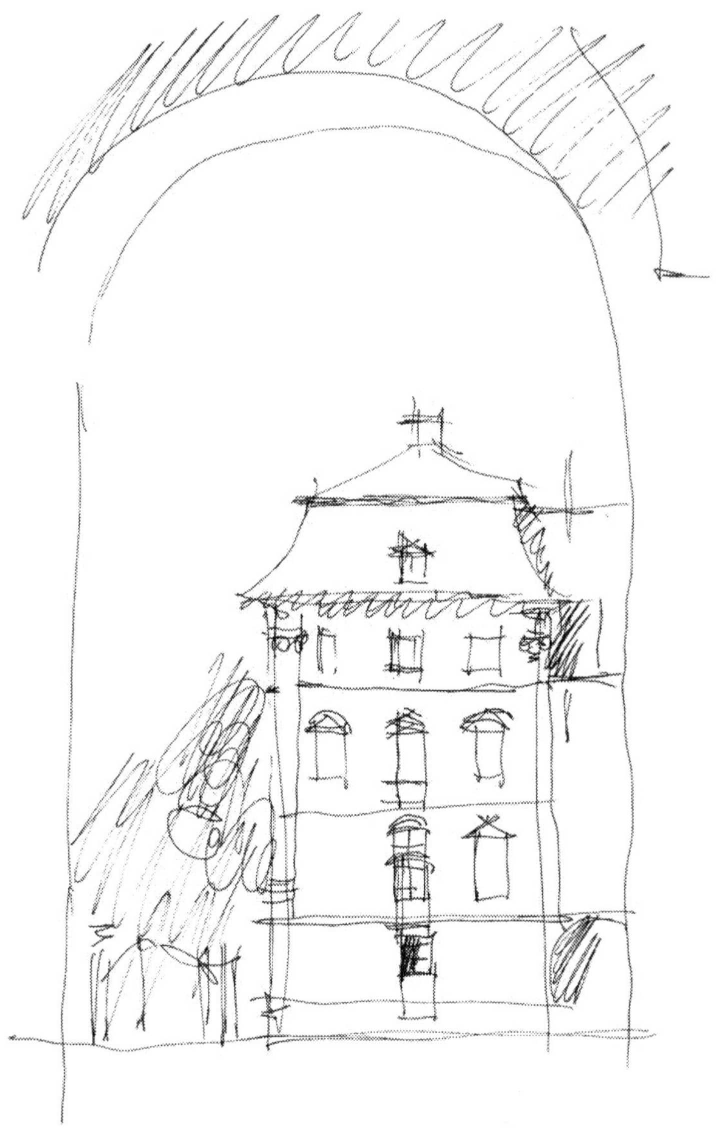

42. Weissenstein. Pavilion at West wing.

And for me Neumann wins hands down. In Weissenstein the three ninety degree turns you have to make on the stair before you enter the Marmor Sahl makes it rather inelegant. The whole thing is brought about by the desire to start in the axis of final entry.
How much more elegant is the stair in Würzburg
The Weissenstein concept asks for a fair bit of space in the depth of the building; for one reason or other, it was not there. The steps down into the Garden room or Grotto have not enough room and are cut into the corridor and look as a make do solution. It looks silly to have a very generous corridor, which at the crucial point of a turn and entrance narrows down because of a level difference that has to be negotiated in the width of the corridor. It might have been a better solution to take the steps inside behind the door. But I believe that that would also have created difficulties in the grotto. Having steps in a hall is not helping the unity of the interior.
Neumann solution of course could be difficult in the elevations but he has resolved those admirably by keeping the stairs free from the defining walls.
The church or chapel could not be visited; again I regretted that I did not bring my introduction.
It was just half past one when I drove my green Peugeot onto the car park" Zum Torturm"
Hans was already there. We had been somewhat generous with driving times. There had not been much traffic on the Autobahn. Sunday morning in Germany does not seem to cause any serious delays. So he was there and had been there for some time. We had a glass of beer and then went to introduce him to Frau Furke. When I arranged the stay for Hans she had asked me if I would like a separate room for my wife's cousin. The excuse I used to visit a girlfriend at boarding school flashed through my mind. We always came in as cousins on a family visit. Until today I still do not know whether the Sisters of Jesus, Maria and Joseph were that naïve or just did not want any fuss.
I decided not to go there and said that I would prefer a separate room if at all possible and it was. I must say that the bed and breakfast arrangements in private houses in Germany is well organised and of a good quality. Good rooms clean and pleasant, good ablutions and generally an "Aufenthaltszimmer" cum breakfast room were there is a T.V., which allows you to see the news and the weather forecast. When we went to "Dass Schiff" in Winterhausen for coffee after a nice meal in "Zum Torturm" they had Ruhetag. So the promised rather dreamy sunset overlooking the Main with coffee and cognac had to be modified into coffee in the "Die ALte Brucke". But the sunset and the rural peaceful evening lived up to expectations.

St. Bartholomä

25 June.
After careful consideration, we moved to Lauternberg or St Bartholomä, and having seen the weather fore cast the night before, we would be camping. My program had further churches south and in the region of München so I had to go south, Hans was not particularly after anything. The distance we had to travel was not that much so we did not go for the Autobahn. Hans and I for that matter had seen enough of it. So we gradually travelled south and had a stop in Rothenburg a.d. Tauber. Images of the town are so much in the mind of everybody as the image of Germany of the fairy tales of Grimm brothers that I do not want to add to the story. It is there, it looks like the postcards and is very well exploited.
Following the secondary roads, we avoided all larger towns and had a relaxed ride until near Aalen we ran into some difficulties to get to Lautern, one of the two places we had picked. Earlier flooding had removed some roads of the face of the earth: "Ausradiert" [98]to use a popular WWII German expression. When we after passing the same "Umleitung", German for "detour", a few times found the camping in Lauternburg, it did not live up to our expectations. After an inspection, we both did not like it so we ended up on the camping in St Bartholomä, a very small village in an attractive region. Still early in the season we had plenty of space and choice. The same went for the evening meal: six Gasthöfe on a population of 2000(?) that is ample choice.
26 June.
Via Heidenheim to Neresheim[99]. It is the last Church of Neumann and not his best, I believe. Of course, one has to make allowances for the fact that he did not supervise the construction. He died in 1753; eight years after his first contacts with the abbot of the abbey and three year after the first stone was laid. Its furnishing never eventuated to the normal extent and probably the extent that Neumann himself had envisaged. It looks bare and white, abstract to a certain extent, but it at the same time allows you to see how Neumann his Vierzehnheiligen concept understood. Here the space and definition relate directly without the mediation of the furniture and decorations. The counterpoint composition is clear, but I am not fully convinced. Above the entablature the integration is there but below there is considerable doubt about what is what. The solid outer wall is clearly visible; the supports for the dome are possibly to close to the wall or too close together? It is not quite the fleeting, fuzzy definition that he achieved in Vierzehn Heiligen. The four bays in the nave and the four bays in the chancel are reduced to two oval spaces in the vault similarly to Vierzehnheiligen. The gallery does curve out in each bay and does not differentiate between the bays that are the centre of a vault oval and the bays that are "squeezed "out. The structure looks static more like a series of ovals supported by four pillars and four double columns for the central dome rather than a fleeting fuzzy definition of a contracting and expanding space. Admittedly, the furnishing could have made a difference but the interior has a classicistic feel. The continuity of Vierzehnheiligen is here a static grouping of two vaults- oval saucer domes- a larger central saucer dome and again two identical oval saucer domes and two almost independent domes as

---

[98] Quotation from A Hittler: Wir wollen Ihre Stätte ausradieren; we will erase your towns from the surface of the earth
[99] B. Neumann. 1745-1792

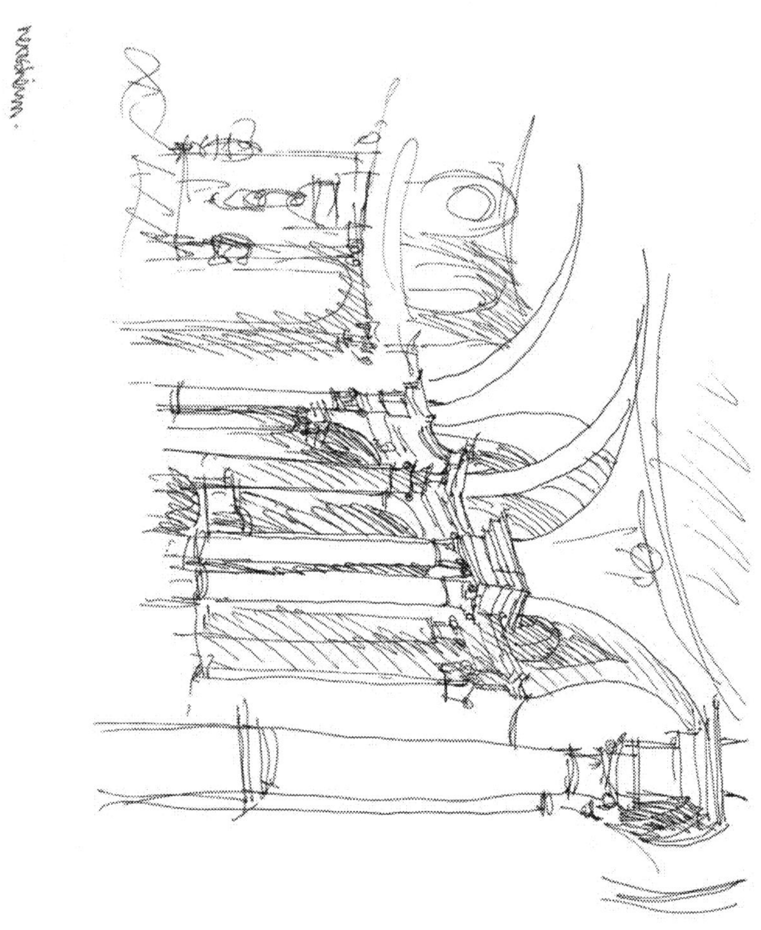

43. Neresheim. Interior towards the East. (for plan refer to page 152)

transept. The counterpoint at ground level is to repetitive to be sensuous. The furnishing is modest, does not grow into one texture with the structure but is attractive. The pulpit is here perfectly balanced by a sculptural composition over the Baptismal Font. To understand Vierzehnheiligen you should see Neresheim first I believe. Neresheim gets a better chance to convince and Vierzehnheiligen will show why I think it is the better of the two: exiting stuff though.
In the afternoon we saw Donauwörth.[100]

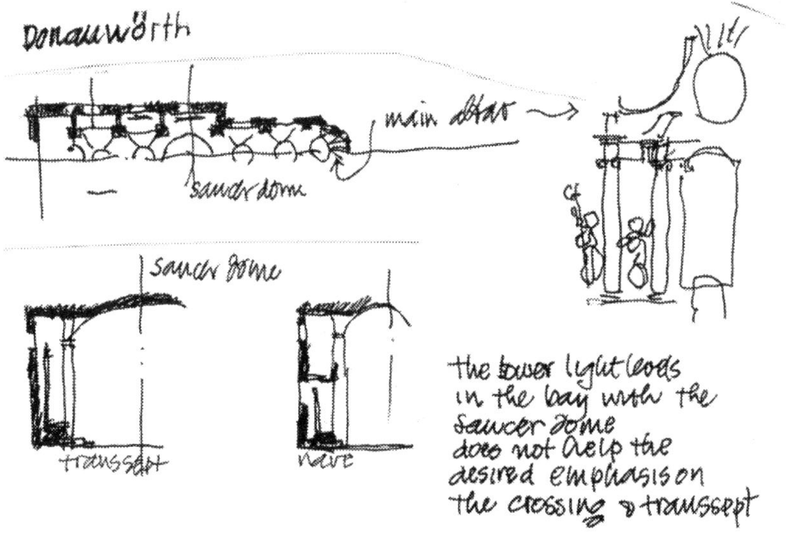

It is a pleasant church nothing revolutionary. The side altars are in red marble with a very agitated gold décor. The round sculpture—angels, saints and putti-- is a bit weird: the flesh is silver and the clothing and symbols in gold. Some of the saints look like characters in an Italian comedy-- Commedia Dell'Arte – with white masks and the almost black holes as eyes, others like skeletons. The combination of gold and silver does not work. The more customary combination of pink for flesh and gold for the clothing and implements is a much more convincing presentation. The biblical description" their faces were radiant white as snow and they shone like the sun" should clearly not be translated in gold and silver. I do not recall to have seen this anywhere and I can see why. The stucco decoration is of a delicate small scale in light yellow and pink. The two narrower bays in the nave have a gallery with windows, on the gallery, and below. The wider bay with the large saucer dome does not produce much effect; the rather much lower light levels caused by the side altars, which take out the lower window, works against the undivided height.

27 June.

We have a rest and a walk around in the hills in the morning. In the afternoon, Hans stays on the camping. I have seen a Peugeot garage in Heidenheim. I am close to 10,000 km and she needs servicing, so I drive to town to make arrangements.
Not everybody is convinced that women are more creative in understanding conversations and social contexts but I am. Women are most of the time more

[100] F. Beer. 1696-1704

imaginative. After I had amply discussed with the mechanic at the reception that my girlfriend the Peugeot 206 needed servicing and had made arrangements for the next day I announced that she now needed a shower. The young man looked rather blank. What was it to him that my girlfriend needed a shower; he could not see how he could help or be of assistance; he would not want to be involved in the sanitary needs of another fellows womenfolk. When I repeated the announcement, the girl in the reception laughed, the young man looked hurt; he apparently was missing something. "Ach" the girl said" Der Her meint dass er eine Autowasche sucht!"[101] Well she knew one in the vicinity so the lime of a trip on a country road to find a highly recommended restaurant soon disappeared and she was as shiny as ever.

28 June.

The servicing of the car was arranged for 9.30 but we brought it in somewhat earlier hoping to speed up procedures. After we had delivered the car and had no indication that they would bring the servicing forward, we crossed the road and had a look around in a Kaufcentrum across. They sold brown liquid as coffee, lots of interesting tools. The German organisation works like clockwork so they serviced the car on the agreed time, not a second earlier. Ordnung muss sein. So it was 10.00 a.m. when we left Heidenheim for Günzburg[102]. The church was closed. We could get in but the whole thing was filled with scaffolding to the extent that you could not see very much of the restoration going on. There was no Kirche führer but the plan looked interesting but hard to make out.

So we continued on to Weltenhausen[103]. There was a Führer and we could get in. It is in a way a rather early church. The altars are on a scheme of clearly defined column with pediment and headpiece. The colour of the interior is in the altars. The whole concept is still a building and furbishing. The frescoes are applied medallions. The church is quite good in itself.

Holzen[104] was the next stop. The Führer has no plan, but I liked the church. The high altar could do with some more daylight but the coordination between the altars is quite good. A feature is the four-life-size evangelists sitting on the entablature in the chancel to illustrate that they are the channels through which the eternal Truth of heaven depicted in the ceiling reaches us mortals on earth. The quality of the sculpture is quite varied. The Mater Dolorosa under the cross is not good enough. The frescoes are still rather static and applied

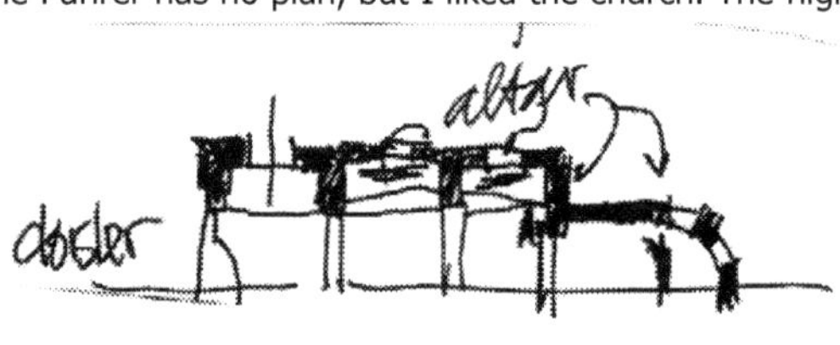

On our way back it rained cats and dogs. Arriving in St Bartholomä the whether improved. We had a whiskey and some cheese and went to Der Stern for our last evening meal. The motherly Wirtin got very embarrassed when I said goodbye" nach Holländisher Art" with three accolades, to the great amusement of the locals. It was a beautiful clear starry night, the end of a few wonderful days. We had good talks on everything catching up on personal insights and changes, days to treasure!

29 June.

---

[101] The gentleman is looking for a car wash.

[102] D. Zimmerman. 1736-1741

[103] M. Thumb. 1670-1687

[104] F. Beer. 1696-1704

The weather cannot be blamed but I felt it was a lousy day. It was a cloudless clear blue sky, the sun was out, and a silvery fog was lifting over the hills behind the pines that shield the camping from the outside. I felt down and decided to let Hans go first. He must have felt that, for he was packed in no time and left me with the leftovers and memories. We embraced and I saw the car disappear around the bend. I took my time to dry the tent pack the gear and get organised. The brilliant day did not change anything, I felt rotten and not really in the mood to get going. The general plan was to end up in or near Isny. I took the easy way out and turned on to the Autobahn, and on a hunch on the spur of the moment I turned of to Leutkirch. The whole system worked. The ladies at the Tourist Verband were very nice and efficient. Within no time, I was on my way to Frauenzell a little village some ten km away from Leutkirch. I had a good room for a decent price. There were at least two Gästhäuser in the village, so for emergencies you could always find something to eat. Leutkirch itself had a fair number of restaurants in an acceptable price range, quite suitable as a base for the region.
After settling in I had diner in "Die Haase Stall" It was a bit sad to be on my own again. I was tired and turned in early.

Leutkirch

30 June.
I had an extensive program to get back on track with some very good churches amongst others 'Die Wieskirche.
I started out at 8.30. with the route sorted out the night before. So it was pretty straightforward to get to Ottobeuren[105]. It is a big church with a front bulging out. It suggests an over tensioned interior that bulges out between the towers and almost bursts through the exterior wall to reveal itself .It looks a sober façade but it has an unusual feature: the entablature supported by four brick red columns curves up over the windows. As the same entablature continues along the towers and jumps up over some windows, it does not strike you at first sight.
The church is very big; about 90 m long and it is light very light. As in Vierzehnheiligen amongst others the half round seemingly structural columns are in pink marble (painted) one shade lighter than the main altar. It is an effective way of tying the interior together. It manages here to bring the long nave to a seemingly comfortable dimension. The whole interior, the frescos in the domes, the decoration and furniture, takes you in and leads you to contemplate the high altar and then back to the individual supporting structures. The very elaborate pulpit is nicely balanced by an equally elaborate sculptural construction over the baptismal font representing the Baptising of Christ in the river Jordan. In most churches there is a sculpture group of the Cross with Mary and St John or St Peter and Mary Magdalene as examples of repenting and repentance. Generally that is not enough mass and attraction to balance the left and right side. In many cases the pulpit cuts somewhat uncomfortably into the vista leading up to the high altar. Not here though; all is well conceived and executed. The quality of the individual pieces is good to very good. It is a very good church, very rich in colours and decoration. It borders on too rich, overdone but the size and height of the interior just carries it.
After such a good start, Irrsee[106] was a disappointment, not the church itself but the fact that it was filled with scaffolding that covered the full left side of the church. Only the famous pulpit in the form of a ship with a rich gold décor and a fascinating blue-green sail held up and manipulated by putti was visible. And without seeing the whole church it was visible that the pulpit was in no way balanced by a cross on the other side. The church was not open to the public. That is the elaborate grilles at the west side were closed. That is hardly ever the case in Germany, other than in Austria were we came across it a several instances. The church itself and its decorations look rather early 18 or late 17th century.
After coffee and cake with whipped cream I stopped at Rottenbuch[107]. It is a rococo refurbishing of a Gothic structure, which I found not as successful as others I have seen. Somehow the narrow nave does not work with the new interior. There are very attractive individual pieces and some very interesting late Gothic sculpture has been retained and that is well worth a visit. The church itself was part of a very gigantic monastic structure, which has been re-inhabited and turned into private houses and public buildings like a Rathaus and a primary school. The settlement is still in development and there is still work going on in large parts of the buildings that are still unoccupied; something to go back to, to see how it works out.

---

[105] J.M. Fischer. 1748-1767
[106] F. Beer. 1699-1704
[107] ?. 1737-1747

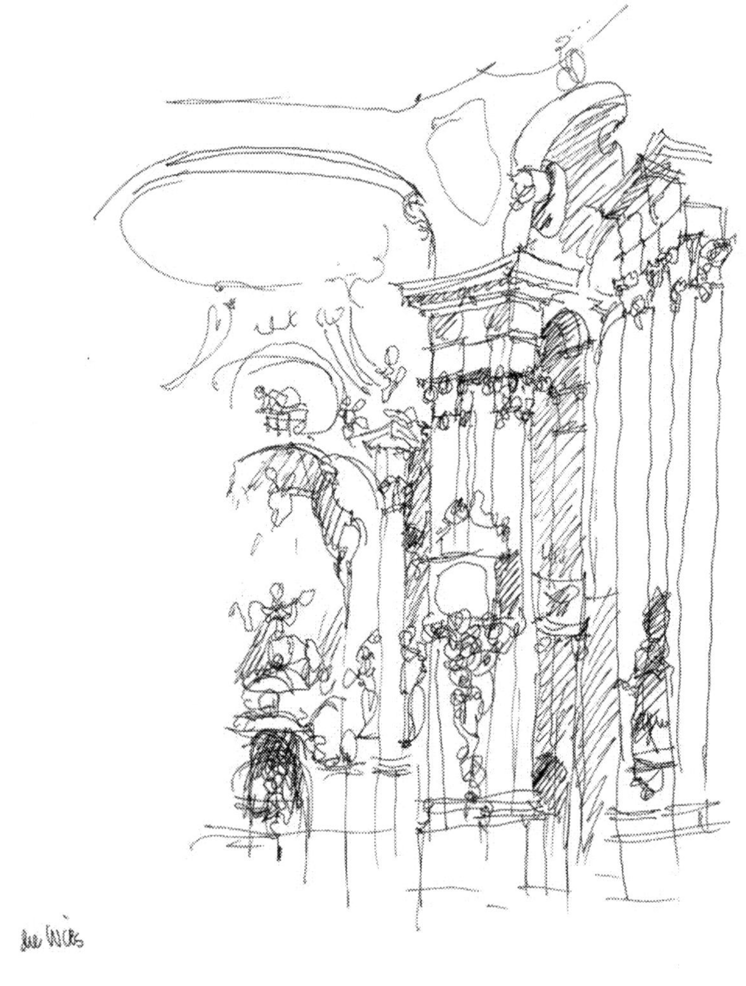

44. The Wiese Kirche towards the East with side altar.(see page 150 for plan)

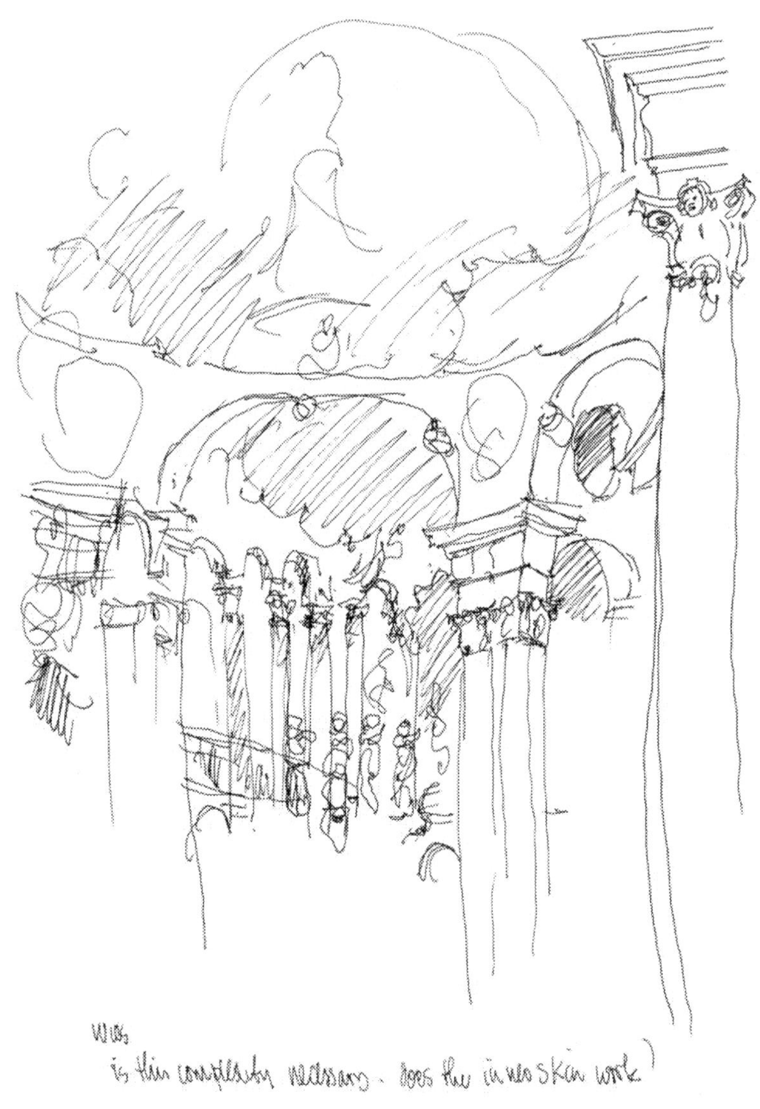

45.The Wieskirche. Chancel

As last on the program of the day: Die Wallfahrtskirche zum gegeiselte Heiland auf der Wiese or the Wies Kirche[108].It is a world heritage building so it should be something. On entering it certainly is something: it is a large space, light, very light. Initially the space escapes analysis. The inner space is defined by a two-layer definition, which bulges out to take in the high altar. There are also some references to a cross with the larger intercolumnium in the left and right side of the central space and the choir gallery and the main altar. It again also refers to the wall pillar church with the normally straight walls defining the nave now bulging out. It certainly is a central dome, be it oval with the sanctuary coming of it, It is a very ornate space; a central space defined by a screen wall formed by a colonnade. As a type it goes back to early Christian times and took the form of such different shapes as the San Vitale, the Hagia Sophia and early basilicas like the San Apollinare en Classe. But the clear organisation and structure of the definition is not what one perceives first in die Wies. It is all more fleeting more alternating between colonnade and wall as the defining element. It is very much lighter more immaterial than Ravenna or the Basilicas, less of this world, more of an outer-world vision.
It is a very refined and accomplished design. The gallery for the choir sits comfortably in the West and is answered by the two galleries or balconies in the sanctuary. In Vierzehn Heiligen I was not quite convinced, but here no questions, it works. It is all very well integrated and balanced. The paired columns refer to each other to form the inner layer of the double skin definition. In section they still suggest a derivation of a wall and reinforce the hint of a perforated wall. They gradually come together and only the last entablature they share fully.
The quality of it all is good very good or superb and the balance is just right: it works. It is one interior space as a vision. But for me it was not Vierzehn Heiligen. It may be my preference. In Vierzehn Heiligen I saw the space and the definition and the perfect balance. In Die Wies I can see the brilliance of the concept the exquisite detailing and dimensioning, but the last bit that makes one go cold or cry or whatever one does when confronted with perfection, that last bit, it was not there for me. I spent a lot of time; it is a feast for the eye and I can see why it is world heritage and Vierzehn Heiligen not, I will come to that later. I paid homage to the genius of Zimmerman, his concept and the realisation of so complex and sensual a spiritual dream.
In Frauenzell I had diner in the Haasestall and a discussion with some of the locals. It was very late when I finally went to bed.

1 July

Sunday; the weather was to clear and the roads will full of Bavarians so I was not quite sure that it was a good idea to go anywhere; I imagined the smaller villages to be totally deserted apart from things going on in the churches. In the end I decided to give it a try anyway and again it turned out different. The roads were pretty much deserted; the sun did come through and it became fairly warm. The route I had planned was unworkable there were too many "Umleitungen".

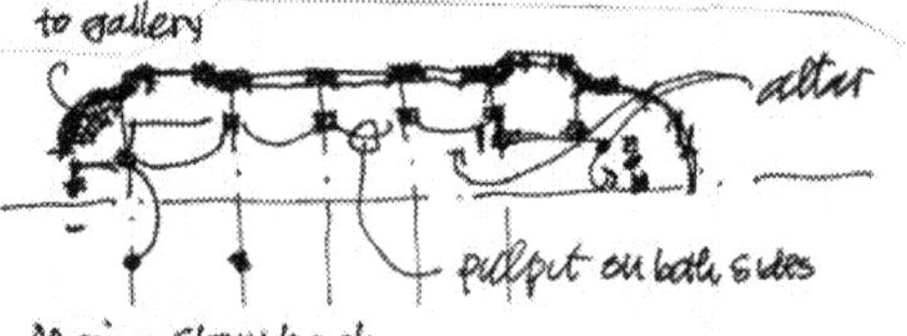

So that part ended in a bit of a mess. Luckily Maria Steinbach[109] is easy to find.

---

108 D. Zimmerman. 1745-1754
109 D. Zimmerman. 1746-1753

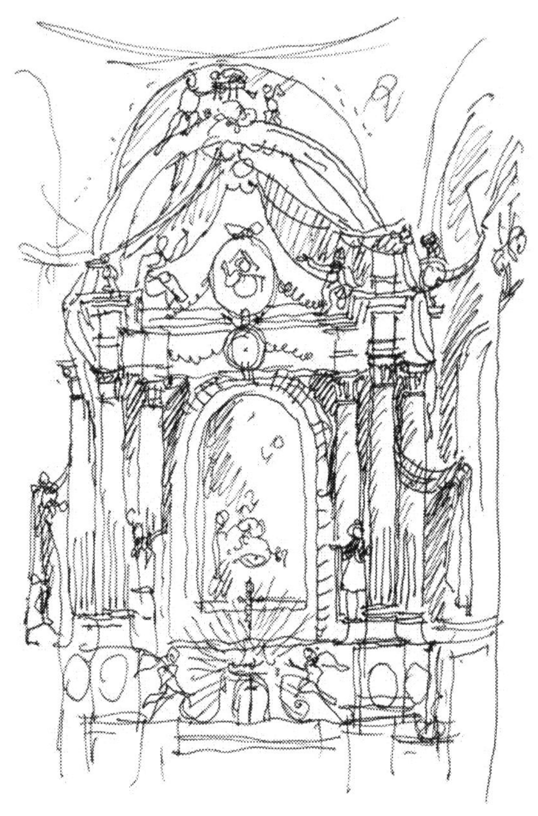

7. Rot an der Rot. High Altar

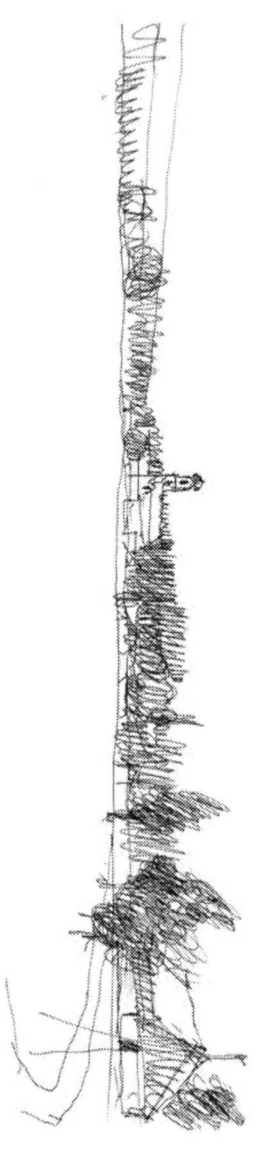

46 Approaching Steinhausen

The church dominates the slightly undulating landscape and the little settlement around it. The landscape looks very relaxed and unified. It took me some time to work out why. The roads generally have no drainage ditches and fencing is not necessary in the agricultural environment; they look rather casual and less formalised and very much part of the landscape. It looks very informal. I like it; it suggests something like seeking ones own way through the land and over the hills without formed roads just a track here and there. The church is quite good. All structural members are marbled a lighter red than the main altar and that works well to unify the interior. The church has a gallery running all the way around which necessitates the cutting the wall pillars. The marbled pilaster group now almost appears freestanding and starts to work as a screen in the manner as die Wies and Steinhausen,

It is a nice space the furnishing is good and the whole is well integrated. The pulpit problem is resolved by having one on the right and on the left side- very unusual accessible from the gallery. The treatment of both is low key.

From there to Rot an der Rot[110] a five bay wall pillar which could be easily mistaken for an early church- late 1600—early 1700. In fact it is a very late and conservative church (1781-1786) The Kirchenführer characterises it as Classicistic. It looks however so much like what one could expect in late sixteen hundred that it would be more like a very early Neo Baroque church. But the interior is clearly designed to work towards a main overall effect culminating in the high Altar. There are lots of nice, a bit sentimental putti fiddling around with drapery and, like all the sculpture, realistically coloured. There has been a fair bit of early furniture incorporated (choir stalls), which contributes towards the conservative or early appearance. The lighting in the church through the window, which are high up in the walls and the way in which the light is incorporated in the high altar give away that this is not an early church. The stucco decorations and the frescoes in formal frames reminded me of much later 19th century work; an interesting church.

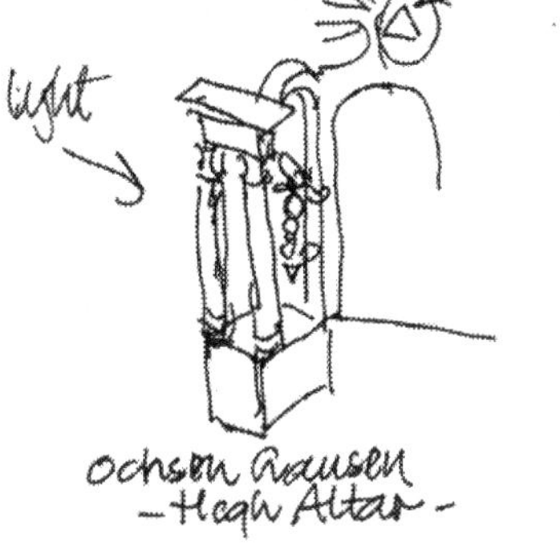

The rest of the day was taken up by two Gothic refurbishing in Ochsenhausen[111] and Gutenzell[112]. Gutenzell is under restoration and investigation. That was in many ways interesting to see. They had removed at places the plaster back to the Gothic brickwork. At some places you could see how much plaster was used to create a rococo interior out of a gothic church. How they put that on without extensive cracking is a bit of a secret. From my experience plaster applied in thick and uneven layers cracks badly. I have read somewhere that that reinforcing plaster with horsehair was common practice. I have come across tiles set in clay mortar reinforced with horse hair, but never come across it in Plaster. I will investigate this plaster matter and plaster sculpture further when at home. Gutenzell was a monastery, which again has been

---

110 F.Beer. 1781-1786

111 (?). 1725-1727

112 D. Zimmerman. 1755-1756

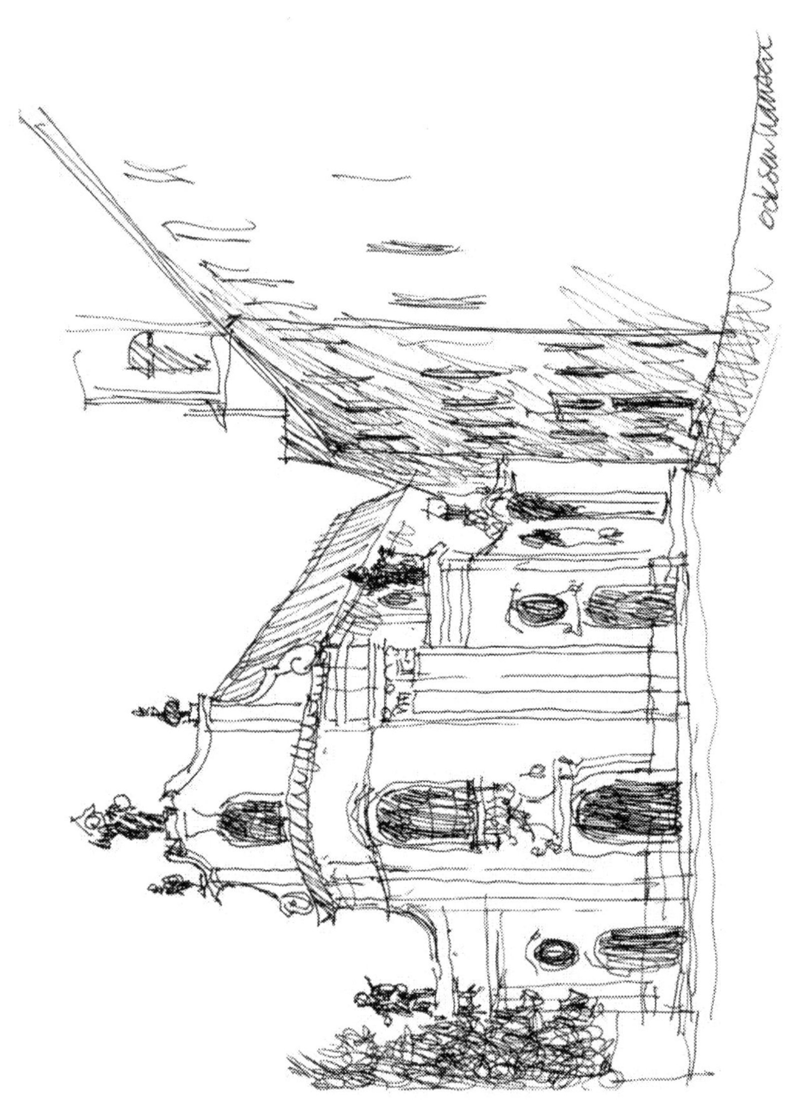

48. Ochsenhausen

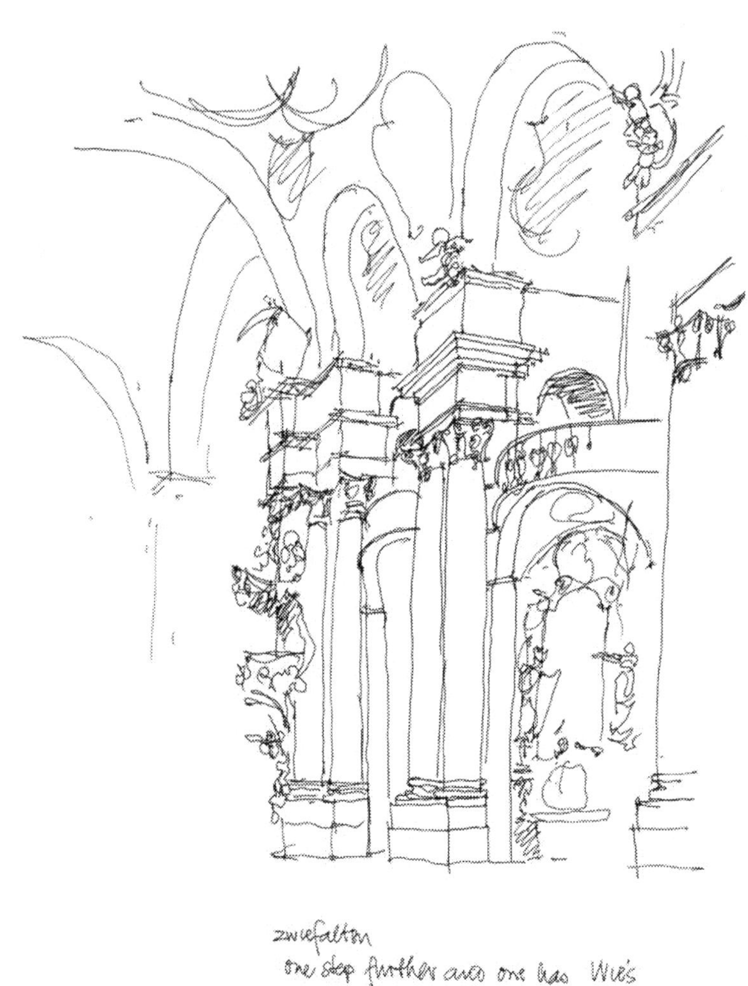

49. Zwiefalten. Nave.

converted in private homes within the walls of the monastery (after the secularisation in 1803?). Ochsenhausen is another Gothic refurbishment. Here the Gothic origins and space are clearly visible. It has however some interesting features, which made the visit worthwhile.

2 July.

It is now very much a routine: shower, shave, breakfast prepare route sheet of how to get where. Today's first stop is Zwiefalten[113], and it is a surprise! From Zwiefalten to Wies is a small step. In the plan this is not visible. It looks like an ordinary wall pillar church with oval dome and a longer choir to accommodate choir stalls for the monks. The overall impression on entering is different. The wall pillars are shaped as double columns and the entablature does not run back to the wall but suggests a block. The galleries swing out and are low enough to allow for a large window. The altars in the side chapels between the wall pillars are not placed against the perimeter wall but against the west face of the wall pillars. They are entirely or partly visible upon entering and cover the entire wall from floor to the vault of the gallery. The transverse walls are completely annihilated. The galleries swing out elegantly; the pulpit is balanced by a group built up around the Prophet Ezekiel. The High Altar is the centre of the composition and all leads to it. The central dome is only noticeable by its fresco, which shows the geometrical form of the circle. The frescos in the nave are in cartouches. The edge of the cartouches is made relative by overlaps of stuccowork up and into the frescos and down by fresco into the stuccowork zone. It is no longer a decorated surface but an opening in the solid ceiling. The step that has been taken in the Wies is to abandon the wall part of the wall pillar completely and tie the freestanding double columns back to the perimeter wall by an arch at vault level. Maria Steinbach still follows the scheme of Zwiefalten. The next step of the Wies is to abandon the concept of a nave with parallel definitions and a sanctuary attached and conceive the church as a nave with varying width and a chancel as a continuation of the central space. The wall pillar concept is clearly transformed into a fuzzy wall or a perimeter wall with a screen wall or colonnade as the definition of the space. In Zwiefalten it is still clear that, however light the structure, it is still seen as a wall pillar church and not as a fuzzy wall i.e. a wall enriched with a freestanding colonnade as inside of the definition. The visit later that day to Maria Steinhausen[114] made it all clear. Here the parallelism of the long walls of the nave is abandoned, and the central space an oval defined by a fuzzy wall. The

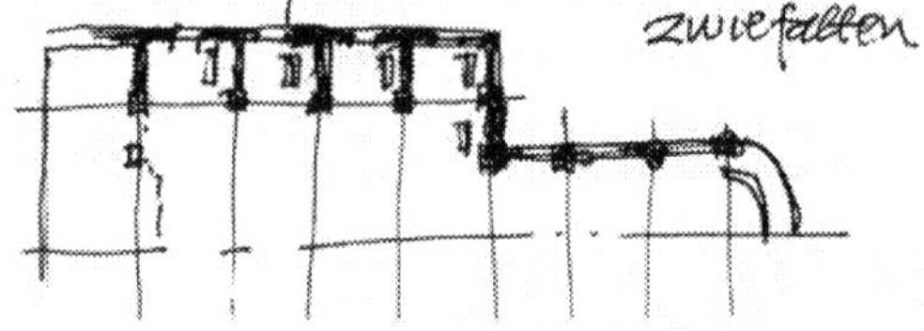

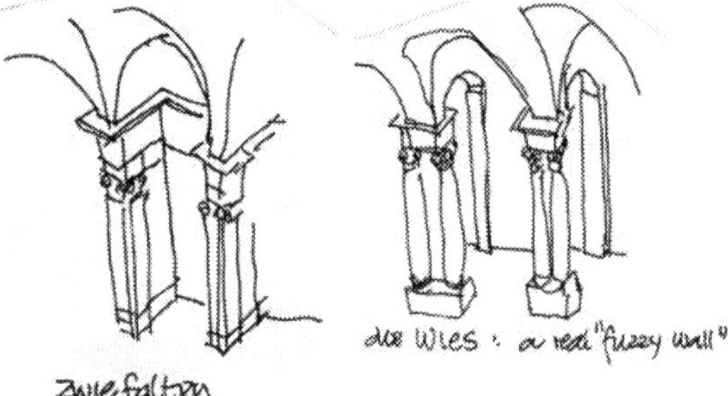

[113] J.M.Fischer.1740-1765

[114] (?) 1728-1733

concept still accepts the sanctuary as an independent or added on space. This is clearly visible upon entering: the columns of the nave cut in the view of the main altar so that it is not visible in its entire width. However accomplished the lead in of the side altars to the high altar is; the altar appears as behind the screen and somewhat outside the space. But we are here comparing works of super class and all are of an unbelievable complexity and refined detailing and colour schemes. The elegant and quiet blue interior of Steinhausen, the gold en richness of Steinbach, the pink and golden vision of Zwiefalten and the warm red and gold of the Wies these interiors are of an everlasting beauty.
In between Zwiefalten and Steinhausen I stopped at Obermarchtal[115] and later in Riedlingen. That proved to be a fortunate intermezzo that allowed me to put some distance between the two giants. As a traditional wall pillar Obermarchtal was enough to keep me looking and also enough to put some distance between the two highlights of the day. And Riedlingen to remind me that not all Rococo is built by a genius or a talented builder. It is ordinary, Riedlingen.

3 July.

I have the feeling that I am coming to conclusions after the high lights yesterday. But to avoid missing something that could add something to the experience I decided to follow the program and went direction München to visit Diessen[116]. Andech[117], Bichl[118]and Schaftlarn[119]. It was one of those days were luck deserts you.

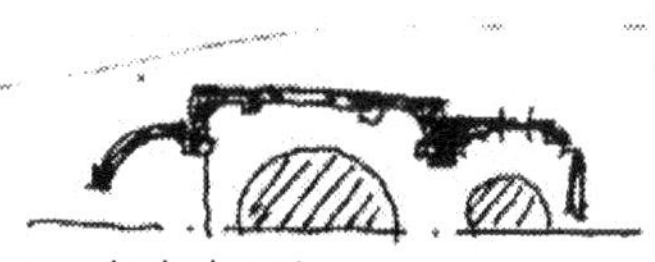

Diessen was worth seeing, Andech was closed for restoration, and Bichl not really worth the drive and Schaftlarn had been closed only a few days ago by the local authorities for reasons of safety. Apparently pieces of the ceiling had come down during use indicating that some repairs were long overdue. So that means closure for the duration of a restoration. I bought a Führer.

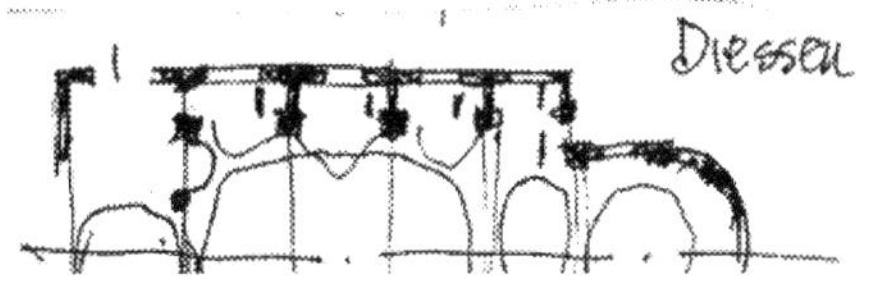

Before I left Herr Rasch- my Gastgeber- had invited me to join him in his weekly outing the Ninepin Bowling Club. There was a decent meal and some fun. We walked down the calm summer evening and when we returned it was a beautiful starry night. I tried some balls but luck was not with me. They took it all very graciously and I did pay my obligatory round of beer when the ball went of the timber strip leading to the target.

4 July.

As it had been a long night, it was well past eight when I awoke. I felt again that it was rounding off time and time to start thinking about the return trip. I wanted to see Ronchamps Notre Dame du Haut. I had to return the Peugeot in Strassbourg on Friday 13 July and my flight to Holland was from Stuttgart on 14 July. I wanted at least one day for Ronchamps. I did not see the need to shift; the whole trip was coming to a conclusion. So it seemed best to take it easy and leave for Ronchamps

---

115 M. Thumb. 1686-1692
116 J.M.Fischer. 1732-1739
117 (?).1751-1755
118 (?)1751-1753
119 F. Curvilles Sr. 1735-1757

on 10 July. That would give me 11 July and 12 July to see Notre Dame du Haut and a bit of that part of France I had never visited before.
So today was an easy day for E-mail sort out a route from Leutkirch to Ronchamps- I had no map of France with me- and walk around in Leutkirch.
Herr Rasch surprised me with fresh wild strawberries that had mysteriously settled on the roof of his garage; they were superb, now I know how strawberries are supposed to taste. I leisurely drifted into Leutkirch to find a launderette or something. The women in the visitor information were as helpful as ever but a launderette that Leutkirch did not have, only some very reliable Reinigungsgeschäfte (laundries). So that had to do. I went back stopped at the church of a neighbouring village and of Frauenzell- nothing of great interest- and collected my laundry, made a list and back to town. The lady said it would be ready Friday morning. Then to the public Library where was Internet access the Tourist information had indicated. There where two computers one with Internet on; and of course two youngsters were playing around on it. The staff was quite helpful, cleared the computer for me so that I could get the mail out. I found the route planner but unfortunately you could not print from that computer. So the whole procedures needed to be repeated on the staff computer with of course all facilities. But in the end I had a good description of the route shortest in time. It runs over the Autoschnellwege in Schwitzerland. There is no really practical connection from that part of Germany to France. He printed out the map and the description and timetable. It should take only three and a half hour to get to Ronchamps. On the merit of that I bought a bottle of Spanish sherry and cheese for aperitifs. I will walk to the Haasestal to eat their Haasigoreng. It sounds interesting. Tomorrow back to München or to Weissenau and Weingarten.
5 July.
General direction München to have a look at the last churches. After Vierzehnheiligen, Zwiefalten, Wies and Steinbach it all looks a bit "been there ";I know now what can be achieved, but to get the overall view that was the original intention I went. I could have saved myself the trouble. The first one I had on the program Grafrath was closed for restoration. So on to Fürstenfeldbrucke; not much better also under restoration. Than to Altomunster to see Maria Birnbaum[120] in the vicinity. The church wasn't closed. The interior is rather simple: a central dome one main axis from West to East the fit out is extraordinary. The exterior is weird. It has a distinct oriental flavour with its domes and towers. The main tower is in the west. The Transepts are smaller towers; the choir is worked up into a dome structure with a cut of side against which a separately roofed apse is built. It was a quiet afternoon, no one around and the weather was good so I took my time to draw the exterior.

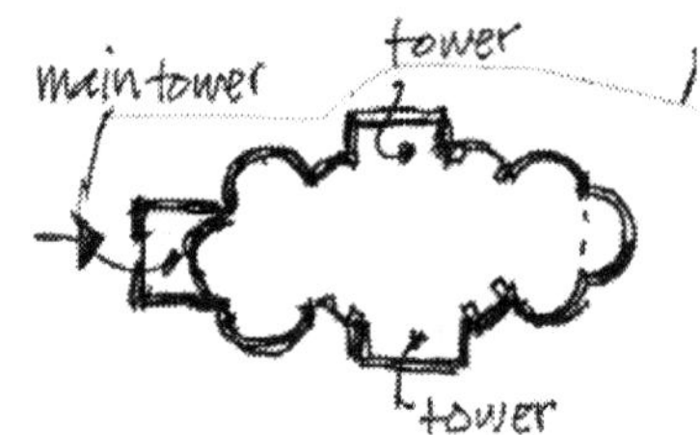

At home I had a sherry and went to the Italian in Leutkirch better and cheaper than in Frauenzell.
To morrow to Weissenau and Weingarten and that will be it. Conclusions and new questions will be the result.
6 July. I had time enough; my washing was not ready before ten. When I arrived at the shop the lady told me that it had been to hot to do anything yesterday afternoon, so she hadn't done it.

[120] C. Pader. 1661-1665

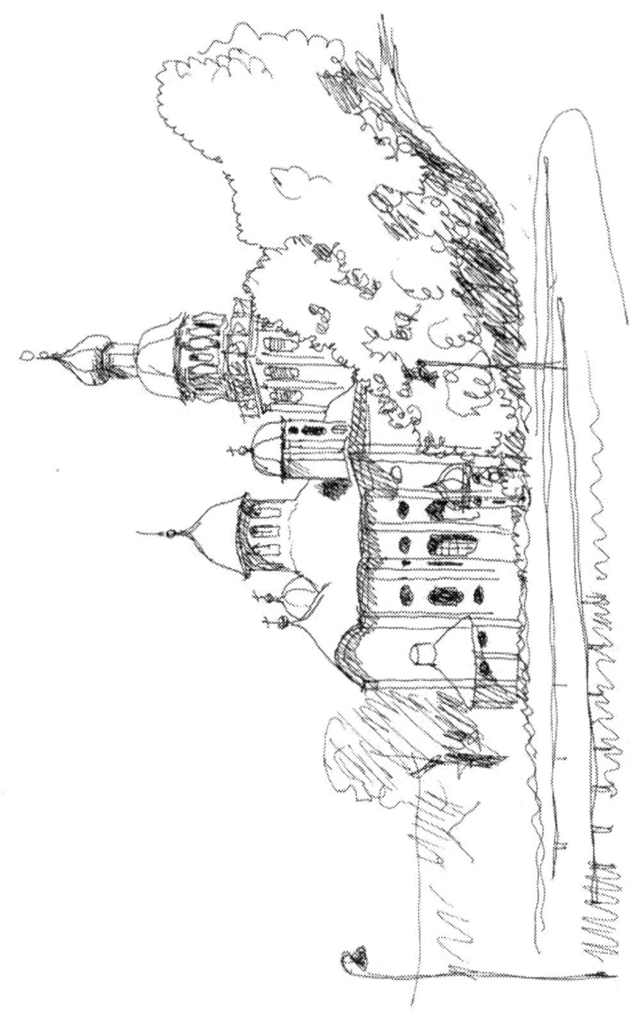

50. Maria Birnbaum.

She was doing it now and it would be ready later. That did not really matter, I had to be in Leutkirch late in the afternoon and would collect it then. But I ended up in a protracted conversation about how things have changed over time and overpopulation deterioration of public behaviour, depopulation of the rural land Germany had changed beyond recognition all those foreigners, not that she hated them but...

At last off to Ravensburg, Weissenau[121] as expected nothing new. So on to Weingarten[122]. After getting carried away by lunchtime traffic; Ravensburg is rather so that Weingarten is more ore less part of it. Signposting was not the best- the locals know their way around- and the traffic was hectic. However, in the end I found parking and a local who could point me to the church. It is an extraordinary large church. It is good to see it after Wies. The wall pillars are decorated at the end with three Corinthian lesenes and the entablature they carry does not run back to the wall: they look detached. The galleries between the pillars swing back in and are not visible in the view on entering. The central dome still stands in the way of an integration of the interior. But a beautiful church, very light and soberly decorated with quality and in the furnishing and the frescoes. On my way back I decided to drop in on Isney the place I originally had in mind instead of Leutkirch. It is bigger than Leutkirch with its wall and ramparts still in tact. Somehow it did not appeal to me It must have been good luck or- more in keeping with the Rococo theme- my guardian angel that made me stop at Leutkirch at the last moment.

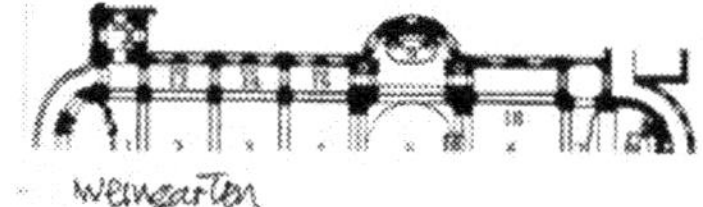

Isny, the old town is not as much tidied up as Leutkirch. I did not feel like an Eiskaffee so I sort of drifted into the R.C. church[123]. Rather plain on the outside is it a revelation on the inside. It looks like a refurbished Hall church, but the Kirchenführer does not mention it. The Church had a long building period and it could be that the foundations of the old Gothic church have been reused. It is a well unified interior and the angled side altars lead in to the High altar. The furnishings and the painting are of good quality. Isney has achieved what the Wies also achieves. One undivided interior with a sanctuary, the refurbishing of the rather dull plan- the führer says 1660- has come up with an exciting experience. The plan is a rectangle divided into three aisles of equal width, in total 8 bays long. The western most bay has a freestanding gallery or mezzanine for the choir and organ. The last three bays are raised and form the sanctuary with the high altar and side altars. The columns are transformed into slender square supports with on all four sides a wall pillar with a free rococo Corinthian capital and entablature block. The four choir pillars each have a modest side altar and two further more substantial side altars angle out from the perimeter wall towards the high altar. They close what otherwise would have been a rather empty north and south aisle. The rib less cross vaulting is elegantly covered by frescoes that change the vault in an undulating plane opening up to the sky and heaven. Entering from the west the church does not show all its richness; only the high altar and the pulpit are visible. Approaching the east the richness of the décor opens up and takes you in. And the quality of most of the furnishing is very good. When half way up the nave the whole interior is visible and it is good. The lightness and the unity are a very nice surprise.

---

121 F.Beer. 1717-1724

122 (?) 1717-1724

123 Architect unknown. Various campaigns.

7 July.

I will be off to Ronchamps via Basel, no more Rococo. Somehow I feel that I can identify with what they- the architects and principals- were trying to achieve. I will have some time the coming days to let it all sink in and formulate a tentative resume. It has been quite an experience and worthwhile in more than one way, but now it is the end of visiting churches. Only one more church; Ronchamps! I have looked forward to be able to see Ronchamps after I did an analysis of the church as part of an evaluation of Modern Architecture. I am keen to see how my interpretation based on drawings and photos is supported by the real thing. But this is an encore an unrelated thing. I am not certain that I will include it in this story "Venturing into Rococo". This venture is over; the trip has come to an end. There is very little to do. I spent the day visiting some smaller churches in the direct vicinity. They are charming but after the great interiors of the recent days, there is nothing to add. Tomorrow Sunday I'll go for a long walk in the forest south of Frauenzell and start getting organised. Monday will be some shopping in Leutkirch and e-mailing and then Tuesday 10 July off to Ronchamps!

I expect to arrive there early in the afternoon, in time to find a place to stay. On 13 July, I will leave for Strassbourg to return the Peugeot after something like 12000 km. I will buy my train ticket Strassbourg- Stuttgart Airport here in Leutkirch and get some insight how early I have to leave Strassbourg to catch my plane back to Holland.

8 July.

Walk in the forest south of Frauenzell to review.

9 July

I did some final shopping and E-mail in Leutkirch and bought a train ticket from Strassbourg to Stuttgart Airport. It seems to be quite easy to get to Stuttgart Airport in time from Strassbourg. If all goes well I'll have an hour or so on the airport.

10 July

Off to France and Ronchamps

Ronchamp.

The fastest way to Ronchamp appeared to be through Schweitz to Basel and from there into France to Belfort. From Belfort the route to Vesoul ran trough Ronchamp my map said, so that should be a piece of cake.

It all went like clockwork and by the time I neared Basel it was still morning; I could be in Ronchamp around one or two and lunch in the local.

But in Basel they had embarked on major road reconstructions of the through routes. It looked as if they were going to put most of it under ground. So there were endless temporary arrangements with the usual ad hoc signage, deviations and a lot of traffic with huge trucks. I apparently missed an arrow- I recall seeing something but a truck blocked my view- pointing to Germany France Mulhouse. When I came through Basel I gradually grew somewhat uncertain. It all was very much Schwitzerland while Basel should be right on the border. A large sign convinced me that wherever I was going it was not out but further into Schweitz. So the next exit I left the motorway and entered again in the opposite direction. The next sign confirmed that I was going to Basel. This time I saw the sign and took the right turn, missed the direct route to Belfort but found myself on the Autobahn to Freiburg and a bit further the connection into France and Belfort.

It was well past one when I left Belfort to take the N19 to Ronchamp.

But they had changed it. The former N 19 was now a Departementale and a new Route Nationale ran direct to Vesoul bypassing Ronchamp. It took me some time to understand what was happening but with the assistance of a local I got to Ronchamp. The local police informed that there was a hotel opposite the church and quite good he said. La Pomme d'Or was indeed opposite the church and a typical French Hotel annex restaurant bar and local pub. The prices were quite acceptable; the room new and with all necessary amenities and the hotel had plenty of vacancies. I booked in had a glass of beer and went for a walk to investigate the town and its amenities.

Ronchamp is on the bank of a rivulet that flows into the Ognon which again ends up in the Saône. The former N19 and the railway line follow the same valley. The railway is raised on a massive early 1900 viaduct. It consists of huge brick retaining walls which where roads have to pass show large brick arches. Ronchamp is not very much more then one street parallel to the railway and the river. It was once a thriving mining village but the mine is closed and it must have been a quiet backwater with a pilgrimage church of local importance since. When the pilgrimage church was turned into a ruin by artillery the only reason for people to come to Ronchamp evaporated. In 1950 Le Corbusier accepted the commission to build a new pilgrimage church for the Miracle Statue of Notre Dame du Haut a not very exciting statue of the Virgin and Child from early 1500. This must have been the stroke of good luck that saved the village from total oblivion.

Ronchamp is a typical street settlement along the former N19 running through the valley of the brook as does the railway line. The valley is not very wide and does not encourage any other form of settlement. The road connecting Ronchamp to the new road from Belfort to Vesoul meets the old road at the East end of an incongruously large open space or square south of the old N19. The town hall or Mairie aligned along the connecting road forms the East closure of the square. At the western end it narrows down to a few shops. The South side is taken up by a Neogothic church and a community hall. The North side is a closed front of shops and one or two bars and the Pomme d'Or. Some efforts had been made to give the unformed space some coherence by a rather ambitious scheme which comprised a distinctive paving pattern which was to cover the square and some of the areas behind the church and community hall and meet up with a park development along the banks of the stream. It also envisaged street furniture and lighting. Somehow it still looks unfinished and the development along the banks has never really amounted to much. It looks like a somewhat desperate gesture of grandeur which sits forlorn in what is an unformed and somewhat empty space. East of the bar of La Pomme d'Or the road leading to the pilgrimage church pierces trough the massive brickwork of the railway viaduct. I resisted the temptation to drive up and have a look at the church right away.

It was late in the afternoon and the drive from Leutkirch combined with the chaos in Basel did have an effect and made me decide to stay in town and go up the next morning and take my time. By the time I had finished my walk around the village it was a decent time to go for an aperitif. After a shower I installed myself in the bar with a glass of beer and the local news paper to get ready for the evening meal. I hate being the first in a restaurant, it all looks so lonely and especially when you are on your own the room somehow seem to take on vast proportions. When I finally went there where quite a few single males, travelling sales men I suppose, trying to eat and read at the same time. For me that does not work.

It was a very decent meal as one would expect in a provincial town and I slept well on in it.

The next morning it was overcast, but still dry. I had given it some thought and decided to walk up to Notre Dame du Haut. It was not to far, a few kilometres up hill. My experience in Germany and Austria had taught me that it is an effective way to prepare you for the experience. After breakfast I walked to the bank to change some D marks into francs and stepped trough the gateway, the large arch of the railway viaduct on to the road to the Notre Dame. Almost immediately after the viaduct the road turned into pine forests. It was dead silent and no traffic. On my way up only one car from behind passed me, for the rest it was the silent of the forest.

It started to drizzle a bit not much but enough to get wet. I donned my jacket, a very light nylon or rayon which I had bought in Krems to replace my old military style jacket and continued my climb through the silence of the morning.

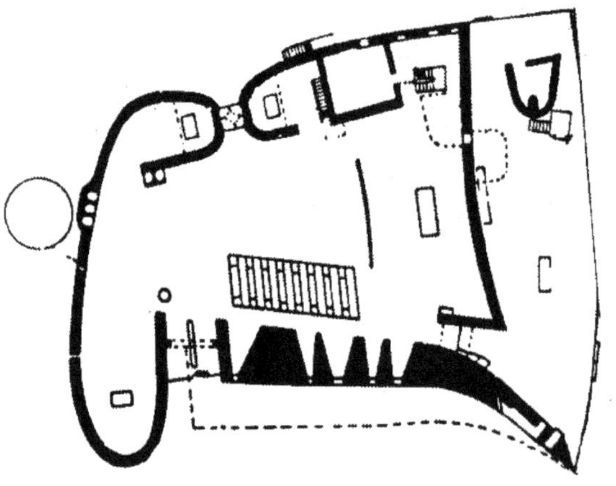

Plan de la chapelle

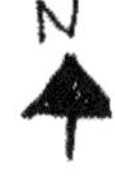

Face ouest ▷

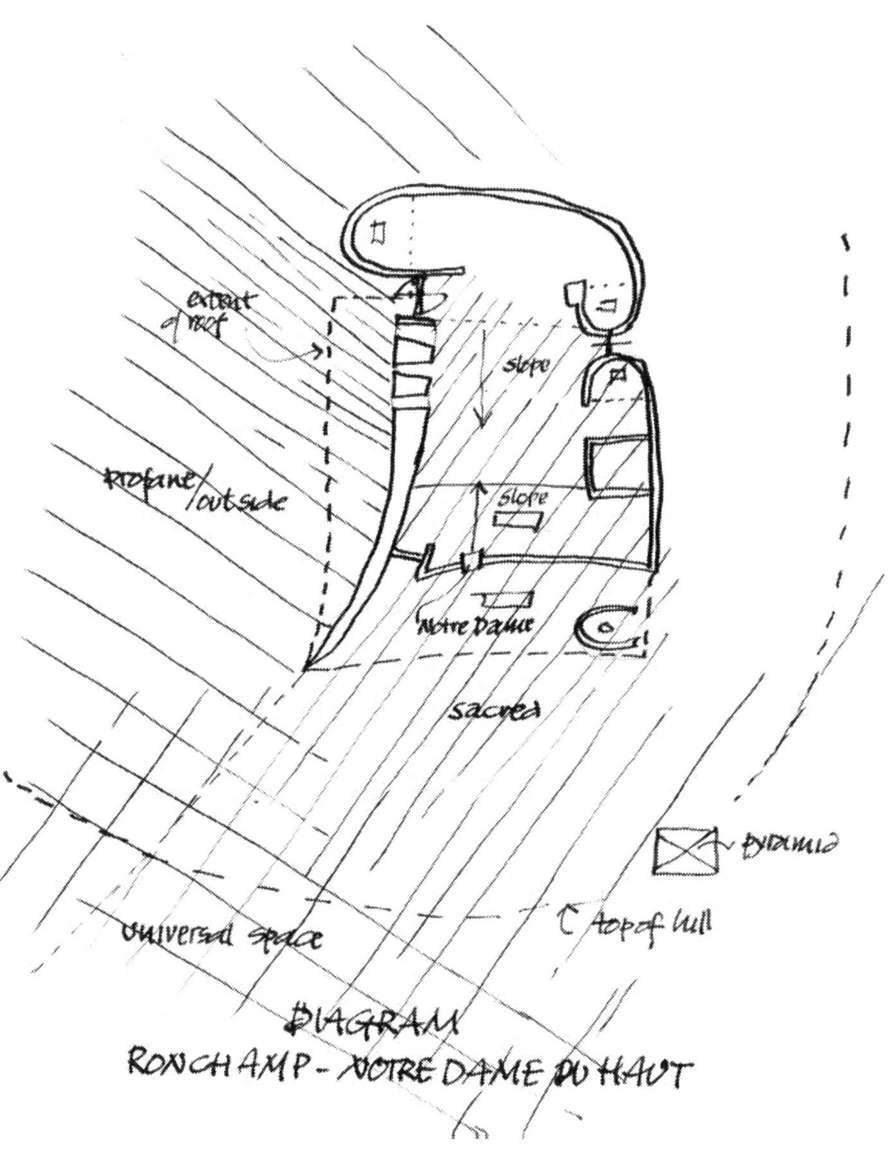

51. Diagrammatic analysis of the chapel.

For an earlier writing I had studied Le Corbusier's church in detail and looked forward to see where I had misjudged the building and its situation.

Although its space concept is thoroughly modern and views space as a continuum of potential in which a building is the concentration and actualisation of some aspects of the universal potential of space, in its forms the church does not fit in with the normal forms of Modernism. Superficially it looks more related to Mendelsohn's Eisenstein Turm than to the Savoy Villa in Poissy. The curved shapes and massive walls look expressionistic and sculptural rather than functional. And of course if Modern means Functionalist in the narrow stylistic sense then Ronchamp is not Modern. If on the other hand Modernism means a space concept that views space as a continuum in which buildings are places where some aspects of the potential of the universal space are realised it is thoroughly and essentially Modern and that sens also Functionalist. It actualises the potential of space to serve any human activity or function.

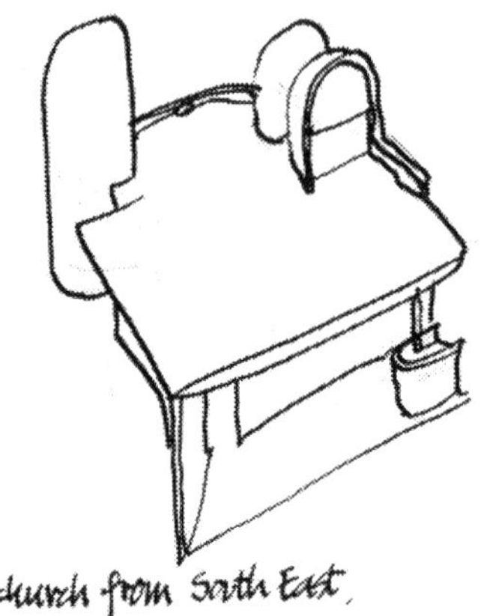

church from South East.

The South wall starts off in the South- East roughly running North-East and curving to the South comes down while increasing in thickness to a massive 5 - 6 meter. It grows out of the universal space and gradually intensifies the separation between this and the other side. The separation gradually takes on the parting of the profane and the sacral aspect of space. Coming in from high and gradually changing from thin and vertical to massif and horizontal it grows out of the gradual condensing of the unformed space into a division between sacred space north and the profane space south of the wall. Thus, the open air area east of the building is sacred, church. The wall comes to an abrupt end at the big vertical element at the South West corner leaving something like a 5 meter gap as the main entrance. The massive overhanging roof is shaped like a rock suggesting a feeling of going in and under. The door pivoting on one central pivot is a real entrance into a mysterious and intense space. Entering from the bright outdoors the interior is dark. To the right the window with the Miracle Statue is the first source of light then the light coming through the stained windows and the slot under the slab of rock that forms the ceiling. To the left the south wall is washed with high light white from the chapel of the Holy Sacrament end and red from the chapel in the west. The structure marks realisation particularisation of the profane and sacred potential of universal space divided and gradually pushed apart by the massive South wall. Behind the wall under the large rock that form the roof it forms the

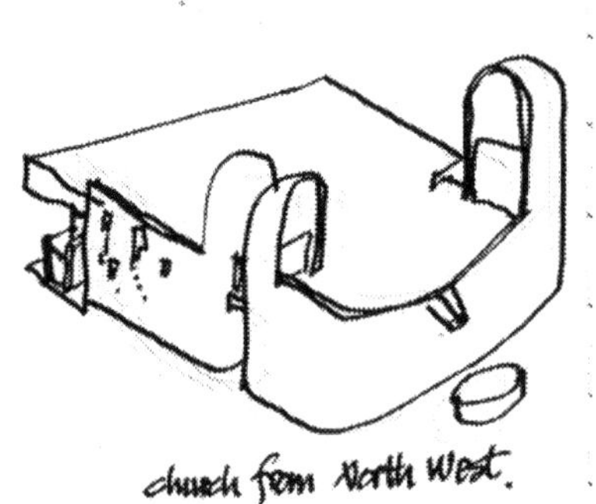

church from North West.

contact between the sacred of the sky and light and the sacred aspects of the earth and life. In the West there is the high light; in the east is the vision of the Mother appearing in the dark subterranean half-light.
To me the chapel had been an eye-opener in the sense that it showed me that the functionalism of the Modern Movement was but a way to come to understand the change that our consciousness was going through in our relation to the world. The real issue for the late 19th and 20th century architects and architecture had been the forming of places that showed space as continuous from inside to outside and at the same time differentiating the inside from the outside as particular and specific against universal and unspecific, as the actualised potential of the universal space with endless potential to be a place for whatever activity or aspect of our life we might choose.
Climbing up, all these thought went through my head and being certain that I was right in my analysis my first desire was to confirm my views in the real built environment. When I reached the summit the rain had stopped; it was still overcast but a much lighter grey sky with a neutral non directional light. I paid my ten franc entrance fee and bought the booklet on the church.
The main South entrance was closed and I walked around the West past the huge gargoyle and water receptacle to the North entrance between the two minor towers into what should be the space of the sky. I was not quite prepared for the experience; the interior is of an earthy intimacy and peaceful silence. On my right hand the light washed wall that curls into the chapels under the two west towers on my left The floor slopes gradually down not much but noticeable till the rail for the Holy Communion on the transition from the part for the lay people and the chancel with the altar. From the Communion Rail the floor slopes up again. This subtle refinement heightens the feeling of going down into a subterranean cavity a sacred cave. To the right of the altar high op in the east wall along the protective heavy wall with the stained glass a large ray of light falls down into the dark space. In the light I faintly see a shape an apparition and I know more than I see that it is the Virgin Mother. I sit down on the last of the pews and let it all come over me.
It is as I expected, but much more intense, much more emotional. I forget all that I had worked out and thought on going up and let it all come over me and let myself dissipate into the space. I can not help thinking of all women I have ever known and see them in the Virgin Mother, Queen of the Earth, the woman goddess, the power of the earth, protective and beyond understanding. I think of the little blond girl I loved in silence, who never knew I loved her. I think of all the girls and young women who I felt had her eyes going right through me guessing my most secret thoughts. I think of the Greek woman who gave me what she could give. I think of them all and feel them all present in a calm serene and loving way. They know it all; they know that I did not want to hurt; I only did not know any better. I feel grateful for what they gave and ready to accept the grace of "la Benie entres tous femmes". The stained glass windows refer to the Litany of the Virgin Mary, the Stella Maris and use those words I have repeated so often and now here gain real meaning. It is a sacred place devoted to the power of life and the Earth, the Great Mother, She who has been before I was and will be after I have long returned to the earth from which I came.
I sat there for a long time just being enveloped in the dark warm cave and let it all come over me.
Then I turned around and went to the two towers of light, light that washed the inside of the West wall. The chapel on the South tower, the highest of them all had in it an altar washed with the most beautiful light from high up. It was on a one step up platform; against the inner wall sat a female dressed in grey a long skirt with some sort of a headscarf. I thought of her as a nun or something praying or meditating, a

continuous attention to the Devine. There seems to be always someone there to honour the Devine; for when I visited the church again next day there was again a female figure sitting silently in the chapel praying.
I spent some two hours there inside and when I came out the weather was clearing. I walked around looked at the outdoor church and sat on the pyramid of meditation. While I was thinking nothing it all fell into place. I could see what the Rococo churches had been trying to convey and how it all fitted in and how Ronchamp is different and the same.
This will need some explanation and for that we will have to go back a bit. When talking about the Rococo Churches we often observed how in those churches the earth meets or better opens up towards heaven represented in the frescos on the ceilings and saucer domes and how the heavens come down along the High altar devoted to the patron of the church and the side altars through saintly intervention. There we said the heavens open up and the earth meets with the eternal, which is high up in the intellectual sphere of understanding Gods essence and his plans for us. That also happens in Ronchamp. The West of the light towers meets with the earth space of the East. But it all happens in the same space on the same level on the same level of reality, inside the cave of the female Goddess the Virgin Mother.
In a Rococo Church it is different. Inside a relatively sober and solid exterior which is totally of this world we enter and find that the space loses its relation to the exterior; its definitions are layered and fuzzy, the size of the space is hard to guess and its location unrelated to the outside. It looks like a scene that gradually builds up from the entrance in the West to the climax of the High Altar in the East. The whole of the interior is one environment wherein structure and decoration are fused into one and develop from East to West into a climax where vault i.e. heaven and floor i.e. earth are connected in one vertical uprising and descending whirl of light, shapes and colours. The solidity of the structure seems to become ethereal, less solid; the structure opens up with height, at ceiling level we look into an other world, as corporeal as ours, more perfect less heavy and material. In this world we see Gods mysteries and the eternal truths and how we humans can attain this blissful life in heaven. The church as a space teaches us that the world as imperfect and hard as it may be is but a cover for the real world of Gods Grace and Beauty, his love for us and how this reality is open to us all in the Church. It all radiates triumphant confidence of being very certain of the validity of the scene. Architecturally, it is the confidence of finally having surpassed the Classics in the understanding and use of the orders the true elements of real beauty.
In this space concept the world can be know and is known in Gods revelation, there is no mystery no question. Believe and follow Gods precepts visible and taught in his church and all will be revealed.
The same triumphant self-assuredness radiates from the Church in Arras. It is less extravagant in its movements but it radiates the same confidence in the eternal truth and validity of its principles. We can and will unveil the secrets of this world. It is in essence a matter of measure. In the arts we have discovered the laws of perfection as first found by the Classics and it is all a matter of measure and proportion. But there is more we have surpassed the Classics by careful study of laws of proportion; science of number will give access to the real and true beauty. This road is not along intuition but of study and science combined with real talent. There is but one true beauty and we now have mastered the secrets. We are on top of the world; all mystery is in principle reducible to a problem that by measuring can be mastered.
That is where the two churches have the same concept of the world; our world can be understood fully and in essence we have grasped its secrets. There is only one

reality and that reality is known and can be comprehended. There is no mystery, only things we do not know as yet.
Arras proclaims that this world is solidly material and can be known. After all it is but a complex watch, beautifully crafted by the Great Watchmaker, a perfect structure designed by the Great Architect. Devising the proper proportions we can create the universal and true beauty and equal or surpass the beauty of the creation. Descartes had confined the spiritual and mystery to the realm outside reality. All that is has dimension and can be represented in number. It is just a matter of time before we can predict what will happen and change the course of events.
Würzburg proclaims the same; the real structure of this world is or can be known. It is spiritual and hidden in this material forms we see with our eyes. And even more; this hidden Truth is given to us in Gods revelation. We know what will happen to us and we know how to avoid all disasters in the eternal life. It differs from Arras that the reality is spiritual and mysteriously hidden in the material cover, only to be revealed inside the Church to those who by the Grace of God have Faith, believe and follow his path.
We know the world and this is the only world, the best possible and we are on top we are master of or fate we control it through our science or through the Grace of God and his revealing the Essential and Eternal Truth to us.
Here is it that Ronchamp differs. It is a sacred space as are Arras and Würzburg. But it is not a proud exposure of the true structure of the world. It intensifies the mystery of this world in the unseen qualities of the universal space and it's potential. It shows how in this world the warm dark, bodily side meets and needs the light, immaterial side of light and consciousness to be fully human. It shows how this world is made of light and darkness and that we have to live it. Ronchamp is for a classical Roman Catholic heretic. The building is a space devoted to the Virgin Mother. It is her space where she meets as equal with the Male Light of clarity and consciousness; together they uphold the world; its essence made visible in the Sacred Place.
Ronchamp has the mysterious half dark with bright reds and blues in the light through the stained glass; it shares that with the Gothic Notre Dame in Chartres. It is the emotional connection to the Earth and the Mother. With the eighteenth century it shares its acceptance of light and understanding of ideas and concepts. It differs from both in that it shows that both are needed to not understand the reality but be able to live in this world. Ronchamp does not ask to be grasped in all its detail. It just wants you to go into its sacred Cave and let it happen.
When I finally went back it was clearing and a watery sun gradually came out. Somehow I felt lighter inside and at peace.
The afternoon I spent sorting out my luggage, throwing away things no longer needed and regrouping and repacking for transport. I was ready for the last stretch, the route to Strassbourg was not too complicated and the place where I had to return the car looked easy to find. The train ticket from Strassbourg to Stuttgart I had bought in Leutkirch and it should be easy to find a hotel near the station. I later found out that I had been lucky to arrive so early, late in the afternoon the press train following the Tour de France invaded the area of the station and took up most of the accommodation near the station.
The next morning after breakfast the sun was out. I decided to drive up and see how the church would be in the sun.
I was not disappointed; apart from more intense contrasts in light and dark the interior was not changed. The light openings are mostly concealed and not present in the interior. Only the window with the Miracle Statue is a real opening in the wall. The more intense light only enhanced the effect. She was even more of an apparition out of another world our inner world.

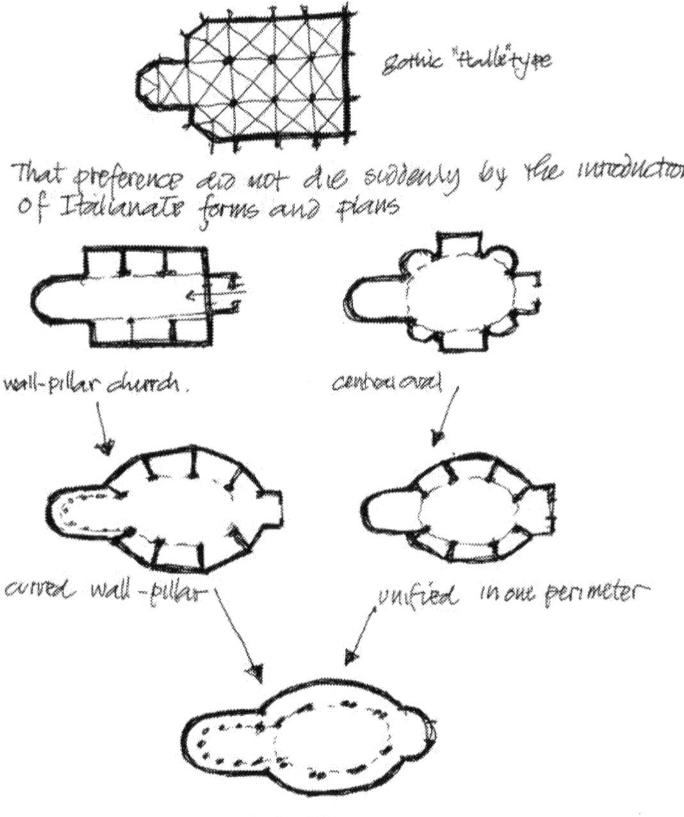

52. Formal analysis of Die Wieskirche

When we started out on our ventures we considered the hypothesis supported by many and amongst them my guide John Bourke that the Il Gesu by Vignola, being the Mother Church for the Jesuit Order, was the main source of inspiration. Now that we have seen a good many churches we should be able discuss this aspect and support our opinion with our own observations. To assist our memory: Il Gesu is a wall pillar church which means that in stead of side aisles the church has on each side of the nave a row of niches separated by heavy walls. They end up in the nave disguised as columns. It is a feature that occurs in Gothic churches when the very deep buttresses required to give lateral support to the vault are brought into the church by shifting the outside wall to the outer edge of the buttresses thus creating a series of rectangular rooms open to the aisle. In Il Gesu they support the heavy barrel vault. The church further features a transept that does not extend beyond the width of the church and a dome over the crossing. There is a one bay chancel with a square closure. The barrel vault was originally divided into bays corresponding with the articulation in bays of the nave. The late 1600 decorations have obfuscated the structural clarity of the original design.

The analysis of the churches I visited shows a rich collection of different plans and cross sections. The group does include a very large number of wall pillar churches of which some have a dome sometimes combined with a transept or a transept-like square bay but these are not the majority of churches. The walls connecting the pillars in the nave with the perimeter wall are very often perforated and in the later churches in Bavaria it is increasingly unclear wether it is a wall pilar or three aisle plan with the side aisles very narrow and subordinate.

There are a good many that are based on a central oval or circle with an arrangement of eight square and round niches or conches from the main space. The central dome is often supported on pairs of double columns or pilasters.

Invariably the churches visited where a lot lighter than either the San Andrea or Il Gesu, especially the later churches are very light not withstanding that the windows are concealed or not at all stressed in the interior.

There are one or two that have the alternating narrower and wider bay like Il Gesu. Generally none of the churches I visited suggested a connection with the Italian examples.

There is a general tendency to have galleries running over the side aisles connected or linked by an increasing perforation of the wall component of the wall pillar, a feature that is not characteristic for Italian churches of the seventeenth century. It does however occur in the late Gothic churches in Germany.

The churches generally do not evoke an Italian feel resembling the interior of Il Gesu. On the basis of my observations I am convinced that Il Gesu is not an important source of inspiration of the vast majority of the Austrian and South German churches of the seventeenth and eighteenth century.

I believe that there are a few things that help understand what the architects were after.

First there is the late Gothic tradition of Germany and more specifically Southern Germany which favoured clear well lit and unobstructed interiors like the Halle type.

It is a three aisled church with the vault in all three aisles at the same height. The aisles are generally of equal width and the spatial concept is far removed from the classic Gothic concept. It is more like one big hall with a sanctuary or chancel of modest dimensions as an extension of the central aisle. There are some churches of this type which have been refurbished in Rococo and generally the space does work well with the much later decoration.

As a second influence is the need to come to grips with the imported Italianate style from late 1500 onwards. This introduced some new types of ground plan which are

typical for the Italian architecture of that time. One frequently used is a central oval with the long axis from East to West covered by a dome, which towards the 18th century tends to become very shallow a saucer dome. The dome is supported on often eight sets of paired columns separating conches or rectangular niches. The East rectangle is often lengthened to takes the chancel while the West bay forms the entrance with the gallery for organ and choir. The other square niches on the shorter axis resemble something like a transept. Very often the diagonal niches are narrower.
Amongst the churches discussed there is a very large number loosely based on the above scheme without clearly pointing towards an Italian example. There is also a relatively small group that in plan remind suggest some resemblance with the Santa Maria in Campitelli by Rainaldi. They show a similar narrowing towards the east and no direct repetition of a standard bay. These churches are generally of modest dimensions (e.g. Maria Plain). There further is a large group that is not really a wall pillar type. They are best described as a rectangular hall with a pilaster articulation sometimes suggesting bays and sometimes the freer of irregular bays.

What they all have in common is the tendency to create one unobstructed space with a chancel in some form in the East.

The churches that could be regarded as based on the wall pillar plan the wall pillars gradually are treated as a screen wall, which conceals the windows from view when entering from the west, and create an interior without boundary without a separating, detached from the exterior.

It is very difficult to maintain that one or a limited number of Italian churches were the driving examples.

Of course like everywhere in Europe the introduction of Italian style elements during the Mannerist period demanded different approaches to plan development

It is equally clear that the South German Gothic tradition of large unobstructed well lit spaces influenced the choice ground plan deemed suitable.

The refurbishment of some late Gothic interiors in the Rococo period shows how well the two go together.

The whole development is fully visible in Die Wies Kirche. It in my view not the best but it is typical and of an extremely high quality and rightly incorporated in the UN World Heritage. It might illustrate the foregoing by revisiting Die Wies Kirche by Zimmerman, followed by a discussion of Vierzehn Heiligen and Neresheim by Balthasar Neumann. The ground plan of the Wies Kirche shows how the nave concept based on the wall pillar plan combined with the central oval in the hands of a very talented architect results in something which is unique.

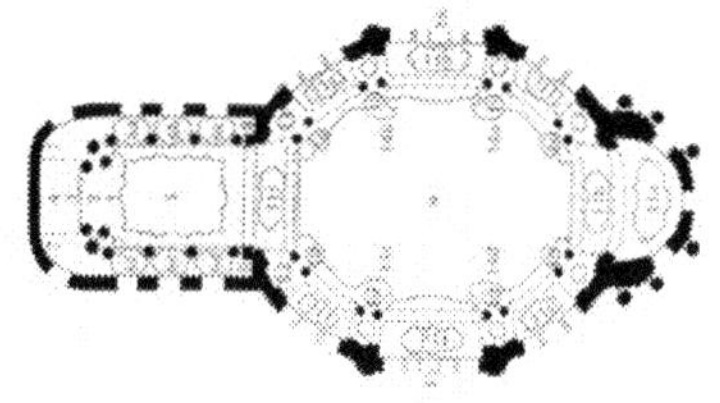

To understand the concept one can take as starting point the scheme used for many of the oval churches (Karlskirche in Wien, Maria Dreiechen, and Weltenburg) or simple hall church of the wall pillar type.

From the oval you make the niches of the same depth and perforate the separating walls to the extent that only the paired columns at the oval remain and connect them above the entablature back to the perimeter wall. In the Chancel you introduce a screen of columns and the plan now is what we have in Die Wies.

Starting from the wall pillar hall following the concept of Zwiefalten and Maria Steinbach by perforating the walls so that only the paired columns remain tied back to the outer wall one only needs to curve the parallel walls out and the ground plan is in essence what Die Wies shows.

Die Wies brings two types that have been used extensively together into one very accomplished concept.
On entering one is not drawn into the question of the exact shape of the interior. It is a fleeting space dissipating into the fuzzy wall. The colonnade of the screen effectively draws the attention away from the light entering openings to the light as it is taken up by the interior. The interior takes us to the climax of the High Altar in the east. The interior is not so much a developing vision as a revelation. The whole interior is fully visible upon entering but fully not comprehendible in its structure. There is no gradual leading into the climax of the High Altar with the Miracle Statue, the revelation is instantaneous not gradual. It is overpowering in the richness of visual stimuli that do not appear as individual forms but a point of increased intensity in the whole experience.
There is a third group of churched based roughly on the traditional plan of the Latin cross. It is a relatively small group some full wall pillar type and others with the wall pillars reduced to pilasters articulating the nave (Maria Taferl). Balthasar Neumann built Gossweinstein's Dreifaltigkeits Kirche on the scheme and in Vierzehnheiligen he had to design for the foundations that were all ready in place after his successor had changed his central type to a Latin cross. At about the same time he designed Neresheim, which is also based on a cross.

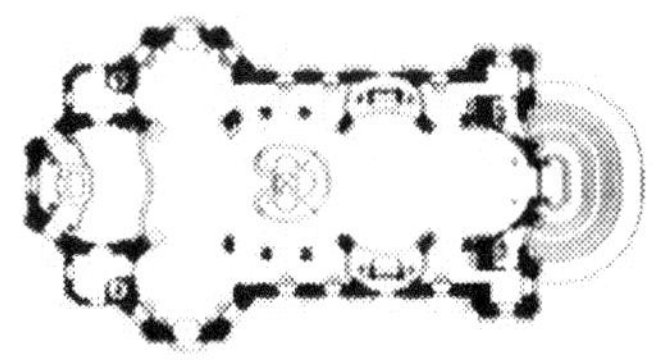

These two churches are interesting because they can be read as the architects comments on both plans.
Vierzehnheiligen is the more complex of the two. Being reappointed as the architect Neumann clearly wanted to save the concept of the altar of the 14 Saints as the climax of the church. That was no longer possible as the lengthened foundations had put the crypt and altar of the 14 Saints solidly in the nave between the crossing and the entrance in the west. So he had to work with that. In the vault however using a configuration already, though not so fully and effectively, was used in Banz by Dietzenhofer. The trick that you combine one bay and two half bays on either side for one unit in the vault. This means that every second bay has a centre of the vault. The in-between bays are part of two bays in the vault
In Vierzehnheiligen Neumann allocated the second bay to the first saucer dome and to the largest dome over the altar for the Saints. The crossing he allocated half to the dome over the Saints and the other half went to the dome over the chancel.
The arms of the transept now acquire a much greater independence. The second bay, with also no specific centre in the vaulting has been given a similar shape as the arms of the transept and likewise a smaller secondary dome.
The church now in its vaulting shows a main scheme, which over the main axis shows a centralised plan. From west, the sequence is one smaller oval over the West, the largest oval over the altar of the saints and the third covering the chancel.

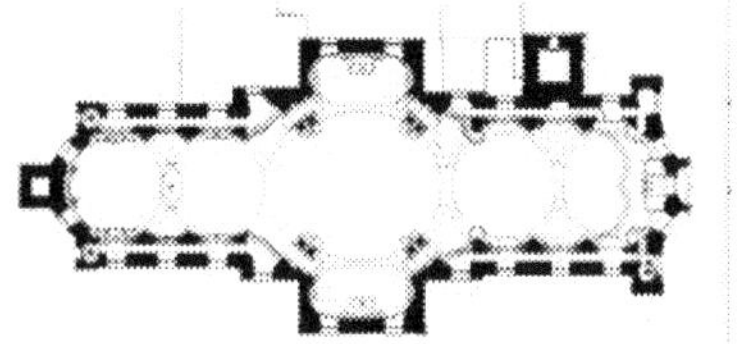

Parallel to the main axis there is the progression from the smaller side spaces of bay two over the larger side domes of the arms of the transept which leads you to the hight altar in the east.
On entering this complexity is not clearly visible. It unfolds while gradually progressing and going through the church a few times.

Neresheim uses the same tricks but is less complex and straight forward. The transepts are solidly tied to the main axis and with the large central dome supported by 4 groups of paired column preceded in the west by two smaller domes and followed after the transept by two smaller domes over the chancel is more static. The decoration of Neresheim was not in any way influenced by Neumann who died shortly after the work commenced. How he envisaged the interior we can only guess. As it stands now we can only see how Neumann in Vierzehnheiligen distributed his eight columns supporting the primary dome in two groups evenly space to hide that he had no transept there. In Neresheim he put his eight columns where they traditionally had been in groups of two on a square with the central dome resting on them and the nave and the transept of equal width connected to the four sides.

The interior in Neresheim although not immediately readable is of a predictable

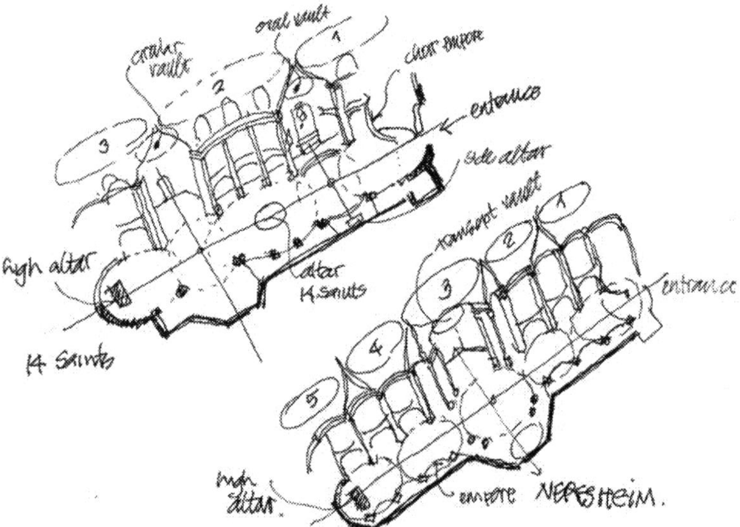

concept and somewhat tame compared to Vierzehnheiligen. As the design follows on Vierzehnheiligen it is possible that Neumann regarded Vierzehnheiligen as a not too bad effort to save a concept bungled by the architect who followed him after his dismissal. The somewhat unfortunate history of Neumann's commission gave us a masterpiece of spatial complexity and a true Rococo work of great class.

GLOSSARY

Aedicule	a shrine framed by two columns and a pediment supported on an entablature. In the wider sense : the framing of a door, window or other opening with two columns, piers or pilasters supporting a gable, lintel, plaque or entablature and pediment.
Aisle	part of a church, hall or other building parallel to the main span and divided from it by an arcade of piers or columns or, in rare cases by a screen wall
Ambulatory	a semicircular or polygonal aisle enclosing an apse or a straight ended sanctuary, originally used for processional purposes
Apse	vaulted circular or polygonal termination, usually to a chancel or chapel
Arcade	range of arches carried on piers or columns, either free-standing or blind i.e. attached to a wall.
Architrave	Lintel spanning from one column to the next
Baroque	the Art and Architecture of the seventeenth and part of the eighteenth century. It is characterized by great emphasis on spatial effects, the effect of sculptural decorations and grand scale compositions which includes vast outdoor areas (Versailles). The extent to which these characteristics are visible varies considerably over entire Europe, so that some scholars do not accept the reality of Baroque Architecture for France, England and Northern (protestant) Europe.
Barrel vault	a vault of semi circular or semi ellipsoidal cross section.
Bay	a vertical division of the exterior or interior of a building, marked not by walls but by fenestration, an order, buttress, units of vaulting, roof compartments and the like.
Byzantine	Art and Architecture of the East Roman or Byzantine Empire and more particular from the sixth century onwards till the fall of Constantinople in 1453.
Chancel	that part of the east end of a church in which the main altar is placed, reserved for clergy and choir, the continuation of the nave east of the crossing.
Classicism	also Neo-Classicism. The revival or return to the principles of Classical Architecture from ca 1750 onwards in France and spreading to the remainder of Europe and the U.S.A till late 1800 or early 1900 (U.S.A. England)
Column	a vertical member of an order usually with base and capital
Conch	a semicircular niche, surmounted by a half dome.
Corinthian	a fluted column on a base consisting of torus and hollow and a capital composed of acanthus leaves
Crossing	the space at the intersection of nave, chancel and transepts, often surmounted by a dome or crossing tower.
Dome	a vault of even curvature on a circular base and supported by a cylinder (drum). The section can be semicircular, segmental, pointed or bulbous.
Early Christian	the Art and Architecture of both halves of the Roman empire from ca, 200 AD till about 500 AD in the East. In the West due to the dissolution of the Roman power little is known until the Carolingian Renaissance round 800 AD leading into Early Romanesque.

Entablature — the upper part of an order consisting of architrave, freeze and cornice.

Gallery — an upper storey over an aisle opening to the nave.

Gothic — The Art and Architecture in Western Europe between early 1100 (St Denis) till about 1400 in Italy and late 1500 in the remainder of Europe. It is the architecture of the pointed arch, the rib vault and flying buttresses. It creates highly integrated interior spaces by repeating a few basic spatial units covered by rib vaults. Rib vaults allow the use of the same vaulting technique over a large variety of spatial units (squares, rectangles, trapeziums, triangles. In its last forms in Germany and England the vault is an undulating plane supported by pillars of columns.

Groin vault — vault formed by the intersection of two barrel vaults.

Intercolumnium — Space between two columns

Lesene — pilaster without base and capital.

Mannerism — the style current in Italy from early 1500 (Michael Angelo) to around 1600. It is characterised by a highly individual use of the elements of the elements of the Classical Architecture. It appears to aim at exploring the expressive potential of the Classical forms and derived variations. (Maniera (Italian): manner, fashion)

Nartex — a transverse vestibule preceding the nave and aisles as an eso-nartex or preceding the façade as an exo-nartex.

Net vault — a vault whose ribs form a network of lozenges of varying shape and size

Order — a set of base, column and entablature with specific characteristics like Doric, Ionic, Corinthian.

Pediment — a low pitched gable above a portico and similar features above windows and doors. It may be straight sided or curved segmentally. In an open top or broken apex pediment the sides stop before the apex; an open bed or broken bed pediment shows a gap in the base moulding.

Pilaster — a shallow pier or rectangular column projecting only slightly from a wall with a capital and base confirm with the freestanding columns and piers.

Putti — plural of putto (Italian for child,) especially child or baby like cherubs

Renaissance — is now understood to be the Italian Art and Architecture from ca. 1420 onward to the beginning of the sixteenth century. Earlier the term included the Art and Architecture in Europe of the sixteenth to the end of the eighteenth century.

Retable — a superstructure found since 11th century, either painted or carved, on the rear of the altar or on its own pedestal behind the altar, especially one with carved figures in the corpus or central part and carved and or painted wings.

Rib vault — vault formed by arches, pointed, circular or oval, springing from supports meeting in a centre with curved infill panels between the arches.

Rococo — By some scholars not regarded as a style in its own right but as the final phase of Baroque. Rococo is represented in France and to a much lesser degree in England and the Northern European countries as an interior decoration style, light in colour and weight with a preference for asymmetrical compositions. In the

	Austria- Hungarian Empire, the Schwiss Republic and Southern Germany it however denotes Architecture of sometimes great complexity, exuberantly light interiors characterised by a fusion between structure and decoration, in a relatively sober exterior
Romanesque	the Art and Architecture in Western Europe from its early beginnings in the Carolingian Renaissance till the advent of Gothic. It is characterized by clear and easily comprehended schemes of layout and elevations. The sculptural decorations are concentrated round the entrances and the capitals. It favours the round arch and uses barrel vaulting and or groin vaults over units square in plan
Sanctuary	the area around the main altar in a church.
Saucer dome	a segmental dome without drum.
Vault	an arched ceiling or roof of stone, brick or concrete, sometimes imitated in wood or plaster
Wall pillar	a pillar supporting the ceiling of the nave and connected to the exterior wall by a wall, thus dividing the aisles in separate mostly rectangular niches.

MAP

The following map shows the area covered by the Ventures. The cities chosen as home base are underlined. The churches monasteries and other sites visited are indicated by a black round surmounted by a cross.

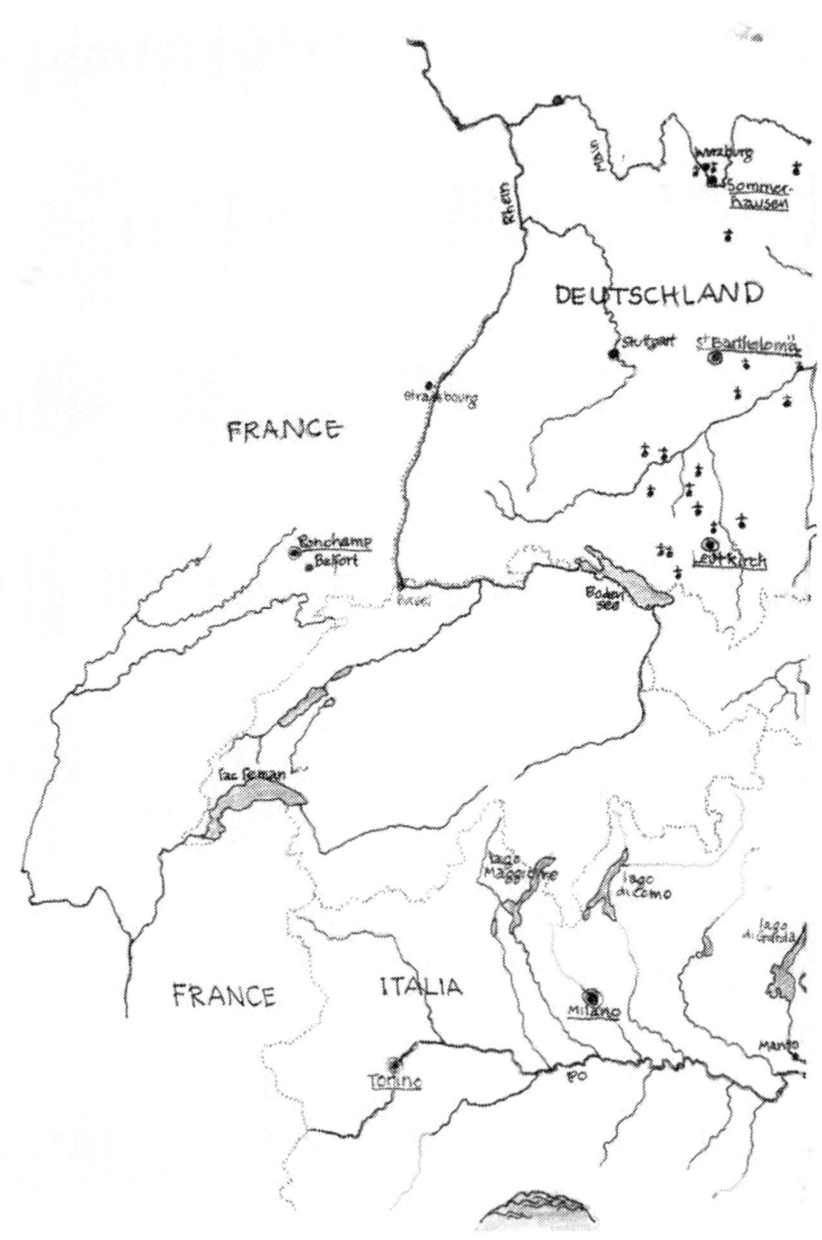
Main
Rhein
Sommer-
hausen
DEUTSCHLAND
St Bartholomä
FRANCE
Ronchamp
Belfort
Leutkirch
Boden
see
lago
Maggiore
lago
di Como
FRANCE
ITALIA
Milano
Torino
Po

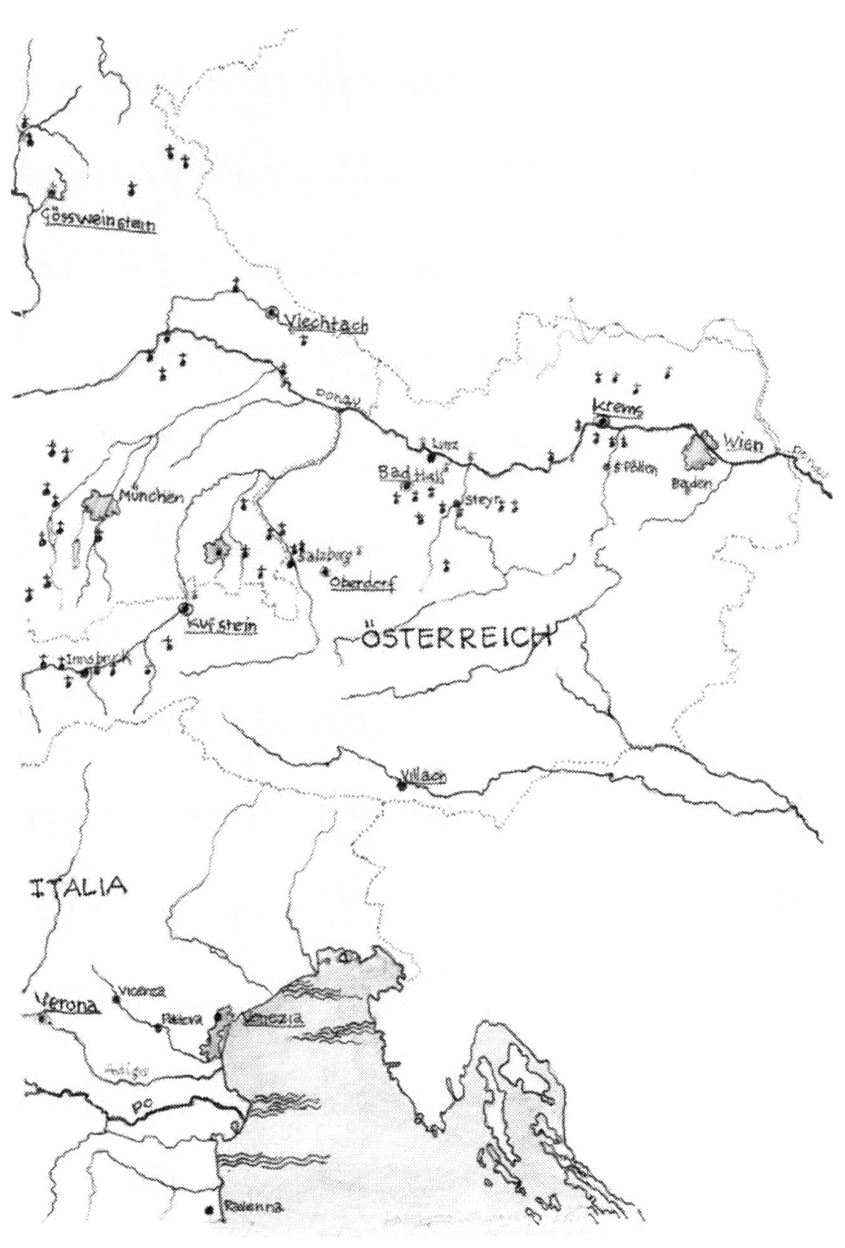
Gössweinstein
Viechtach
Donau
Krems
Wien
Linz
Bad Hall
St Pölten
Baden
München
Steyr
Salzburg
Oberndorf
Kufstein
ÖSTERREICH
Innsbruck
Villach
ITALIA
Verona
Vicenza
Padova
Venezia
Po
Ravenna

www.ingramcontent.com/pod-product-compliance
Ingram Content Group UK Ltd.
Pitfield, Milton Keynes, MK11 3LW, UK
UKHW012220240726
13966UKWH00003B/872

9 781847 539526